HOW TO PLAN, SUBCONTRACT
AND
BUILD YOUR DREAM HOUSE

Everything you need to know to avoid
the pitfalls and the rip-offs.

What you must know that nobody wants
to tell you.

Save up to 50,000.00 Dollars or more
as your own General Contractor.

WARREN V. JAEGER

TROJAN HOMES PUBLISHING CO.

TROJAN

HOW TO PLAN, SUBCONTRACT AND BUILD YOUR DREAM HOUSE
Copyright © 1998
By Warren V. Jaeger

Published by Trojan Homes Publishing Co. Box 176 LaGrangeville, N.Y. 12540

This book is intended to provide accurate and authoritative information in regard to the subject matter covered. It is sold with the understanding that the author and/or publisher is not engaged in giving Legal, Architectural, Engineering or other professional service. If legal, Architectural, Engineering or other professional advice is required, the services of a competent professional practitioner should be obtained.

Library of Congress Catalog Card Number: 95-78686

ISBN 0-9647824-0-5

Printed in the United States of America

TABLE OF CONTENTS

TABLE OF CONTENTS

TABLE OF CONTENTS

SUBCONTRACTORS

Working yourself - Cutting Down the Mess - Finding Subs - Hiring Subs - Beating the One Shot Deal Rule 29, Pay Subs Fast - Rule 30, No Beer - Form of the Agreement - Rule 31, The Key To the Contract Supervising Subs - Rule 32, - Praise

CLEARING THE LAND

Building Permit - Rule 33, Kowtow - Staking Out - Roughing Out the Location - Clearing - Rule 34, Avoid Chainsaws - Rule 35, Forget the Firewood - Stabilizing the Access - Preparing the House Site

LAYING OUT THE FOOTINGS

Diagrams - Computations - Fig. 1 - Fig.2 - Fig. 3 - Fig.4 - Fig.5&6 - Fig.7 - Fig.8 - Fig. 9, Laying Out On the Ground - Rule 36, Don't Panic

BUILDING THE FOOTINGS

Width of the Trench - Setting the Elevations - Fig. 10 - Marking the Layout - Digging - Using the Transit - Fig.11 - Setting Grade Stakes - Footing Inspection - Ordering Concrete - Pouring the Footings

STARTING THE FOUNDATION

Ordering Block - Laying Out For the Block - Sub Grade Insulation - The Water Service Line Backfilling Rule 37, Push uphill - Rule 38, Better high Than Low - The Full Basement Foundation - Fig. 12 - The Footings - Backfilling - Layout For the Block - Setting the Block

DEALING WITH DRAINAGE AND GROUNDWATER

Rule 39, The Hole Fills With Water - Footing Drains - Rule 40, Worthless Drains - Under Slab Drains Surface Drainage

FINISHING THE FOUNDATION

Plumbing Waste Lines - Preparing For the Slab - The Basement Floor Drain - The Vapor Barrier Reinforcing Wire Mesh - Concrete Shrinkage - Rule 41, Dry Concrete Slowly - Screeds and Screeding - Hooking the Mesh - Floating the concrete - Troweling and Finishing - Completing the Block Work - Rule 42, Don't Backfill Without Weight on the Foundation

TABLE OF CONTENTS

HEATING, VENTILATING AND AIR CONDITIONING

Choosing the Heating System - The Oil Burner - The Gas Burner - Electric Heat - The Heat Pump Geothermal Design - Principles of Heat Pump System Design - Air Circulation - Rule 49, Don't Oversize Duct Design - Balancing - Duct Layout - Rule 50, No Sound or Motion - Rule 51, - Bad Design Increases Costs - Under Slab Ducts - Basement Ducts - Feeding the Second Floor - Insulated Ducts - Rule 52, Ducts Loose Heat, Increase Costs - Refrigerant Lines - Auxiliary Heat - Solar Heat - Passive Solar - Wood Stoves - Fireplaces - The Ultimate Lazy Man's Fireplace

ELECTRICAL WIRING

Introduction - A Basic Concept of Electricity - Power - Utility Company Service - Type of Power Supplied - The Main Disconnect - The Distribution Panel - The Three Wire System - Electrical Shocks Rule 54, Never Touch - Ground Faults - The GFI - Murder in the Bath Tub - Appliance Circuits - Large Appliance Circuits - Convenience Receptacles - Lighting Outlets - Recessed Ceiling Lights - Rule 55, Recessed Lights Are Trouble - Kitchen Lighting - Bathroom Lighting - New Lighting Styles - Rule 56, Visit Showrooms Early - Telephone Wiring - Cable TV - Rule 57, Plan Ahead - Emergency Generator Systems- The Emergency Panel - Hooking Up the Generator

PLUMBING

Sewer Connection - Cleanouts - The Trap - The Piping - Septic Connection - The Leaching Fields Effluent Lift Pump - Pump Alarm - Effluent Pump Wiring - Rule 58, Song and Dance - The Lockout Public water Connection - Well Water Service - The Pitless Adaptor - Well Pressure System - Gas Service LNG and Propane - Gas Usage Interior Gas Piping - Hot Water Baseboard Systems - Zone Circulation Noise Control - Air Binding and Bleeding - Piping in an Overhang - Domestic Hot Water - Interior Drain Line Noise - Toilet Connections - Water Piping - Rule 59, Test Lines - The Air Cushion - Under Sink Connections - Water Conservation - Whirlpool Tubs

INSULATION

How Insulation Works - Rule 60, No Heat - Fiberglass Batts - Paper Faced Batts - Crushing - Convection Air Infiltration - Deformity Behind Wires - The Right Way - Moisture Migration - The Vapor Barrier Insulating Ceilings - Interior Walls - Floors - Attic Spaces - Miscellaneous Insulation - Air Infiltration Remedies - Cathedral Ceilings - Basement And Garage Access Doors - Hiring The Subcontractor - Rule 61, Save Money

DRYWALL AND TAPING

Wallboard Types - Fastening the Wallboard - Screwing It Up - Ceilings - Walls - End Joints - Curves and Corners - Soffits - Taping - Skimming - Sanding - Hiring The Drywall Contractor - Taking The Count - Rule 62, Check Count - Rough Door Openings - Making The Agreement - Sheetrock Delivery

INSIDE FINISHING

Trimmers - Underlayment - Bathrooms - The Kitchen - Interior Stairs - The Second Floor Nose - Interior Doors - Door Materials - Pre Hung Doors - Door Operation - Rule 63, Nomenclature - Types of Door Assemblies - Interior Hardware - Door Swing Conflicts - Door and Base Moldings - Cornice Moldings Window Sills - False Ceiling Beams - Closet Shelves and Poles

CABINETRY AND APPLIANCES

Buying Your Kitchen - Bathroom Vanities - Installation - Appliances - The Refrigerator - Rule 65, Don't put Ref. - The Range And Oven - The - Microwave - The One Piece Multi Unit - The Exhaust Hood - The Dishwasher - The Garbage Disposall - The Garbage Compactor - Ordering Cabinets And Appliances Rule 66, Order in Advance - Appliance Servicing - Outlet Warehouses

FLOORING

Hardwood Flooring - Tile Flooring - Marble And Granite - Vinyl Flooring - Wall To Wall Carpet Buying Carpet - Rule 67, Double Check

PAINTING AND DECORATING

Staining - Painting Ceilings - Wall Paint - Color - Buying Colored Paint - Wall Paper - Architectural Mirrors

FINISHING UP

Patios - Rule 68, Double Check - Walkways - Decks - Concrete Retaining Walls - Fieldstone Retaining Walls - The Driveway - Landscaping - The Lawn - Final Cleanup

SCHEDULING

The Critical Path - Making Your Schedule - The Critical Path Steps - Get The Building Permit - Mark Out House And Driveway Location - Clear And Grade - Layout For Footings - Excavate Footings - Site Development - Set Grade Stakes - Get Footing Inspection - Pour Footings - Lay The Block - Insulate The Foundation - Backfill The Foundation - NOTE - Well And Septic - Water Line - Under Slab Plumbing Site Work - Under Slab Plumbing Inspection - Pour The Slab - Framing - Duct Work - Roofing And Siding - Plumbing And Electrical Wiring - Electrical And Plumbing Inspection - Insulation - Exterior Finishing - Insulation Inspection - Drywall Installation And Taping - Underlayment And Interior Trim Install Interior Stairs - Tile Work - Install Cabinetry - Interior Painting - Landscaping - Vinyl Flooring Appliance Delivery - Finish Plumbing And Electric - HVAC Equipment - Hanging Interior And Exterior Lighting Fixtures - Carpet Installation - Duct Louvers And Trim - Hardwood Floor Finishing - Final Inspection for C.O. - Rule 69, Anticipate

FOREWORD

Over many years I have written thousands of pages of business letters, articles, evaluations, project descriptions and patent documents.

I make no claim to any literary style, but I do hope that I have developed the ability to explain things clearly, understandably and in plain English.

There is always the danger however, when explaining something familiar, one will fail to anticipate questions that come to the mind of the reader, leaving him wondering on a particular point.

Should this happen, please write to me in care of the Publisher, and I will endeavor to provide you with an answer or clarification.

I suggest that you read this book from start to finish so that you will be familiar with the scope of the information contained. Then I would read it again and thereafter refer to it as necessary as a continuing guide.

I am sure the information in this book will save you thousands of dollars, hours and hours of wasted time, and help you avoid mistakes, pitfalls and hassles.

GOOD LUCK!

Warren V. Jaeger
LaGrangeville, N.Y.

INTRODUCTION

THE INDIVIDUAL YOU

In the early 90s, the so called experts pronounced doom and gloom for wannabe home owners: "Prices will drop below 50%", "Buying or building a home in the 90s will not be a good investment", "Better buy bonds", and "Remember the savings and loan debacle".

But one thing we can be reasonably sure of is that the experts are invariably wrong. They are wrong because they are only number crunchers. They don't understand the psychological dynamics of home ownership.

"The great American dream", is alive and well. It is still the only way to satisfy our most basic desires: A place of our own, a place of privacy, a place to create, a place to grow a family, and most importantly, a place to be safe. Not only safe from crime and violence, but also emotionally safe; a haven from the cares and strife of the outside world. These desires have driven humankind since the first cave was occupied, and the first mud hut was built.

You want to build your own home because you not only feel and understand the emotional reasons, but also because you need even more. You want your home to express your individuality, to show the world your uniqueness, to express and fulfill your own special personality. Whether it's the swimming pool, the tennis court, the garden, the work shop, the studio, the dog kennels, the model railroad, the place to display art, or that really great gourmet kitchen, above all you want your home to be of you, and by you. Because you are an individualist, you cannot picture yourself living in a house that was someone else's.

There are many nice development houses, but no single one has all the features you want. If only you could combine some of them. But of course you can, you can build! You've got plenty of ideas. What an exciting undertaking! What a challenge! But how to start?

Building a home can be, and should be, an exciting, and rewarding experience. All too often, when undertaken by people who have not taken the trouble to learn what they are

1

doing, it becomes a nightmare. Hassles, arguments, things unforeseen, and things overlooked, controversy and mistakes, all turn what ought to be a happy experience, into a horror.

In the following pages I will tell you in clear easy to understand language, how to avoid the mistakes. I will give you rules to follow. When a rule is given it is gospel, it is carved in stone. Don't skip it. Don't ignore it. Don't think it can't happen to you because it can.

Every rule given was derived from a problem that occurred because the principal in the rule was either not understood, or not followed. Each rule is derived from my many years as a designer and builder of custom homes, and as it is with most of life's lessons, it cost me to learn it. That's why I made it a rule. Heed it and it won't cost you.

NOT ONLY CAN YOU BUILD YOUR DREAM HOME, NOT ONLY CAN YOU EXPERIENCE THE EXCITEMENT AND SATISFACTION OF BEING YOUR OWN BUILDER, BUT BY ACTING AS YOUR OWN GENERAL CONTRACTOR, YOU CAN SAVE 30, 40, 50,000 DOLLARS OR MORE BY ELIMINATING THE BUILDERS MARKUP.

PART ONE

SELECTING AND EVALUATING
A BUILDING SITE

CHAPTER 1

LOOKING AT LAND

DO YOUR HOMEWORK.

Don't take things for granted. Don't take someone else's word without making sure it's true.

A few years ago a client came to me to design and build a unique contemporary home on a rocky but beautiful lot in a wealthy suburb. Before starting a design, I always examine the land to learn it's characteristics that might affect the design. At my request, the client took me to the site which was on a lovely dirt road in a beautiful wooded area. "What I particularly like about this location" he said, "is that there are only eleven lots in a row on one side of the road. The land behind the lots and across the road, is a permanent nature conservancy." He told me that the broker had come out with him, with the subdivision map, and shown him where the lots were located. The particular lot he was interested in, the broker explained, began at a small culvert which ran under the road, and extended to the right, a distance of some three hundred feet. The client showed me where the culvert was, and we walked the land together. There were several rock outcroppings and a small area between, which was not large enough to site a house. I told him I thought we could use the rock as an attractive back ground, but without a doubt some extensive blasting would be necessary. Of course blasting is very expensive. The client however, said he liked the lot so well, that he would be willing to bear the extra cost. We worked out a preliminary design and budget, and agreed to go forward. The client was a lawyer and an assistant District Attorney in New York City. He said, that although real estate was not his field, he had read up on the subject, and would handle the contract to purchase the land himself. Later, when the purchase was completed, he boasted about how he had checked every clause, and all the fine print, putting the seller's lawyer through his paces.

Before starting a job, I always require the owner of the land to have a licensed surveyor stake out the corners and lines of the property, so that the exact placement of the house can be determined. The client hired the surveyor, who had done the subdivision map, and when the lot had been staked out, he called me.

I went to the lot, found the culvert, and looked and looked, but I could not find the surveyors stakes. Returning to my office, I called the client, telling him that the surveyor had not staked the lot after all. He called the surveyor who assured him that he had staked the lot, and suggested that I meet him the following morning at the main road near the property. We would go to the lot together, and the surveyor would show me the points he had staked. As arranged, we met the next morning, and drove to the site, with me leading in my car. When I stopped at the lot, I noticed in my mirror that the surveyor was not behind me. I got out of my car, and saw that the surveyor was getting out of his car about a half mile back on the road. In that instant, I had a flash of understanding, and knew what had happened.

The client's lot was next to last, at the other end of the row of eleven lots. Sure enough, the surveyor had staked out the proper lot in accordance with the lot number he had been given by the client. Believe it or not, when the broker showed the lot to the client, she held the map upside down, and told the client that lot #10, which they were looking at, was lot #2.

With all the care the client had taken over the contract and purchase, the entire transaction was based on an unverified assumption, that the lot he looked at, and wanted to buy, was lot #2 in the subdivision, when in actuality, he was looking at lot #10.

Well, the end of the story was, that I called the client, and could not resist telling him that I had met the surveyor, and that I had good news and bad news for him. "What's the bad news?" he asked. I said, "do you remember how you told me about all the precautions you took in the contract, and what a great job you did?. How you checked and double checked? Well there is only one problem, you bought the wrong lot'." A long silence ensued followed by a single explosive four letter word." What's the good news?" he finally asked. I told him that he must have stepped in his four letter word, and that luck was with him, because if we reversed the plans to the opposite hand, (mirror image), the house would fit perfectly on the lot, and he would save the $15,000.00 we had budgeted for blasting, as it would not be necessary. Fortunately, this story had a happy ending, but if it had been reversed, and the client was suddenly confronted with a large additional expense he couldn't afford, all his plans would have gone down in flames.

RULE NUMBER 2

NEVER ACCEPT TECHNICAL INFORMATION GIVEN BY A BROKER WITHOUT CHECKING IT OUT.

Remember, a real estate broker is not a surveyor; is not an engineer; is not an architect; is not a lawyer; is not a builder, but is a sales person anxious to make a sale.

When buying a building lot, in the binder agreement prior to signing a formal contract, always require that the seller have the lot staked out by a licensed surveyor so that you may see exactly where the lot is, and how the side lines run. Standing in a road with a subdivision map in your hands, it is virtually impossible, to tell accurately, the direction of the side lot lines. This information is absolutely crucial, in eliminating unpleasant surprises, after the lot has been purchased.

RULE NUMBER 3

NEVER ACCEPT AN OWNERS CLAIM WHERE THE BOUNDARIES OF HIS LAND ARE.

One time, a client who owned a building lot about a hundred miles away from where he lived, decided to build a house on the lot for speculation. He felt the market in the area was active, and after owning the lot for fourteen years, the time to cash in had come.

He took me to the lot, and walked me about, showing me the boundaries of the land. There was a particularly lovely spot toward one side of the lot which he envisioned as the site for the house. It indeed was lovely land, and in a good area. He told me how over the years he would drive up to look at his lot every few months. He enjoyed the ride to the country, and would bring his family along to picnic on the property. He didn't have a copy of the deed, but told me the property was about four acres in size. He agreed to pay the costs for me to search the county records, obtain a copy of the deed, and have a surveyor stake out the lot. Needless to say, there were a few surprises. The lot turned out to be only two acres, and there was a deed restriction that forbid building within 100 feet of any lot line. This effectively reduced the possible building area to less than an acre. Of course the nice location wasn't even on the property. It's not that the fellow lied, he was just subject to a syndrome that infects every land owner. Every time he went to see his property, he remembered it as being a little larger than the last time. Over the years the land had grown in his mind to twice it's actual size.

This is an immutable rule about people who own land. When a person owns a lot next to a vacant lot, every time he cuts his lawn, he cuts a few inches further onto the adjacent lot. He doesn't do it consciously, it just seems to him that that's where the line is. Everyone without exception, who lives on land next to a vacant lot, after a few years, has incorporated ten to twenty feet of land he doesn't own, into his lawn. If you are looking at a lot next to a lawn, be assured that the lot line lies in the grass. If you send a surveyor to stake the lot many people become irate. "How dare you drive those stakes in my lawn? That's my property, I'm certain of it. Get off my land!" is not an exaggerated reaction.

RULE NUMBER 4

POSSESSIVENESS OVER LAND BRINGS OUT THE WORST IN PEOPLE.

You must expect it and allow for it. People resent construction on land next to them that has been vacant for a time. They will fight against it; they will erect barbed wire; they will vandalize the construction. They will even be possessive over land they don't own.

A client purchased a six acre parcel in an area of wealthy estates and summer homes. Next to the property was a lovely contemporary summer home that belonged to a big time New York doctor. When I examined the land I noticed that at great effort, someone had constructed pathways outlined with fieldstone, throughout the lot. I brought this to the attention of my client and asked him what he wanted me to do. "Go ahead and bulldoze them" he said, "this land has been on the market for years, if someone wanted it they had plenty of opportunity to buy it!"

The next day we started to clear the house site with a bulldozer. We hadn't worked for more than a few minutes, when a man came running up the hill toward us, from the direction of the summer home. He was frantically waving his arms. I knew what was coming so I walked toward him to appear polite. "What are you doing?" he screamed, "You are destroying all my walking paths; you have no right to do that". I explained that my client had purchased the property, and hired me to build a house on it. "He can't buy this land, he never even came to talk to me about it." he replied. Unreasonable you say? No one would act like that? I am afraid it is all too typical.

Now that I've gotten your attention, and shown you a few of the pitfalls lurking in the labyrinth you have chosen to travel, we will move on to some specifics, so that you will anticipate and avoid the danger. In the next chapter we'll talk about the detailed steps in choosing a building lot and evaluating it's suitability.

CHAPTER 2

POLITICAL AND SOCIAL
CONSIDERATIONS

In choosing a place to build your home there are two categories of information to consider. The first is what I call the political and social climate, and the second is the particular physical and topographical characteristics of the land which will affect the way in which you build, and the cost of doing so.

LOCATION

Location! Location! Location!. The three most important rules of real estate. I'm sure you have heard this caveat many, many times. It is repeated so often, because it is so true. Nothing is more important in determining the desirability, and therefor the value of a building site than it's location. Let's look at the factors one by one.

ZONING

Here's where you will start to apply rule number 1, "DO YOUR HOMEWORK." If you are not intimately familiar with the area in which you are looking for a site, it is essential to become familiar, so that you can make informed judgments. Find the local stationary, drug or book store, and buy a street map of the area. Study it and cruise around a bit so that you can begin to get a "feel".

Next, meet the bureaucracy. Go to the City Hall, the Town Hall, or the Village Hall, serving the locale. Look around. See what the people look like. See if they seem to be busy and industrious, or are hanging about drinking coffee. Is the building modern, up to date, and well maintained, or is it old, run down, and dirty? This can tell you much about the economic level of the community, and whether the area residents are involved, want improvements, and are willing to pay for them.

A quiet, rural, slow area may be what you are looking for. That's fine too, but don't expect the road in front of the lot you're considering, to be repaved any time soon. While you're in the Town Hall, go to the Town Clerk's office, and purchase a zoning map and a copy of the zoning ordinance. The Town or municipal area, will be divided into zones in accordance with the type of use permitted. The usual categories are industrial, commercial or business, residential, and business-residential. Residential zones are usually divided by the minimum size of building lot required, such as residential half acre, residential one acre, residential two acre, residential three acre, residential five acre and larger sites.

There are usually exceptions or special zones for public facilities, such as power stations, dumps, schools, hospitals and nursing homes, garages for municipal facilities., airports, helipads, etc. Don't put a lot of faith in agricultural zones. As an area grows they are usually rezoned into higher uses.

In suburban areas there are certain distances from the lot lines, in which building is not permitted. It is essential to look these up in the zoning ordinance, so that you may make sure there is enough room to build the type of home you contemplate.

In cities, the divisions are usually in blocks, composed of lots. Usually building is permitted right to the lot lines although there are exceptions. In San Francisco, for instance, there is a requirement for a minimum of a one inch space between all building.

Make sure that you not only learn the zoning of the land you are interested in, but also where the zone boundaries are in relation to that land, and what the adjacent zoning is.

A fellow once bought a building lot in a subdivision adjacent to a large tract of undeveloped land. He thought he would enjoy lovely woods in his back yard forever. Several years later, when he heard that an apartment complex was proposed for the vacant land, and a large building would be only a hundred feet from his rear boundary, he was shocked. He couldn't believe that this beautiful wooded area, which he had enjoyed for so long, and on which he paid no taxes, was going to be taken away from him. What did he do? Why of course he did what every red blooded American suburbanite would do, he organized his neighbors, and they descended en masse, on the local planning board to oppose the development.

This reaction does nothing but cause expense, delay, anger and hard feelings for all parties involved. If the zoning on the adjacent parcel remained the same since the fellow bought his lot, the courts hold, that he knew, or should have known, the zoning of the adjacent parcel, and should have expected it to eventually be developed accordingly.

RULE NUMBER 5

THE LAST MAN IN TOWN ALWAYS WANTS TO BE THE LAST MAN IN TOWN.

People who relocate to a new area by taking advantage of development already done in that area, thereafter oppose any further development of the same kind.

If you attend a planning board public hearing on a proposed new sub-division you will hear over and over the following plaint. "We moved to this area because of it's quiet and rural atmosphere. If this development is permitted there will be overcrowding in the schools, too much traffic on the roads, depletion of the water table, and pollution of existing water supplies." What these people are saying, is that an owner of land should not be permitted to develop his land, even though the ordinance allows it, because the one who owned the land next to him, did it first. However, he should still own the land, and pay the taxes, so the neighbors may continue to enjoy it as free scenery. What is amazing, is the absolute sincerity, and belief in the justice of their position, these people display.

They have also learned that a good way to oppose a project is on environmental grounds. They suddenly become nature lovers as they never were before, and wear on their faces an expression of self righteous devout belief in this new higher calling.

Frequently, local boards bowing to the pressure of the opposition, deny a proposed development even though it meets all the legal requirements, unless of course, the developer, is a member in good standing, of the local "Old Boy Network."

If the developer is not "one of the boys" he must go to State court, in which after great expense, and years of delay, he will doubtless prevail.

RULE NUMBER 6

LEARN ABOUT ADJACENT ZONING.

If you buy land adjacent to, or near land zoned for another purpose which is undesirable to you, you must assume that eventually that land will be developed for that purpose, and you will have no legitimate complaint.

If you want to build, and have seclusion and total privacy, then you must buy enough acreage to buffer against future development.

FLOOD PLAINS

If the land you are considering is anywhere near a stream, a brook, a lake, a river, or salt water estuaries, marshes, bays, sounds, or the ocean front, it is essential that you know whether it is in a flood plain, or tidal plain.

Often building is permitted in these areas but there are special requirements concerning what you build, and how you build it, particularly with respect to the elevation of the ground floor and the elevation of the lowest opening in the structure.

Since the disastrous floods in the mid west in 1993, many locales will be reconsidering their flood plain rules. THE FEDERAL EMERGENCY MANAGEMENT AGENCY has prepared official flood plain maps of the entire country. These are usually referred to as FEMA maps. The Town Clerk, Zoning Administrator, or Building Inspector's office of the community in which the land you are considering is located, have these maps. Examine them, and determine whether the land is in a flood plain. Remember that these maps are to the scale of a thousand feet to the inch. The thickness of a pencil line can be ten to twenty feet. Unless there are compelling reasons, if the land is in a flood plain, my best advice is to look for another site.

Trying to build in a flood plain is tricky business which should be left to the experienced professional. However, you may be considering a larger parcel, which has a stream or brook on it. There may be a flood plain area along the brook, but most of the land is not in a flood plain, and has suitable building locations. You still must tread carefully.

If you are considering obtaining a mortgage in order to build, when you apply to a bank, they will send an appraiser to look at the land. If there is any water on the site, or near the site, the appraiser will request a flood plain report. This report is obtained usually, from a private reporting company which specializes in examining and interpreting, FEMA maps.

Although you may think the proposed building location is not in the flood plain, the reporting company may say it is. Even if you send them actual survey data showing the site is not in a flood plain, if it is a close call, they will protect themselves, and say it is. Then the bank will require you to obtain flood insurance. This is difficult and costly to obtain. Engineering and survey information is required by FEMA which is the insurer.

If the field survey shows that the building site is not in the flood plain you may be faced with a further dilemma. The bank will not waive the insurance requirement unless you can get the reporting agency to amend it's report. Rather than amend their report, they will tell you to get a finding from FEMA. That means you will have to go to FEMA and get them to verify that your building site is truly not in a flood plain. Dealing with a federal agency can involve endless red tape, delay, and expense. If the reporting company says that the site is in a flood plain, but your detailed survey data shows that it is not, you are in a further pickle. You won't be able to get the flood insurance because you can't show that the site is actually in a flood plain. A real catch 22.

RULE NUMBER 7

BEWARE FLOOD PLAINS.

If you are buying land, and there is any question about a flood plain, make sure your contract provides for cancellation if your chosen lending institution requires you to obtain flood insurance to build the house on the land in the location you want. You must also check for special requirements in the local building ordinance. You should check with the State Environmental Protection Agency for any special permit requirements.

Similarly, if you are considering ocean or beach front property, be very, very careful. Do not proceed without guidance from a Professional Engineer.

WETLANDS

Wetlands can be another dangerous pitfall. If there are any wet areas, ponds or swamps on or near the land you are considering, you must check it out carefully.

State environmental agencies have prepared wetland maps of all the state land. Copies of these maps should be available for your inspection in the local Zoning or Building Office. If they are not, you will have to enquire of the state environmental agency. If there is a designated wet land area, you may not build in it, and it may require special permits to be allowed to build within a certain distance from it.

Most states designate wetlands that are larger than a certain minimum size. If they are designated, they will appear on the wetland maps with a reference letter and/or number. Sometimes the local authority has designated smaller areas, not designated by the State, as local wetlands. You must check this out with the local Zoning and Building Office.

Concerning the seashore, the State may also have designated certain protected areas in which building is limited or forbidden entirely. The famous Lucas case in South Carolina, after five years of litigation, was decided in July 1993. Mr. Lucas owned two beach front lots. When he wanted to build on them he found that the state had passed an environmental law forbidding construction that close to the ocean. The fifth amendment in the U.S. Constitution states that private property shall not be taken for public use without compensation. The restrictions on the land, obviating any useful purpose, was viewed by the court as "a taking" of private property, even though the ownership of the property remained with Mr. Lucas. Mr. Lucas was awarded 1.5 million dollars, and the State received the property.

The incredible ending is that once the State owned the property they then sold it for development purposes. Arguing that the fact that there is a house on either side, and in between the lots, makes it logical, to use the land for development. How do you like that one?

Unless you inherited the land, or bought it years before at a cheap price, avoid these problems like the plague. Look elsewhere!

DEED RESTRICTIONS

When a developer buys a large parcel of raw land, and creates a subdivision, it means that in accordance with the zoning ordinance, and with the approval of the local Planning Board, and sometimes the Zoning Board, or the Town Board, he has laid out streets on the land, and created building lots fronting along the streets. He is also responsible for having the utilities installed in the roadway, and performing the preliminary and final paving of the roads.

In order to protect the saleability of the individual lots, the developer will usually create deed restrictions. These are rules recited in the deed, or incorporated in the deed by reference to a certain filed document, enumerating the restrictions that are to apply to all of the lots in the subdivision.

If a purchaser buys a lot in the subdivision, especially early in the development, and intends to build let's say, a 2500 square foot house, he does not want to later on, find that someone buys the lot next to him and builds a 1000 square foot house of much less value. In order to prevent this problem, and others like it, the developer establishes deed restrictions. Usually they will require the construction of a house of not less than a minimum number of square feet. Sometimes the number of stories is prescribed. On occasion, if the developer is trying to market, say a community of early American architecture, the deed restrictions will also restrict the type of materials to be used on the exterior, and even some of the architectural features.

Other restrictions will be for the purpose of preventing nuisance behavior, such as loud music blaring from a window, or repairing a truck in the driveway, hanging wash on an outside line, or harboring certain animals. Frequently, the number, size and/or weight of pets is limited.

RULE NUMBER 8

WHEN BUYING LAND YOU MUST READ THE PRIOR DEED WITH YOUR OWN EYES.

If there are deed restrictions, they will be recited in the deed, or the deed will refer to another filed document.

Once I contracted to design and build a unique contemporary house which was to go on a lot the client had just purchased. A few days after we started the job, the man who owned the neighboring house, came over and engaged me in conversation. He was interested in knowing what kind of a house was going up, and what the people were like. When I mentioned that the house would be 1500 square feet, he asked me if I knew that there were deed restrictions on the lots in that development, which required a minimum of 2000 square feet. I told him that I didn't know about it and that I was sure my client didn't know it either.

I called my client and he became very upset because his lawyer, who handled his purchase, had never told him about any deed restrictions. He called the lawyer and asked him about the problem. The lawyer said, "Wait a minute let me look in the file." Shortly he said, "Oh yes, there are deed restrictions, didn't I ever tell you about them?"

The upshot was, that we had to redesign the house, making it larger, to comply with the deed restrictions, and the client had to apply for a mortgage all over again. Fortunately he could afford the additional cost, otherwise he might have found that he bought a lot on which he could not afford to build.

EASEMENTS

An easement is the right of someone, who is not the owner of a piece of land, to use that land for a specific purpose.

Usually an easement is created by agreement between the owner of the land, and someone else. Such easements are recorded, and either recited in the deed, or referenced in the deed.

It is not uncommon for an owner to grant to another abutting owner the right to pass over his property for access to the second owners land.

The easement may be general or created over a specific surveyed route.

When a property owner has an easement across the land of another for access, he does not automatically have the right to install utilities through the easement. It must be specified.

Easements may run with the land, that is, remain in effect no matter who owns the land, or they may run for a specific term, or for the use of a specific person.

Frequently in development land, there are easements created to allow utility companies to install facilities either over or under the land. Drainage easements may be created to allow the passage of drainage from a road across the intervening land to a stream. Drainage easements are usually created on the property line between two lots so as not to restrict the use of the lot. Often a drainage easement will require that the drainage be piped underground for a specified distance back from the road. In subdivisions it is common, to create a general easement, allowing drainage from any lot, to run on any other lot. This is to preclude arguments between adjacent lot owners, over a question of whether the water from one persons lot is running on to another's.

Easements may also be created in another way, without being in writing. These are called easements by prescription, usage or adverse possession. If a person uses the land of another openly, so as to be seen by all, exclusively, in the sense that he is the only one engaging in the particular use, and continuously, without interruption for a statutory period of time, usually between ten and twenty years, an easement right has been acquired.

When Rockerfeller Center was built in New York City, some of the land was used for a street which is one block long, and runs between buildings. In order for this street to remain privately owned, and not become a public thoroughfare by usage, once a year, the street is barricaded and no traffic is permitted, in order that the usage is not continuous.

In another famous case, a man who owned a news stand near the corner of a vacant lot, used the lot every day, as a short cut to his news stand. When eventually a large sky scraper was proposed, which would take in the small vacant lot, the news stand owner claimed that he had an easement right across the vacant land, which he had been using openly and continuously for more than twenty years.

The entire immense project was brought to a standstill, while the land owner tried to get the news stand owner to back off. But he refused money, and stood adamantly upon his right. Eventually someone had a bright idea. They offered to build the man a new news stand, inside the lobby of the new building, where he would be in out of the weather and could still follow the same route to work inside the building. The news stand owner was so pleased by the idea that he could continue his business inside in comfort. and out of the weather, that he happily agreed, and the project was able to go forward.

When following Rule 8, "Read the deed with your own eyes", if a formal easement has been granted, it will be recited or referenced in the deed. The possibility of an easement by prescription or usage, can usually be discovered by examination of the property itself. If roads, paths, storage areas, hunting shacks, and the like are discovered, they should be further investigated to determine whether an easement by prescription has been created.

LAND TAXES

While visiting the City or Town Hall gathering information, it would also be useful to drop in at the Tax Assessor's office. If you can tell them an approximate size and cost of your proposed home, they can give you an estimate of your probable real estate taxes, and tell you what services, you may expect to receive, in return.

ACCESS AND TRAVEL

The first thing you did when we began was to buy a local map. As you have been moving about you've begun to get a feel for the local roads and streets. If you will be commuting, ask where the nearest railroad station is. Go there and find out about schedules for trains you are likely to use. It's also a good idea to check that the parking facilities at the station are adequate. You don't want a surprise, the first time you show up in the morning to take the train, to find that the parking lots are full, and you have to cruise around the local streets trying to find a space and avoid a ticket.

If you travel a lot, find out where the nearest major airport is, and how long it takes to get there. Check on feeder lines and limo services, as well.

If you plan to commute by car, there is nothing better, than to drive the commuting route, at the time you usually would be going. This will give you a good idea of traffic conditions, and the time it will take you, to get to work.

SCHOOLS

If you are planning to have children, or already have children of school age, the local school system will be of prime importance to you. Usually in areas where the education level of the population is high, such as you might find where hi-tech business is located, or where educational or medical facilities are prominent, parents take a more active interest in their school system. They demand, and get, good schools and facilities, and are willing to pay for them. In these areas therefor, you can expect higher school taxes.

I am a great believer in seeing things with my own eyes, whenever possible. I recommend calling the local school district office, and asking for information and an inspection tour, of the schools your children are likely to attend. There is nothing like first hand information.

If you are distant from the area you are considering, go to your public library and ask to see a book titled, PUBLIC SCHOOLS USA, A comparative guide to school districts, 2nd Edition published by PETERSON'S GUIDES, and you will find useful information.

HOSPITALS AND MEDICAL SERVICES

This is always an area of interest, especially if older people are in the household. Look in the local Yellow Pages. There is usually a section listing medical practitioners by specialty. See if there are doctors specializing in the areas of your concern. Check where they are located, and how much traveling is involved to use their services. Do the same for hospitals. The Yellow Pages will list the nearest ones.

Again, seeing with your own eyes has no substitute. Drive to the nearest hospital and look it over. Check the building, and it's maintenance. Ask to see a list of the affiliated doctors and their specialties. Ask about diagnostic equipment. Do they have a CAT scan? Can they do an MRI? Do they have laser equipment? Do they have a kidney unit? You might want to check out the maternity facilities. Above all, don't be bashful. Ask questions. Most people are more than happy to answer you, and are flattered by your interest in what they do.

It's also a good idea to inquire about ambulance services. Some communities run their own local services. Hospitals run their own, and there are usually private ambulances as well.

POLICE AND SAFETY

If you want to know about the crime level in an area, the best thing is to go to the local police station, and ask about home security recommendations. This is a good way to start a conversation about crime in the area. Once again, personal enquiry, will usually obtain plenty of good information.

It is also worth while to understand the local police structure and jurisdictions. Municipalities, usually have their own police force. Many Townships, also have some local police. In some locales, the County Sheriff's Department is the main agency. In all areas, there is always back up by the State Police. Of course, it's always a good idea to get all the pertinent phone numbers. You should also inquire, whether the locality has a 911 emergency service operating.

RECREATION

Recreation facilities are usually provided by all the political divisions, City, Town, County and State. The local Chamber of Commerce is a good source of information in this area. They will have pamphlets describing the local cultural interests, historic sites, state parks, camping and boating facilities, parks, beaches, golf courses etc.

Once again the yellow pages will yield information about the availability of gyms, health clubs, tennis courts etc.

FIRE PROTECTION

POLITICAL AND SOCIAL CONSIDERATIONS

While you are checking out the bureaucracy, it's important to learn the facts about fire protection. Is there a municipally supported fire department or is it a volunteer department? Is a crew always on duty or is it strictly on call? The following factors will affect the cost of your fire insurance: How far from your property is it to the nearest fire house? Are there fire hydrants? If there are no hydrants, how far is it to the nearest, lake, pond or stream from which water could be pumped? This must be close enough for the hoses to reach.

If you are planning to build in the country, it is a good idea to check the availability of a water source in case of fire.

THE TELEPHONE BOOK

Today, the telephone book offers a lot of information besides phone numbers. My telephone book has a special section called "The Blue Pages", which gives all government information. It lists the location and number of City, Town, County, and Federal agencies by section.

My phone book also has another section called the "Community Pages". Here's what's listed:.

Historical sites and landmarks.
Educational and cultural sites.
Galleries.
Arts and Theaters.
State Parks.
Local parks and recreational areas.
Camping.
Boating.
Golf courses.
Shopping malls and districts.
Transportation including:
    Airports,
    Rail lines
    Bus facilities.

ARCHITECTURAL REVIEW

Some communities have a requirement for architectural review before a building permit is issued. The community may be trying to maintain a particular historical appearance, and will want new construction to conform to special characteristics. It would be a grievous error to purchase a piece of land on which you intend to build a contemporary home to find that only early American designs will be approved.

The historical look is becoming more and more important to many communities. In New England the look may be that of a whaling village, or a colonial town with brick sidewalks and gas lights.

In the south west, adobe construction might be the desired style. Make sure whether or not there are any local architectural requirements before starting the design process.

CHAPTER 3

WATER SUPPLY AND SEWAGE DISPOSAL

WATER SUPPLY

Nothing is more crucial to the viability of any building site, than a reliable source of potable water. This must be carefully investigated before any land purchase is finalized.

In rural areas, it may still be possible to draw good water from a stream or lake. However in any city or suburban area, the water supply must be approved. by the local Board of Health. Even if the local Board of Health does not have this requirement, when a mortgage is being obtained, the lending institution, before closing and finalizing any mortgage, will require proof of potable water. This is usually a coliform test performed by a qualified laboratory or the Board of Health.

In cities and many suburban areas there is a public water system. In evaluating a lot, being told by the broker that the lot has "water and sewer" is not enough. There may be pitfalls. Most lot buyers don't know what to ask and assume that a normal situation exists which will be learned when a plumber is hired to install the water service.

In subdivisions which are to be served by public water supply, the developer is responsible for the installation of the water mains in the roads. He is also responsible for the installation of the "laterals". A lateral is a line which connects to the main in the street, and runs laterally into the property, ending in what is usually called a curb box. A curb box is nothing more than a valve for turning the water on and off, which is buried below the frost line. These curb boxes are required to be appropriately marked. This is usually done with a post which is on the valve, and protrudes several feet above ground. The top of the post is painted blue to indicate water. This marks the point from which you will run your water line to the house.

WATER SUPPLY AND SEWAGE DISPOSAL

At a certain point in the development, after the water lines have been installed, and the roads paved, the roads are dedicated to the City or Town. That means the land under the roads and the improvements, become owned by the public entity.

Sometimes during the installation of the water lines, the contractor doing the work fails to install all the laterals. This frequently occurs near the end of dead end roads. This kind of cheating is not uncommon, and may not be discovered by the developer or the inspecting authority.

Here's what can happen that nobody wants to tell you!

I purchased a building lot in a subdivision, where the development map showed there were water and sewer laterals installed into the lot, about ten feet past the property line. There weren't any markers for the laterals, but because the development was six or seven years old, I assumed that they had just rotted out or were knocked over. When we were ready to install the water line to the house, I had a backhoe dig in the place where the map showed the water lateral to be. After a half day of work we had not been able to find either the water or the sewer lateral. I instructed the back hoe operator to start at one side of the lot and dig a continuous trench across the entire front of the lot. The trench was at the outer edge of the lot right next to the edge of the black top road. Doing this, I felt sure that the laterals would be found, as perhaps they were not extended into the lot as the plans showed. After another half day of digging no laterals were found, and I was forced to conclude that they had never been installed.

When the water mains and laterals are installed by the developer, it is required that the work be inspected and tested before backfilling of the trenches. The inspection is made either by the Board of Health, or the Building Department. This is done in anticipation of the fact, that eventually the roads and the water system will become the property of the Town, and that thereafter they would be a Town responsibility. Obviously in this case someone had failed to do their job properly.

When I could not find the laterals, I called the Town Building Department and requested that the Town install the laterals which were missing, and which were their responsibility.

The Town Engineer came to the site and verified that the laterals were missing. He then told me that the Town would not install the laterals, and that if I wanted them, I would have to install them myself. My only other option, was to sue the Town, a matter which could take a long time to conclude, and which could cost more in legal fees than the cost of installing the laterals.

I had to obtain a special permit to open the street, and also post a bond for the repair of the black top paving. When I was done, I had spent about five hundred dollars on wasted backhoe digging, and another fifteen hundred for permits, digging, connecting to the main under pressure, and repairing the road. On a house that was selling then for about $50,000.00, the additional $2,000.00 expense put a huge dent in my profit margin.

RULE NUMBER 9

WHEN BUYING A BUILDING LOT THAT IS SUPPOSED TO HAVE UTILITY LATERALS, ALWAYS PROVIDE IN THE CONTRACT, THAT IF THE LATERALS DON'T EXIST, THE SELLER MUST PAY FOR THE COST OF THEIR INSTALLATION.

When a broker tells you that a lot has water and sewer, he doesn't want to tell you what you might have to do to connect to them. It is also possible that the Town might have a moratorium on hooking into the system due to overload on existing capacity. Make sure this is not the case before buying the lot.

WELL DRILLING

If there is no public water supply, you will have to drill a well. Availability of sub surface water varies greatly across the country. The best thing to do is to talk to local well drillers who have drilled wells nearby, and who have a general idea of what will be necessary at your particular site. It's also a good idea to talk to people living near by, and find out what kind of well they have, how deep it is, and how good the water is.

In the Northeast, the underlying land is composed of stratified rock of various types. Although areas can be found on the land particularly where a spring is evident, and a shallow well can be dug, as was done by our ancestors, today because of all the chemical pollutants which abound, water supplies taken from bodies of water at or near the surface, are no longer considered safe. Such a water supply may not be permitted by the Board of Health having jurisdiction, unless expensive purification facilities are installed.

One alternative is to drill an artesian well. This type of well is a hole, usually six inches in diameter, which is drilled down through the underground rock strata.

There are extensive fissures and crevices, which run horizontally between the layers of the stratified rock. Water runs through these fissures, and as the well cavity passes through, a little of the water running through each strata will seep into the well.

The well is drilled deeper and deeper, penetrating more and more water bearing strata, until the cumulative seepage adds up to a satisfactory water supply. It is desirable that this supply be able to maintain a continuous flow of at least five gallons per minute.

Usually in an area, there is a typical depth, where most of the water laden veins are located, and wells on adjacent lots will be approximately the same depth. Of course this is not guaranteed; there are exceptions. The veins may slope upward or downward.

Because of the abundance of subsurface water in this kind of area, the well location is usually chosen for convenience, rather than by any judgment of which is a better or poorer spot to find water.

Modern well drilling equipment consists of a drilling tower which is carried horizontally on a large truck, and which is erected to an upright position at the location of the well. The tower holds the drilling motor which rotates a shaft, and hammers at the same time.

The drill bit, which is the same type used in drilling oil wells, called a rotary bit, is threaded onto the shaft of the drilling motor. Usually an 8" bit is used to start. The bit is lowered to the ground and rotated, starting the hole. Initially the bit is held in place by a steel collar. The bit is rotated and hammered until the motor can be lowered no further in the tower.

The bit is held in place and the motor shaft is unscrewed from it. The motor traverses to a rack holding a series of twenty foot long drill rods. It screws to the top of a rod, and then traverses back over the bit and screws the bottom of the rod onto the bit. The drill motor is now at the top of the tower with a twenty foot long drill rod hanging down and connected at the bottom to the bit.

The drill motor can now be made to rotate and hammer again, drilling the bit with the twenty foot extension into the ground until the motor is at the bottom of the tower again. The process is repeated, and twenty foot long extensions continue to be added as the bit drills deeper and deeper.

Initially, the bit is drilling through soft material; top soil, sub soil, gravel, clay etc. until the bed rock is reached. The drill is then withdrawn from the ground by reversing the process of adding the rods. A hollow steel pipe, called the casing, is lowered into the hole and seated into the bed rock. The joint into the rock is sealed with cement. The casing keeps the soft material at the top of the hole from collapsing into the well. The casing is sealed into the rock, so that any seepage down through the soft material from the surface, cannot enter, and contaminate the well.

After the casing is set, a smaller 6" drill, that fits inside the casing, is lowered down to the rock. The drilling is then started again, adding drill rods as the well goes deeper. As the drill rotates, water and compressed air are pumped down into the well through the center of the rods. The water acts as a lubricant for the bit as it grinds away the rock. The compressed air blows the resultant mud and grit to the surface, emptying the hole of the ground up material.

The well driller keeps a log as he drills. He notes in the log, the rods as they are added, and the type and nature of the material coming to the surface from the successive depths. When the water coming out at the top of the casing, seems to be more than the amount being pumped down, the driller will test the well.

The test is done in an unsophisticated but very effective manner. The driller, using a shovel, will make a dam around the casing so as to contain the water coming out of the top. He will place a small length of pipe through the top edge of the dam, so that the water will run out of the dammed area through the pipe. He will then put a one gallon container under the outlet of the pipe, and time how many seconds it takes to fill the container. Dividing that resultant time into sixty, yields the approximate gallons per minute flow.

As the well is being drilled there are judgments to be made in terms of the cost of drilling, against water acquired. The cost of drilling a well, is based on a fixed price per foot which may be greater or lesser, depending on the type of rock being drilled. The drill bits are expensive, and wear out after a certain amount of drilling. The bit wears faster in hard granite for example, than it would in softer shale. Consequently, the per foot price for drilling in granite is higher. The casing installed, is also charged for by the foot.

Example:

A well is 200 feet deep. Water was first acquired at 150 ft. By 200 ft. there is a three gal./min. flow. It appears that in another 50 ft. the desired 5 gal./min. will be achieved. At 250 ft., 5 gal is achieved.

Question:

Should the drilling continue?

Answer:

As acquisition has been regular, there is a good chance that if another twenty foot rod is drilled in, a safety margin may be achieved. In times of drought, the water table may lower, and the well flow may lessen. It is good to have the extra flow, and under ordinary conditions it's worth while to invest in the extra drilling.

Example:

A little water was acquired at 100 ft. No more was hit until 220 ft., when another 1 gal/min. was obtained. The well is now at 360 ft., and there is 3 gal/min.

Question:

What to do?

Answer:

It might take a couple of hundred feet more to get 5 gall min., or it might not be obtained at all. At this point the drilling is stopped and the rods are pulled. The water will rise in the well because of the underground static pressure. The water rises to 40 ft. from the top. That means that there is a column of water in the well, 320 feet high. The well holds about one and a half gallons of water to the foot, so there are 480 gallons of water stored in the well. This storage can be used as a reserve.

Let's say we are using water at the rate of 5 gal/min., which is about the full flow of a garden hose. If the well gains 3 gal/min., there is a deficit of 2 gal/min., which will gradually lower the level in the well. In three hours, 360 gallons which was stored in the well, will be used up, and the pumping should be stopped. A well should never be emptied to the bottom, because mud and silt which has deposited at the bottom of the well becomes stirred up, and the water will be muddy for a day or more.

The well can sustain a flow of 5 gal/min. for three hours, which is much more than ordinary household usage. If water is used to sprinkle the lawn, a cycle of two hours on and two hours off would be recommended. The decision then, is not to drill any deeper.

Example:

The drill has reached a depth of 360 ft. and no water has been acquired.

Question:

What to do?

Answer:

One option is to pull the drill out and start in another location. If you do that, you will have spent over $2000.00 on a dry hole in the ground which is of no use. It is more likely than not, that if you drill a second hole it will go to the same depth as the first one without hitting water.

On the other hand, if you keep drilling the first well, the water might only be down another ten feet. The odds are in favor of continuing the drilling.

RULE NUMBER 10

BE PRESENT DURING THE DRILLING OF THE WELL, SO THAT YOU CAN PARTICIPATE IN THE DECISIONS, AND UNDERSTAND HOW THE FINAL DEPTH WAS DETERMINED.

By and large, well drillers are honest. However, there is that occasional one, who will rip you off, and charge you for drilling deeper than he actually did. He may cheat on the amount of casing as well. If you were present you saw how much casing was put in. If you are present when the drilling is finished, you need only to count the drill rods as they are removed from the well. Each rod is twenty feet long. Add ten feet more for the length of the bit, and you will know the depth of the well, and how much you should be charged for.

WELL POINTS

In other parts of the country, there may be a known water table below the ground, sufficiently shallow that a well may be made by driving a point rather than drilling. A point is a special pipe with a pointed steel tip and protected screens on the side. The point is usually screwed on to the end of two inch pipe and hammered into the ground. Lengths can be added in the same fashion as described for drilling. Water can be pumped right out of a water table in this fashion, when the sub surface material holding the water (the aquifer) is very porous. In other areas, there might not be an underground aquifer, but rather, the water may run under the ground in veins like streams.

DIVINING

In such cases it is necessary to divine the location of the underground water. There is sophisticated electronic equipment which can locate underground water, by measuring minute changes in the electrical magnetic field of the ground. There is also the option of hiring the services of a "Water diviner". This is a person, who has the ability to locate underground water by holding some object or device in their hands. The traditional device is a forked branch cut from a fruit bearing tree. Cherry branches are popular for this purpose. One branch of the fork is held in each hand with the joined part pointing forward. The diviner walks back and forth over the search area. When over water, the forked branch rotates in the hands of the diviner, and the common end points downward. This is an unexplained phenomenon, but good diviners have a remarkable success rate. Some diviners use other objects instead of a forked branch. There is a successful diviner in England who uses a pair of pliers. Some diviners use pieces of metal or wire, and other unusual materials that they have found to work for them.

I can remember as a child eight or nine years old, visiting an uncle's farm with my family. My uncle had just dug a new well, and had located the water by divining. A discussion about divining ensued and we all went outside to try our hand. I can remember vividly, walking forward with the wye of a forked cherry branch grasped tightly in my hands. I was astonished when the branch began to twist downward pointing at the ground. I held with all my might but the branch nevertheless turned, even twisting off the bark. My uncle confirmed that I was actually standing over the area where he had found water.

Many years later, I learned another method of divining. With this method I was regularly able to locate buried water mains and laterals. Here's how to do it. Straighten two wire coat hangers, and cut two straight lengths of wire, each about two feet long. Bend one end of each rod to a ninety degree angle so the bent part is about four inches long. Grasp a four inch end in each hand, and hold the rods in front of you pointing forward just as you would hold a pair of guns. The extended rods should be parallel. The wire is so thin that it will rotate freely in your hands.

Don't try to grip so tightly that the wires can't turn. Now walk forward slowly over your test area with the wires extended forward and parallel. If the wires, without your controlling them, turn inward toward each other and cross, you will be directly above water. It never failed for me, maybe it will work for you.

WATER QUALITY

The quality of water obtained from wells will vary greatly, but it is a certainty that it will contain dissolved minerals. This is called "hard water". There is water softening equipment, which can remove most of the dissolved minerals, especially calcium, and soften the water. The water softening equipment people will be glad to test your water to determine the degree of hardness.

Sometimes well water will contain sulfur. When you turn the water on it smells like rotten eggs. This may be unpleasant, but it is not unhealthy.

WATER SOFTENING

Many people do not have their water softened, because they believe the dissolved minerals in the water are beneficial, and give the water a good taste. Hard water will not lather soap nearly as well as soft water, and tends to form residues with detergents. The minerals in hard water over time, may deposit in the water pipes eventually clogging them.

When water is supplied by a public water system, the water is usually soft because it is drawn from reservoirs which collect rain water. Sometimes the water supplied by a public system will be drawn from a river. This water will also tend to be soft.

Some public water systems do draw water from wells, and in this case the water will be hard. In all cases of a public water system, the water will be chlorinated, to control a bacteria called E. Colli, which results from sewage, and can be a contaminant that finds its way into the water supply. Chlorination of public water systems is usually required by law.

When drilling a well in areas that use sub surface sewage disposal, it is always necessary to test the water for E. Colli. This can be done by taking a sample to a local laboratory, or Board of Health. As mentioned earlier, the lending institution providing the mortgage will require a satisfactory water test before closing the loan.

SEWAGE DISPOSAL

This is another very important consideration which pertains directly to the particular building site chosen. If there is a public sewer system to which you may attach your sewer line, the matter is much simpler. Remember to check with the sewer district to make sure there is no moratorium on connecting to the sewer system due to overloading at the sewage plant.

Don't forget RULE 9, which pertains to sewer connections as well as water connections.

When connecting a house sewer outlet to the public system, it is desirable that the line run down hill to the point of connection, so that a gravity flow is maintained. The sewer line should have a downward pitch of 1/4" inch to the running foot.

If you are planning to have a basement below the exterior grade, and if you also plan to have plumbing facilities in the basement, make sure that you will have sufficient pitch. If it appears that sufficient pitch is not obtainable without raising the house elevation too high, you will have to use a sewage pump up system. This will add to your construction costs, and future maintenance costs. If the pump goes out of order, or there is a power failure, and you continue to use water, your sewer line will back up. This is a messy business.

If you are purchasing a building lot in a subdivision, that does not have connection to public water and sewer systems, the broker may assure you that the lot is "Board of Health Approved" for a well and septic system. Most people accept that statement as some kind of guarantee that there will be no problem with water and sewer provisions.

What they might not want to tell you for example, is that the wells already drilled in the subdivision, went seven hundred feet deep to reach water, or that the absorption of the soil is very poor, and the septic system that is required is large and expensive.

Once a client came to me to discuss building a home on a lot that he had purchased. We had a number of meetings and arrived at a concept for the house, and a budget cost. I asked if he had a copy of the subdivision map so that I could see what the septic system consisted of. He said he didn't have a copy of the map, but that it was no problem because the broker had assured him that the lot was "Board of Health approved."

I obtained a copy of the map from the County Clerk's office, and examined the septic requirements. The absorption of the soil was so poor that a maximum system was called for. This system would cost about $10,000.00 to build, compared to an average cost at that time, of $2,000.00. When I told the client, he was devastated.

He could not qualify financially for a larger mortgage to cover the additional cost, and as a result he was forced to abandon the idea of building a house. It was a case where he had bought a lot he couldn't afford to build on.

The problem resulted from not knowing the right questions to ask.

RULE NUMBER 11

WHEN YOU ARE TOLD THAT A LOT IS BOARD OF HEALTH APPROVED, MAKE SURE THAT YOU FIND OUT WHAT KIND OF SYSTEM THE APPROVAL REQUIRES AND HOW MUCH IT WILL COST.

Just to say Board of Health approved, is saying very little. Remember when there is bad news, those doing the selling aren't going to tell you.

If you are proposing to buy land that has not been Board of Health approved for a septic system, you should have it done, and know what your sewage disposal system is going to cost before committing to buy the land. Before getting into the testing and design of a system let's look at a typical septic system and see exactly what it is.

SEPTIC SYSTEMS

A Septic system consists of three main elements, the tank, the distribution box, and the fields. A septic tank is a large concrete box, with an inlet hole near the top at one end, and an outlet hole a few inches lower at the other end. Inside the tank are baffles which prevent liquid from flowing directly from the inlet to the outlet. The theory of a septic tank is that it traps solid material, preventing it from flowing out of the tank, so that it will decompose by action of natural bacteria which are normally present. When the material has decomposed to a liquid it is able to flow under the baffles, and through the outlet. It is conducted through a 4" diameter plastic pipe to a distribution box.

The distribution box is a concrete box about two feet square and a foot high. It has an inlet hole and a series of outlet holes all at the same height, but lower than the inlet.

The idea is, that when liquid flows into the distribution box it will reach the level of all the outlet holes at the same time, thus dividing the liquid outflow equally between the outlets.

The outlet holes in the distribution box, are connected to a series of plastic perforated pipes which run under the ground in parallel rows about six feet apart. These pipes are what is referred to as the fields. They are for the purpose of distributing the effluent (the out flowing liquid) over a certain area of the ground where it will be absorbed naturally. The pipes are laid level in a trench two feet wide, and about two feet below the ground surface. Under the pipes is a bed, six inches deep, of 1" diameter stone. Another three inches of stone is placed over the pipes and then the trenches are filled in with the material that was removed. A layer of heavy rosin paper or hay is placed over the stone before backfilling. This is to prevent the earth from filtering down between the stones.

When sewage material enters the tank it displaces an equal volume of effluent which flows out of the tank to the distribution box. It is divided at the distribution box, equally between the lines of the field. It flows through the perforated pipes in the field trenches. The perforations in the pipes are not directly on the bottom but approximately 60 degrees from the perpendicular, or in an eight o'clock and four o'clock position. This enables the liquid to run the full length of the pipe, distributing evenly in the trench rather than running out at the beginning of the pipe. The object is to distribute the liquid evenly over the soil area of the fields, thus maximizing the absorption surface. The liquids not only percolate into the soil to the sides and the bottom of the trenches, but by a kind of wicking action, they are also drawn up toward the surface for evaporation. This evaporation is an important component of the system, accounting for about twenty percent of effluent elimination. If the trenches are too deep in the ground the wicking action cannot occur, substantially decreasing the efficiency of the system.

It can be seen therefor, that the area of the fields is relative to the absorption rate of the soil. If the soil contains a lot of clay, and the absorption is poor, it is necessary to spread the effluent over a larger area. If the soil is sandy, and the absorption is good, a smaller area will suffice. The size of the fields is determined by testing the percolation rate of the soil.

A percolation test is easy to perform. Using an ordinary post hole digger, a hole is made in the ground to a depth between twenty four and thirty inches which is the level of the soil below a trench. The hole is filled with water and the water is allowed to percolate into the ground until it is gone. This is called presoaking, and is done so that the test may be performed in soil that is already wet, which would be the case in a functioning system. A wooden stick or lath is taken, and a nail is driven into the wood six inches from the bottom, and another, seven inches from the bottom. The end of the stick holding the nails is then placed into the hole so that the nails are then at heights of six and seven inches above the bottom of the hole. Water is then poured into the hole until it is exactly even with the top nail. A stop watch is started, and the time is measured until the water level has dropped to the bottom nail. We then have the time it takes for the water to percolate down one inch. In very sandy soil the time can be as low as one to five minutes. Average soil would be about twenty minutes, and poor soil would be forty five minutes to an hour.

WATER SUPPLY AND SEWAGE DISPOSAL

Engineers have worked out tables giving the size of fields required for the various percolation rates. The trench length is usually limited to fifty or sixty feet so that the liquid will travel the entire length. The size of the fields required, is then expressed as the number of runs and the maximum length of each run. For example: five runs at sixty feet, or four runs of fifty feet. The runs are usually spaced six feet apart, but sometimes in poorer soil the spaces are made wider.

There is a second criterion which affects the design of a septic field, and that is the depth of absorptive material below the trench. Obviously if the bottom of the trench is on rock, the system will not function properly because of the lack of permeable material to accept and distribute the liquid. Also the depth to water is a concern. If there is a water table just below the septic trenches then the effluent can enter and pollute that table. Engineers have determined that there should be four to five feet of soil below the bottom of the trenches to distribute and filter the effluent.

Thus we have a second test called the deep hole test. This is nothing more than using a backhoe to dig a hole in the ground where it is proposed to locate the septic fields. If rock or water is encountered at a depth of less than seven feet from the surface, the fields must be elevated. Suppose at a depth of five feet we hit bed rock. There will only be three feet of material below the bottom of the trenches which is a foot less than the minimum necessary. Therefor it is required to build a pad one foot high. The pad is a bed of permeable material such as run of bank gravel or sand. In many areas the gravel or sand must be taken from a bank in which the material has been State approved for use in septic systems. If the gravel has too high a clay content it is not approved.

If our system, based on the percolation tests, is required to be four runs of sixty feet each, then allowing a margin, our pad would be twenty four feet by seventy feet.

We must remember that if we elevate the pad we must also elevate the tank accordingly to maintain pitch. There will be one foot less pitch from the house to the tank. If the ground has any down slope the elevation can be accommodated. If the land is level then either the outlet pipe from the house must be elevated or a pump up system is needed.

In addition to rock and water levels being the reason for building a pad, poor soil percolation is also a reason. Where the percolation is very poor a pad five feet deep may be required so that there will be at least three feet of good absorbing material beneath the trenches. Additionally, if the percolation is poor, a larger field will also be required. A maximum system might require ten runs of fifty feet in a five foot deep fill section or pad. This fill pad would be thirty six feet wide by a hundred ten feet long, and then sloped off at a thirty degree angle. This pad would require approximately eight hundred eighty cubic yards of approved fill. If it costs say, eleven dollars a yard to deliver and place the gravel, the pad alone will cost $9600.00. A big difference from a system that does not require fill.

There's more. If we build a five foot high pad, and the trenches are only two feet deep in the pad, the liquid effluent released into the trenches could leak out the sides of the pad, resulting in surface pollution and a very unpleasant odor. To prevent this, an impermeable material is required to be placed on the sloping sides of the pad. This material would be soil with a high clay content. Frequently the native top soil is adequate for this purpose.

If the pad has been built on a down slope, precautions must also be taken to keep drainage running down hill from flowing onto the pad, and water logging the gravel. Obviously, water logged gravel cannot absorb the effluent run into it. The solution to this problem, is to construct what is called a curtain drain around the uphill side of the pad. A curtain drain is a trench, in this case five feet deep, curving around the uphill side of the pad. Perforated pipe is installed in the bottom of the trench and routed out both sides of the trench until reaching daylight on the down hill slope away from the pad. The trench is filled with 1" stone. If water runs down hill or even through the ground, when it reaches the stone in the trench it seeps to the bottom, and is conducted away by the pipes. A curtain drain is sometimes called a French drain.

The placement of a fill pad requires some artistic appreciation for the natural contours of the land so that it may be blended into the existing slopes, and not be obvious. A five foot high mound in the front lawn is not very attractive, and you will tire of answering people who ask, "Who is buried there?"

It is easy to see that according to the various requirements which a septic system may have, the cost of constructing it can vary by thousands of dollars. That is why I said earlier that when the broker tells you the lot is "Board of Health approved", you have not received any meaningful information.

One thing to remember is this: When percolation and deep tests are made pursuant to a subdivision plan, the location of the tests is chosen for the convenience of the testers. If the test results are poor, the system is designed accordingly. Very often if a lot has an expensive septic system, by testing in other spots a better, and therefor cheaper location may be found.

If the house has a basement in the ground, it is usually required that the septic tank be at least ten feet from the foundation, and the fields a minimum of twenty five feet from the foundation. This is to prevent any possible seepage into the basement.

If there is a stream, pond, lake, or any body of water nearby, it is usually required that the fields be a minimum of a hundred feet from the water.

Where there is a well a distance of one hundred feet is required between the well and the fields. If the well is at a lower elevation than the fields the minimum distance is usually two hundred feet.

If there are storm water drains a minimum spacing of twenty five feet is required.

SEPTIC MAINTENANCE

Although there are cases of septic systems which have worked for twenty or twenty five years without failing, these are the exceptions. To prevent septic problems, regular periodic maintenance should be performed.

The solid material put into the septic tank does not decompose totally. Over time, what is called a crust will form at the top of the tank, and sludge accumulates in the bottom of the tank. When there is too much solid material floating at the top of the tank, the entry of more material into the tank may become obstructed. When that happens the sewer line backs up causing a messy overflow inside the house.

When there is too much sludge it begins to get under the baffles in the tank, and flow into the fields. The sludge getting into the fields tends to clog the pores of the soil stopping the percolation. When the fields become saturated so that they cannot accept any more liquid, a back up will occur. When fields become saturated there is no real remedy, although putting muriatic acid into the system through the distribution box, sometimes helps dissolve the sludge. The only permanent remedy is to build new fields in a new location, or excavate out all the saturated and clogged material and replace it with gravel and a new set of pipes and trenches. This can become very expensive, not to mention the inconvenience of not being able to use any water until repairs are completed.

It is recommended that every two, or three years at the most, you have a commercial septic service pump out the septic tank. This will remove any accumulated crust and sludge before damage occurs. It is also recommended to add bacterial agent to the septic tank every six months. This will augment the natural bacteria so that decomposition of the solids will be maintained.

If your washing machine empties into the septic tank, bacteria should be added more often as detergents tend to kill the natural bacteria. The bacterial agent can be purchased at a hardware store, and can be easily added to the tank by flushing it down the toilet in accordance with the manufacturers recommendation on the package.

Usually when installers put in a septic tank they cover over the access hatch with earth. Years later when a failure occurs, nobody remembers exactly where the septic tank and it's access hatch is located. It becomes necessary to bring in a backhoe and dig around until the tank is found and the hatch uncovered. If it is winter time, and the ground is frozen, jack hammers may be needed. Because their tank has not been left accessible, most people don't bother to pump it out until there is a problem. By then it may be too late, and you could be confronted with a major expense to replace the system.

When properly installed the septic tank is not more than a foot or two below the top of the ground. Have the installer or the builder make a wooden box out of pressure treated lumber to fit around the access cover and come up to the final grade level. An inside dimension of two feet square should be adequate. A steel plate may be placed over the box and secured with a few non rusting screws. The cover should be coated with rust inhibiting paint.

It is thereafter an easy matter to open the septic tank for regular inspection and pumping. Lots of people don't pump their tanks because of the cost. It is a lot cheaper to spend about two hundred dollars every two or three years than eventually spend thousands to replace a failed system. With regular maintenance a properly installed septic system should perform indefinitely.

RULE NUMBER 12

MAKE SURE YOUR SEPTIC TANK HAS AN ACCESS HATCH.

Most people don't know where their septic tank is, how it works, or what maintenance is required. Now you will!

CHAPTER 4

SITE TOPOGRAPHY

Nothing is more important to the eventual aesthetic success of building a house than blending the structure to the land in such a way that the natural flow and lines of the land are maintained, and the house looks as though it belongs where it is. Too often, in order to accommodate a particular design, the land is carved, graded, scooped, and filled to fit up to the foundation. The result is always an intrusive look, as though the house was fighting the landscape, often appearing to be sitting up on a mound.

Site blending, as I call it, is more of an art than a science. Those who are good at it, seem to have a feel for the land and how to work with it. If you are willing to put in the time and effort, you can achieve a good understanding of how to work with the land.

It comes back to "RULE 1, DO YOUR HOMEWORK!" You must spend time on the land, walking and seeing (note I said seeing not looking) the characteristics of the land. See how the land slopes, and particularly note the natural drainage patterns. If you look carefully you will be able to tell how the water runs. Of course, sites differ greatly, and any particular characteristic may be very important on one site, and of small importance on another.

DRAINAGE

Drainage is the key to the evaluation. It's pattern indicates the slopes and contours of the land. If the ground is relatively level, the drainage pattern may be hard to see. Types of vegetation can be a clue. A simple rule is, if you see what I call cabbage growth, that is, low leafy vegetation, it is a good indication that water collects there in the rainy season. What appears to be dry land in the summer can easily be very wet land in the spring. You must really keep your eyes open.

A level lot would appear to be a simpler proposition than a sloping lot, but don't be fooled. It may be more difficult to blend the house to the land, and control the drainage, than it is

29

on a lot with a slope where contours can be adapted and blended to the structure, and drainage patterns more easily redirected.

SITE TOPOGRAPHY

Many years ago I knew a young architect who had been working for a commercial builder as a project manager. He had never practiced full time as an architect. However, he was doing well and decided to build himself a home. He acquired a five acre level, wooded site, and designed a beautiful stucco contemporary home. The building had rounded corners, tubular columns, and high ceilings, with lots of glass. It was attractive and impressive.

He started work in the summer, and by fall the structure was erected, and interior finishing was beginning. For the first time since the job started, there was a heavy and prolonged rainfall. When he came to the site the next morning, he was shocked to find that the first floor slab was under six inches of water.

What he had forgotten to do, was to evaluate the drainage, not only of his own lot, but also of abutting lots. The land was quite wooded and it was difficult to see that the location he had chosen to situate the house, was actually the low point in a very shallow depression about ten acres in size. He forgot to evaluate site drainage, and plan land slopes for the total site. It is a basic rule in home building that the ground around a house should slope away from the foundation for at least thirty feet on all sides. He did this, but failed to notice that his whole site was a low point in a large shallow basin. It had rained enough that the water level in the basin rose higher that his slab, even though the slab was slightly elevated to it's immediate surroundings.

RULE NUMBER 13

WHEN SETTING A SLAB ELEVATION, BETTER TOO HIGH THAN TOO LOW.

If a slab is too low the remedy can be very very costly. If it is too high, additional fill can always be added around the foundation, and blended to the existing grades.

CHAPTER 5

FOUNDATION TYPES

Before discussing further, the siting of a house to the land, it is necessary to talk about different foundation designs. Each different type of foundation has it's own requirements in blending to the site.

The term "basement" is frequently misunderstood, and when used, means different things to different people. A basement is nothing more than the lowest level of a building.

BI-LEVEL

For instance, there is a very popular house design known as a bi-level, hi-ranch or raised ranch, depending on the locale. This is a two story structure, where the lowest story is constructed at grade level. The second story is the living level, and the lower story, the basement. The basement usually contains a one or two car garage and an expansion area which can be finished as additional living space or recreational area. Because the basement is above grade it can be built with windows at ordinary height. The entry to the house is built at the half level between the lower level and the upper level. When entering, you come in at the mid level stair landing and can go either a half flight up to the living level, or a half flight down to the basement level. The space above the landing and the stairs is open, and visually creates the feeling of an entry hall without any square footage being devoted to an entry hall per se.

On the exterior, it is the custom to build a half flight stoop up to the entry. Earth is sloped up against the front of the basement to create the illusion that the basement is partially in the ground.

The bi-level design has a lot of advantages. It does not require an excavation in the ground, except for the footings, so it can be used on land that has not much soil cover over underlying rock. Because the basement is on grade, the lower level provides light and dry expansion space. People who buy this design like the idea that they are getting a full living level on the upper story but still have plenty of expansion room on the basement level. One or two more bedrooms, a family room or a recreation room could be added. The bi-level is comparatively inexpensive to build, but the trade off is a lack of architectural excitement. It is pretty much a box although imaginative use of brick and stone at the entry can dress it up. The roof has a low pitch without breaks or changes.

In some areas the raised ranch has been so extensively built that it has become the symbol of a low cost development house. Despite it's economy and advantages, many people will not build one for that reason.

STRAIGHT RANCH

A straight ranch is similar to a raised ranch except that the entry is at the upper level rather than at mid height. It can be built on a full foundation or on a slab on grade. If built on a full foundation, to avoid a very ungainly look, the foundation needs to be set into the ground at least half way. The basement level can usually still accommodate a two car garage, but the remaining space becomes less attractive. Windows become more difficult and frequently require wells around them because they are below grade. As soon as the foundation goes below grade, dampness and condensation become a problem.

TWO STORY

A two story design is the choice of many people who do not like to have their living space all on one level. They prefer the separation of having bedrooms on the second floor. In much of the country two story designs have been done in early American style and so the designation " Colonial" has become synonymous with two story. Frequently clients would come to me and say, "We don't want a ranch, we want a colonial". Upon questioning however, I found that they really wanted an English Tudor style or a Mediterranean style rather than an Early American style.

Of course the so called Colonial style originated in New England and includes the Cape Cod, the Salt Box, the Garrison House, the Dutch Colonial and a variety of two story structures with gables, half stories, widows walks, and the like.

New England homes were always built with a cellar under the house. Because of that, most clients in the North East consider it a must, to have a full basement under the two story home. They feel that the basement provides inexpensive future expansion space. They picture in their minds, a basement similar to that in a raised ranch which is usable, dry, and windowed. The basement under a two story must go well into the ground, so the entry level is no more than a few steps up from the surrounding grade. If a two story is made too high it has a very awkward and unpleasing appearance.

To these clients I have always pointed out that the basement will have very limited usability. Access to the outside must be by an exterior cellar stairway. I also point out, that in New England homes with an old fashioned cellar, the cellar was used for very special purposes. Storage of food, potatoes and comestibles which kept fresh, in the cool and damp atmosphere of the cellar. By the same token, an in the ground basement will be cool and damp, and not inviting as living space. It is not even good space for storage because things stored in this climate will soon be ruined by rust and mildew.

I once stored a valuable rug in my basement. Several years later when I wanted to use the rug, I found that it had been completely destroyed by rot and mildew.

I have seen many people spend considerable sums of money making a so called finished basement. They envision the party room, or the game room with a ping pong table or exercise equipment. When they are first finished they get used a few times. A party is thrown and it looks like a pretty good idea. However, I have never been in a finished basement more than two years old that wasn't an abandoned area. They collect junk, dust, and all the toys and paraphernalia that can't be put elsewhere. They gradually become a modern version of Grandma's attic. I wondered why this was so. I began to ask people about their use or non use of the finished basement. I'd get answers like, "Oh I don't know, I just like it better upstairs." Or, "I try to get the kids to play down there but they rather keep all their junk in their rooms.

It comes down to a purely psychological reason. People are not comfortable in a basement. The high window wells give them a sense of being underground. The unease is augmented by the slight dampness and smell of mildew. They simply don't feel comfortable in that environment, and avoid spending any prolonged time there. They much rather seek above ground space, where there are windows and daylight. Whether it's a subconscious feeling of being in a dungeon or a grave I don't know, but I do know beyond a doubt, that people given a choice, will not stay in a basement when they don't have to. We'll discuss alternatives later, but for now I'll set forth a rule.

RULE NUMBER 14

FINISHED BASEMENTS ARE A WASTE OF MONEY.

People are generally uneasy in sub grade space and do not enjoy such an ambiance.

SLAB ON GRADE

A fourth style of foundation design is the slab. Depending on the climate, this can be either a slab on grade or a modified slab with frost walls and footings.

In warm climates where the ground does not freeze, slabs can be constructed on grade. The edge of the slab is a footing which goes down into the ground about a foot and rests on crushed stone for stability. Reinforcing rods are installed around the perimeter for strength. The floor and footings are poured of concrete at the same time. This is called a monolithic pour.

If building in a climate where the ground freezes in the winter time, precautions must be taken against frost heave. when water freezes it expands in volume by 4 %. That is why frozen water pipes burst. The same thing happens to soil underlying a footing or a slab. When the ground freezes, the moisture it contains, expands. The power of this expansion is enormous. It can easily lift a footing and the weight of a house. Frost heave can cause cracking of the slab, the foundation, breaking of utility pipes, and distortion of the structure leading to cracked walls, uneven floors, and a host of problems.

MODIFIED SLAB

In order to avoid these consequences, the slab is constructed with footings and frost walls below. This is referred to, as a modified slab. A trench is excavated around the perimeter of the slab to a depth below the frost line. This depth is usually specified by the local Building Department, and is based on depth of frost experience, in that particular locale. A footing of concrete is poured in the bottom of the trench. A standard footing is 16" wide by 8" thick. It provides the same function as a foot, and distributes the weight of the structure over the area of the footing, as it rests on the underlying soil. Most of the time footings are made 24" wide. This is because most excavators only have a 24" wide bucket on their backhoe.

You do not need to pay for the extra concrete to make a 24" footing if you can find an excavator with a 16" bucket on his backhoe.

A frost wall is then built on the footing, rising up to the desired grade level. The frost wall can be built of concrete, or more usually, concrete block. Other footings are constructed inside the perimeter, to support bearing walls or columns. If the ground is compact, these interior footing need not go down to the depth of the perimeter footing, because the interior footings will be protected from frost by the structure above. They may be poured in an 8" deep trench just under the slab elevation. This is called a "haunch". The concrete is poured into the haunch at the same time that the floor is poured. The perimeter of the slab rests on the frost wall. These construction techniques will be discussed more fully later.

CRAWL SPACE

In Crawl space construction, the foundation is actually a series of piers or columns. The columns rest on footings and usually rise a few feet above the grade level. The floor deck is constructed on beams which span across the piers. This is now an obsolete design. It was popular years ago, and used extensively in warmer climates where freezing was not a consideration. It was also used in more northern climates for summer bungalows and cabins, which were not intended for cold weather use. The advantage of crawl space design was that it eliminated the cost of building a basement under the structure, and minimized excavation.

Back in the days, not too long ago, before there were backhoes and excavating machinery, foundations were dug by hand. Digging the footings for piers was much less labor than excavating for a basement. There was also the advantage of keeping the floor off the ground where it would not rot, and be susceptible to insect intrusion. These were also the days when insulating materials were not used. Heating was by a stove, and air conditioning was unknown.

As the use of concrete became more prevalent, and power mixers were developed, poured concrete began to be used for foundations instead of field stone and mortar, or brick and mortar. When the redi-mix concrete truck was developed construction underwent major changes, and poured concrete was extensively used. Poured footings and slabs became easy to build.

You can build a house on a crawl space today but many additional steps would be required. Generally a dirt floor under the crawl space is no longer permitted, and the ground must be covered with at least two inches of concrete or black top.

To insulate the floor, batts of insulation would have to be installed in the floor deck, and the underside of the deck covered with a non rotting material. Plumbing drains, and water and heating pipes in the crawl space, must be protected from freezing. Barriers must be made around the perimeter of the crawl space to keep out animals.

Now that we have at our disposal, backhoes and bull dozers, slab construction is simpler and cheaper than crawl space construction.

Many people labor under the misconception, that slab on grade construction will result in cold and damp floors. Not only is this not true, but a slab on grade provides a warmer floor than a floor over an unheated basement.

With an understanding of the different types of foundation designs, we can now examine how each style fits to various types of topography, so that in evaluating your building site, you will know what "lay of the land" best suits the type of foundation you intend to build.

CHAPTER 6

BLENDING HOUSE TO SITE

UPHILL SLOPE

An uphill slope can produce one of the nicest settings for a home if the common mistakes are avoided. A home which is elevated above the road is more impressive than one below the elevation of the road. If the slope is gentle, the best approach is to notch out the site, by cutting into the uphill slope and moving the removed earth forward to form a level area. You must make sure that the level area allows the positioning of the house far enough in front of the cut out area so that the cut can be graded down from above, and then sloped upward slightly to the rear of the house. This final upward slope is essential in controlling drainage. Water which will run down the hill toward the house must not be allowed to flow against the foundation. This would only result in lots of problems. The final up slope should also be higher in the center, and slope left and right as well. This will direct water flowing down the slope, around the house. If there is also a side slope, it might be necessary to direct the water entirely to one side or the other.

There are other approaches which do not cut into the slope as much. It is my experience that these methods will not give the most pleasing result, but may be utilized only because the builder is trying to avoid some bull dozing expense. In the end it will probably require as much dozer time to push earth up against the front, and cut out at the rear for drainage.

It is always better to set up your building platform (level area) first. You will be much better able to visualize how the house will fit the site when you do this, and it will be easier to plan your drainage. It will also be much easier to dig your footings, working on a level platform.

SLOPES

It is simpler to describe slopes in terms of percentage rather than in angles. A 10%. slope means that the elevation rises 10% of the distance covered. For example, if we go forward ten feet, and at the end we are one foot higher than the starting point, we have had a rise of one foot in 10, which is a ten percent slope. It is much easier to determine these slopes in the field, in terms of percentage. It only requires the use of a builders transit and a measuring stick. Measuring angles requires more sophisticated equipment, and is more difficult to do. It is also difficult to visualize a slope which is expressed in an angular measurement unless you have a lot of experience. Slopes expressed in percentages can be easily paced off on the ground and a rough idea obtained quite easily.

THE TRANSIT OR BUILDERS LEVEL

As long as I have mentioned it, let me explain about a builders transit. A transit is a fancy level that has a sighting lens system so that you can sight along a level line perfectly horizontal to the earth at the point you are located. The sighting system is a telescope so that you will be able to read the numbers on a measuring stick a considerable distance away. It enables you to determine the relative heights of things to each other.

For example, let's say we want to dig a hole in the ground exactly three feet deep. We set up our transit, leveling it by using it's leveling bubbles. We hold our measuring stick, which is nothing more than a long ruler, vertically on top of the point where we want to dig our hole. We sight through the telescope of the transit, and read the height on the ruler which is in the cross hairs of the telescope sight. We see the marking on the ruler is at four feet one inch in the cross hairs. Now we start to dig our hole checking from time to time by holding the measuring stick vertically in the hole, and reading the height on the cross hairs through the telescope. If we read five foot one inch, it means that we have lowered the stick by one foot, and the hole is one foot deep. Therefor, when we hold the stick in the hole, and the reading is seven feet one inch, three feet more than the four foot one inch we started with, then we know we have lowered the stick three feet, and the hole is three feet deep. Notice that when we lower the stick the reading increases by the amount we have lowered it, and if we raise the stick the reading will decrease by the amount we have raised it. It is always a good idea to carry a note book and pencil when doing this work so that you may jot down the various readings. It is easy to get confused and sometimes add when we should subtract, or subtract when we should add. It is a good idea to make a little diagram of what you are doing and mark your readings on the diagram.

FIGURE 1

(Fig. 1.) shows a typical 10%. slope.

FIGURE 2

(Fig. 2) shows how the notch is cut, and the removed material moved forward to create a level platform.

FIGURE 3

(Fig. 3) shows a bi-level house set on the platform. The dotted lines indicate the final grading and blending.

FIGURE 1

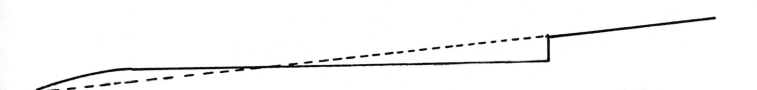

FIGURE 2

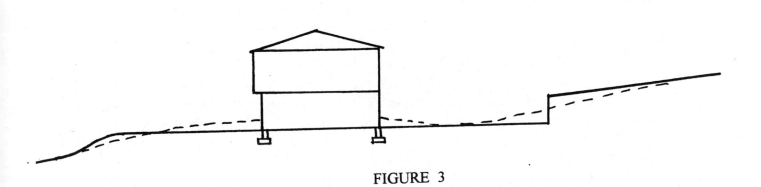

FIGURE 3

FIGURE 4

(Fig. 4) shows a straight ranch on a full foundation. About half of the foundation is set into the ground. This allows enough foundation exposure to have some high windows in the basement.

FIGURE 5

(Fig. 5) illustrates a two story on a full basement with the basement half set into the ground.

FIGURE 6

(Fig. 6) shows a ranch house on a slab.

RULE NUMBER 15

WHENEVER POSSIBLE, LEVEL THE BUILDING PLATFORM FIRST.

This may seem like extra work but in the long run it will be less work. If underlying rock is going to be a problem you will discover it first and be able to plan accordingly. It is very difficult to lay out a foundation on a slope, and equally difficult to dig footings when the machine is not set level.

FIGURE 7

When steeper slopes are involved it may not be possible to cut deep enough to level out our platform due to the problem of underlying rock. (Fig. 7) illustrates a situation in which it was just possible to get into the ground enough to bury the rear of the foundation. In this case the final grade must be done afterwards as shown by the dotted lines.

FIGURE 8

In a case where the depth to rock is very shallow, and the foundation cannot be set into the slope, it becomes necessary to extend the front footings downward below the basement floor. If fill material cannot be gathered on the site, it may be necessary to bring in fill to do the final grading.

Let's take a further look at the situation that occurs in (Fig. 7) and (Fig. 8). which both illustrate a straight ranch on a full foundation. In both cases the front of the foundation is fully exposed. If the foundation is built of poured concrete or concrete blocks the appearance of the house will be extremely ugly and ungainly. I have seen many houses built this way, and they always look like mistakes, which they are.

When confronted by this situation, instead of building the front wall of the foundation from concrete or masonry, you should build it as a regular frame wall. Redesign the entry to come in at the lower level and use an interior stairway to the living level. Add windows in the lower

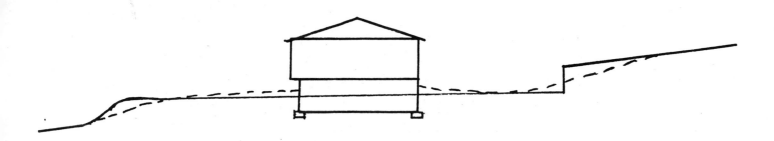

FIGURE 4

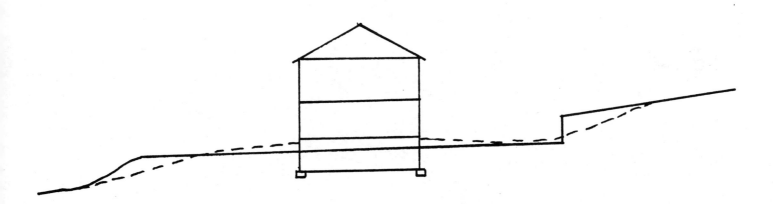

FIGURE 5

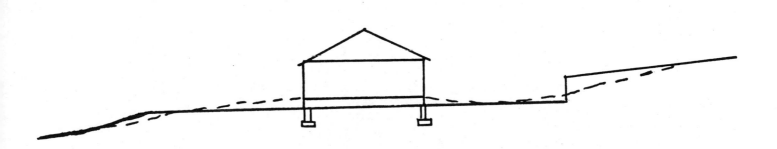

FIGURE 6

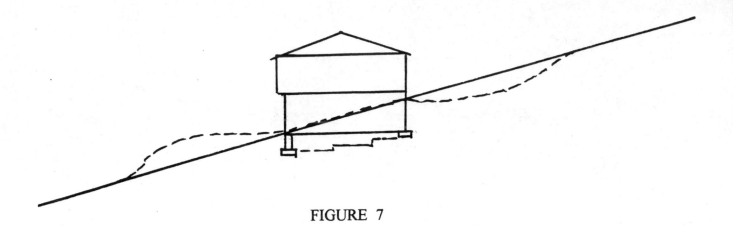

FIGURE 7

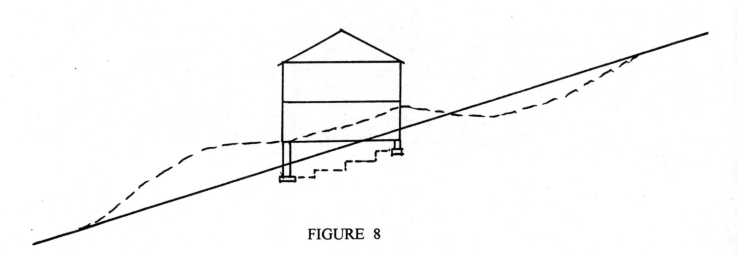

FIGURE 8

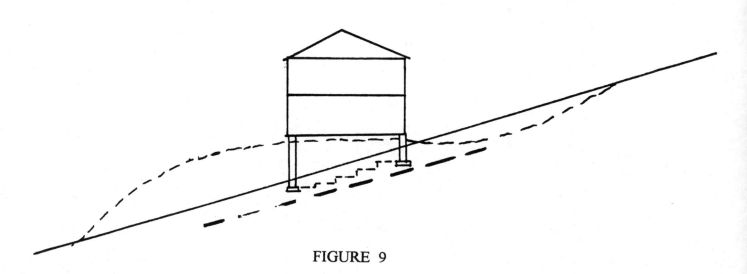

FIGURE 9

level and generally style the house as though it was a two story. This will make the home appear to be set much closer to the ground which always looks so much better.

FIGURE 9

(Fig. 9) Illustrates the placing of a two story house on a steep slope where the underlying rock is only a few feet below the surface. The heavy dashed line indicates the level of the underlying rock. A modified slab on grade is constructed with the footings stepped down following the slope of the rock.

The modified slab is a good solution for building on rock. Remember it is not necessary to dig the footings down below the level of the rock because a certain depth has been prescribed to get below the frost line. A moments reflection will tell that the rock is the best possible footing to have to support a structure, and that we need only to build our vertical frost wall on top of the rock, using the rock as the footing.

DRIVEWAYS

In all the houses with basements that we have situated on an up slope, the basements can be used for a two car garage opening to the end of the foundation. The earth need only be graded at the side to a level slightly lower than the garage floor providing a level area in which to back the car out of the garage. The cut is then brought forward, until it comes out of the slope. It will then follow the downhill incline to the road.

Driveway cuts should always have a slight downhill pitch for drainage. Where the driveway cut is made to the side at the end of the garage, on a steep slope a notch must be cut. If the earth cannot be graded down to the driveway level, it may be necessary to build a retaining wall to hold back the bank. When this type of retaining wall is constructed, a flight of steps is usually incorporated to provide access from the back door down to the garage and driveway level.

DOWNHILL SLOPE

On downhill slopes our objective is somewhat different than it was on uphill slopes. Building on the uphill, it was our purpose to keep the house down to the ground level so as not to look awkward. However, when building on a down hill slope we want to try to keep the house higher and closer to the road elevation. If the slope is gentle we still have the option of using any of our foundation configurations which we can blend accordingly

FIGURE 10

(Fig. 10) Illustrates a ranch on a full basement. In this case by keeping the structure high, we can fill in at the front which will give the ranch a look of being snug to the ground. At the same time we are able to minimize the appearance of the house being lower than the road by adding the fill in front. A further advantage of this configuration is that the basement may be made much more accessible from the rear and therefor more usable. Patio doors and windows may be added in the rear.

With the front and part of the ends below grade, dampness and mildew will still be a problem.

Although the grade level at the rear tends to mitigate the below ground feeling. It is important that good ventilation is provided. This may be accomplished by the use of a circulating air, heating and cooling system. Heat pumps are excellent for this application and we will discuss them further when we talk about heating and cooling systems later on.

FIGURE 11

(Fig. 11) illustrates the blending of a bi-level or raised ranch to a 10% down grade. The height of the house still works to our advantage.

FIGURE 12

(Fig. 12) shows the blending of a modified slab foundation of a one story ranch. The aesthetics of this arrangement are not as pleasing. When observing the house from the road, one sees mostly a lot of roof and shingles. The design of the front elevation tends to be lost. A two story house on a modified slab would look better, and raise the eye level when looking from the road.

On steeper slopes, a full foundation is the only way to achieve a reasonable result, and keep the house from looking as though it is down in the bottom of a hole.

FIGURE 13

(Fig 13) illustrates a two story house with a full foundation on a 30% grade. A step footing is used following the slope. Note that the foundation at the rear extends substantially below the basement floor level. This construction is the same as building a modified slab, and then building the first floor walls of masonry. Actually, the rear of the basement can be of frame construction which is recommended, as it facilitates the installation of patio doors and windows, and provides the cavity for the insulation which otherwise would have to be framed inside the masonry wall.

In this example, if there are no sub grade problems, the basement floor could be lowered to the elevation of the front footing, creating a basement with a high ceiling. However it should be noted that the deeper a foundation wall goes into the ground, the thicker the masonry construction must be to withstand the pressure from the backfilled earth.

When back filling a foundation which is deep in the ground be very careful that the bull dozer or heavy machine does not go closer than eight feet from the foundation. If a heavy machine goes on the soft backfilled material it could squeeze the material against the foundation wall causing it to buckle. Backfilling should not be done until the full weight of the house is on the foundation wall. This will help resist buckling.

The best way to compact backfilled material against a foundation is to fill in about eight inches of earth at a time and then to compact it using a mechanical compacting machine.

We cannot cover every possible configuration in this explanation, however if you understand the principals involved, it only requires a little common sense to apply them to any case. Side to side slopes for instance, can be treated the same as front to rear or rear to front. If

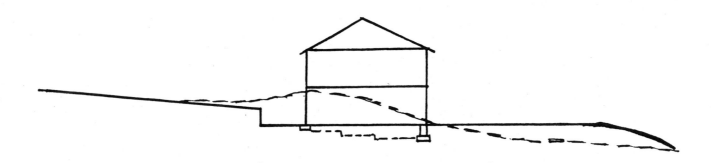

FIGURE 10

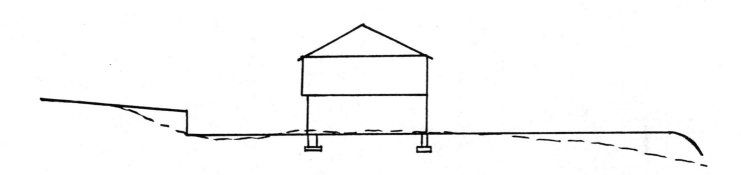

FIGURE 11

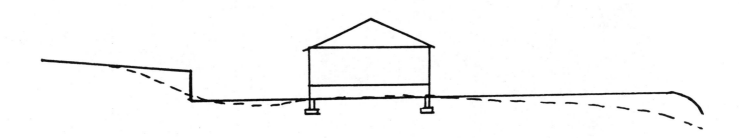

FIGURE 12

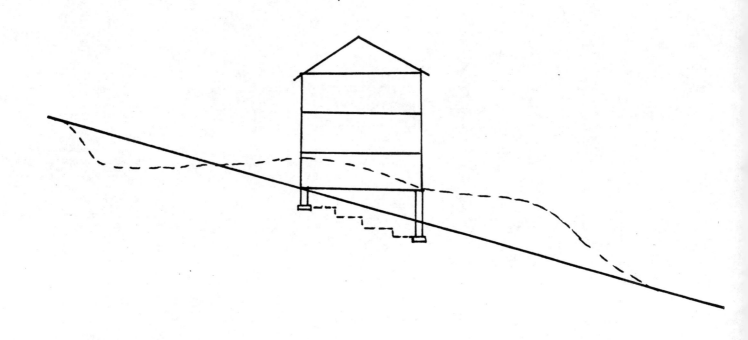

FIGURE 13

you have a front to rear and a side to side slope the principals remain the same. However, remember rule No. 15, It is always better to level the building platform first whenever possible. It will make a lot of things easier.

EXITING THE LOT

In designing your driveway, it is important that where the driveway meets the road, there be a level spot at least the length of the car. This is necessary to insure safe entry onto the road and adequate visibility. If, for instance, your driveway is on an upslope as it meets the road, it will be difficult to see the traffic. If the driveway is wet and slippery it may be hard or impossible to get started on the incline. If you are in an area where there is likely to be snow or freezing rain you might not be able to get out of your driveway, and up the slope under those conditions. When this kind of weather is anticipated, having a level area at the road where you can leave your car is invaluable.

If the slope of the lot is too steep, it may not be possible to build a level platform perpendicular to the road. In such a case, plan your driveway to approach the road at an angle becoming parallel when the grade of the road is reached. This may limit you to exiting your driveway in only one direction so plan accordingly.

PART TWO

PLANNING THE HOME

CHAPTER 7

STYLE AND DETAILS

Now that we have evaluated the building sites we were considering, and made our final selection, it is time to begin planning the actual home.

Up to now you may have had a good general idea of the kind of house you want but now you must begin to get specific. That doesn't mean that you must first determine your floor plan or your exterior design, but it does mean that you must start to focus on the style and details that will determine the final size, shape and appearance of the home.

CLIPPINGS

A good way to begin is to start a clipping collection. Every time you see a picture in a magazine of some detail that you like, or an entire room, clip it out and save it. Don't start to edit or make choices, just clip it out. You might clip a picture of a whole room because you liked a particular window, or the fire place treatment. You like Palladian windows, skylights, lofts, clip it. Maybe you see a particular color combination that takes your eye, or you see a great looking faucet for a kitchen sink. Anything and every thing that catches your attention, save.

You will find some interesting things happen to you. You'll be in a department store where you went to buy some article of clothing, and suddenly you will realize that you're standing in the bath department looking at toilet seats. Isn't that lucite one with the embedded gold coins great? Ask for literature, collect brochures, and while you do, get prices. We're going to want them later on, when we start to put costs together and begin our reality check. But for now, go crazy!

You'll find yourself looking at lighting equipment, appliances, kitchen cabinets, green house windows, smoke detectors and alarm systems. You will become captivated by landscape ads showing brick walks and spacious decks, and look at that cedar Gazebo, wouldn't that look great in the back yard, and it's only $ 15,000.00 delivered.

Of course before you acquired this book, you began buying plan books. You pored over floor plans till your eyes danced. Some are good, some are better, and some are really great, if only......!

RULE 16

PEOPLE WHO SELL PLAN BOOKS ARE IN THE BUSINESS OF SELLING PLAN BOOKS AND PLANS. THEY DO NOT BUILD OR SELL HOUSES.

The renderings in the plan books are designed to attract and appeal. What looks good on paper may not be as good for you in reality.

There is nothing wrong with buying plans. In fact it is an excellent idea. They can be very helpful in determining your final home and are well worth the price for the ideas and starting point they provide. However, do not assume that they must be built exactly as drawn. They can be modified to adjust to your budget and preferences.

English Tudor designs with tons of elegant stone and brick work, hand hewn timbers and custom leaded glass windows are shown. They have great turrets with slate roofs, and all kinds of appealing goodies.

The reality is, that hand laid stone work is very expensive. So is brick work. Slate roofs are out of sight. Complex eaves, curves and trim are all costly to execute. An attractive Tudor design that you find in a plan magazine could illustrate fifty thousand dollars worth of expensive exterior treatments. The same is true of the grand contemporaries and Mediterraneans.

Unless money is no object, you must ask yourself if you want to spend that kind of money on exterior appearance, when the same amount or only half, could pay for a multitude of luxuries on the inside, including more living space.

We do want our homes to be attractive. We do want to impress our friends and relatives. We do want a feeling of satisfaction and accomplishment, when after a hard days work we drive up to our lovely, elegant home.

RULE 17

YOU DON'T HAVE TO THROW MONEY AT THE OUTSIDE OF A HOUSE TO ACHIEVE AN ATTRACTIVE AND ELEGANT APPEARANCE.

Much depends on the artistry of the designer. When the line, form, and proportions of a design are right it is not necessary to hang expensive treatments on the outside. Some imagination with trim and color is all it takes.

If you begin to observe why a certain house looks elegant or cozy or whatever your choice is, you will begin to see why. You will notice the proportions, and the lines, and the little trim accents that give the building it's essential character. Unfortunately there is not room here to teach the elements of good design, but if you will start to look, you will begin to see.

Here is one idea about design. Have you ever heard of the great "Painted Ladies" in San Francisco? If you have not, they are turn of the century Victorian homes that have been restored and painted with imaginative and harmonious color schemes. You can find pictures of these great homes in any library or book store.

There is lots of trim, and color and gingerbread, none of which is very expensive. The secret is in the brilliant unity of the design. Every line leads the eye to the next. Every angle relates to the next. The whole structure projects a visual rhythm and delight. All the elements of the design harmonize, but not at the expense of blandness and dullness.

Every great design has the same quality. Go to the library and get a picture of Frank Lloyd Wright's great masterpiece, "Falling Waters". Look at it from the depth of your soul, and the hand of artistry will touch you. You may not be able to do it, but like pornography, you will know it when you see it. Try, reach out, extend yourself, and a new appreciation of architectural beauty will be yours.

WHAT YOU ALREADY KNOW

A vast resource in this endeavor lies in what you already know. You doubtless have lived in a variety of homes over time, and have formed opinions about what you like and what you don't like. Sit down with pencil and paper and, reminisce. Jot down the things you liked, and the things you did not. Note the rooms that seemed appropriate in size and those that were too small. Was there a closet that was especially good or a pantry that was so so handy? Put it all down.

Next, it's important to establish a good sense of the size of things. Most people go way off in this regard. They usually think a bathroom takes less space than it actually does, but that the living room must be larger than it needs to be. Get a good 16 foot builders tape and start measuring things. Especially measure rooms that are furnished. Put down the size of the room and then add your comments, such as, "When I open the dining room table the chairs are cramped against the wall. Another two feet in length would make it right. The living room is too long, if I put the couches against the walls, the furniture is too spread out to have a good conversational group. If I move them closer, the space behind the couch, between it and the windows, doesn't look right". Try to decide what change in size will fix the objection. Keep writing down the dimensions of the rooms. Now you may note some problems that you are not sure how to fix. Don't worry, you are not an expert designer and your experience is limited. However, when you finally consult with an experienced designer you will know what you want, and the designer will probably be able to figure out how to achieve it.

If you are planning a pool table or a ping pong table, check the manufacturers recommendation as to the space required. Most people do not allow enough room around these tables for their proper and comfortable use.

Study entrance halls. Look for the conflicts with the way the doors swing. Keep on measuring and recording your impressions. These notes are going to be invaluable in avoiding mistakes that you would regret after your new house is finished.

THE ATTACHED GARAGE

The attached garage is a popular alternative to a "garage under". The attached garage extends the size and lines of the home, adding variety to the roof lines, and in general enhancing the appearance. Eliminating an in ground basement, and building on a slab, not only will improve the way the house snugs to the land, but will also save money that can be applied to the attached garage.

An attached garage affords the opportunity to create an attic space above. A garage attic can provide good, dry, and usable storage space that is much better than the damp space of an inground basement. When planning the garage, consider making the garage say, ten feet deeper. This can create an invaluable storage space for all the tools, bikes and paraphernalia that one accumulates. In a well planned house the kitchen usually is adjacent to the garage so that additional space in the garage can be used for things like a mud room, laundry, pantry, potting room and many others.

ATTICS

Don't overlook the potential of a good attic. Today, the access to an attic is usually by means of a pull down stairway. Try to go back to the old way of having an attic staircase. This one thing alone can vastly increase the value of an attic. Raising the pitch of an attic roof can create a great deal of usable space with a very small increase in cost. The labor is virtually the same except for the additional roofing.

Remember how we described the slope of a lot in terms of the percentage of grade. Well the pitch of a roof is expressed in somewhat the same manner. A roof pitch is expressed in the number of inches the roof rises vertically for every twelve inches of horizontal distance. A roof that rises 3" vertically for every 12" horizontal distance is referred to as a three inch pitch or a three on twelve pitch. Expressing the pitch in this manner, rather than in angles, enables the carpenters to easily cut the angles of the roof beams by using their carpenters square which is marked out in inches. They can lay the square on a beam to be cut and duplicate the exact pitch required.

A three inch pitch is usually the lowest pitch used for a shingle roof. A lesser pitch might allow water to back up under the shingles, especially if snow is melting on the roof.

To create a good usable attic space a minimum of a nine inch pitch is necessary but a twelve inch pitch, sometimes called a "Full Pitch", is very much better, and costs very little more to build. Depending on the design, gables and dormers can further enhance the usability of attic space.

In a two story design, it is frequently possible to create access from the second floor to an attic over the attached garage. This can make a great children's playroom.

RULE 18

ATTICS PROVIDE VALUABLE, USABLE, ADDITIONAL SPACE AT LOW COST.

Remember. where there are budget constraints, the attic can be finished or developed at a later time.

LOFTS

A loft is another way of making attic space usable. The loft is generally used in contemporary designs where a cathedral ceiling is over a living room or family room. A loft can create very appealing secondary living space, such as a music area, or a library. Add some skylights and a loft can become an artist's studio. Lofts can be reached by using conventional stairs or a spiral stairway is frequently an excellent solution. A loft can be made to access a full attic over the garage, creating a very interesting and economical arrangement for a family room.

FENESTRATION

Fenestration is a fancy word for windows, which is another subject requiring some thought on your part. Window selection will depend a lot on the style of the design. In a colonial design you might want windows with divided panes, while for a Tudor you would prefer diamond panes. These effects are readily available, and can be achieved with a removable wood grill, which is the most attractive, or with double glazed windows that have the dividers located between the panes of glass. These are reasonably attractive and do not have to be removed to clean the window.

In current design the Palladian window is very popular. This is a window that has a semi circular section on top. They may be clear or divided in accordance with the style. These windows are very lovely and create a wonderful feeling of light and space. However the trade off is, that the use of such a window requires a high ceiling. They are also a little costly and require more costly custom made window treatments.

Glass area is used more extensively in contemporary designs where an indoor outdoor feeling is desired. It is important however, not to overdo, especially when privacy is not complete. It can result in a fish bowl effect, where the occupants of the home feel exposed and on display.

RULE 19

DO NOT CREATE LARGE WINDOW AREAS ON THE NORTH SIDE IN COLD CLIMATES OR ON THE SOUTH SIDE IN HOT CLIMATES.

Despite the extravagant claims of some window manufacturers, windows are very poor insulators. Low emissivity glass known as type E glass, gives only a very slight increase in insulating value. Not only do north facing windows lose a lot of heat, but they also create drafts, and draw body heat when you sit near them. In warm climates it is obvious that you want to avoid the direct rays of the sun which can overheat a home. Rather, situate your windows on the shady side of the house.

These exposures should also be kept in mind when selecting a lot, unless the lot is large enough to permit any orientation of the house you choose.

CHAPTER 8

ROOMS AND THEIR ARRANGEMENT

Now that you are developing a good clipping file of style and details, and a lot of good notes and measurements, it is time to consider the number and nature of the rooms you want to have in your home. Of course, the number of rooms will determine the size of the house, and the size will determine the cost. For purposes of this discussion we will talk about an average size house between two and three thousand square feet.

FUNCTION

Before you can determine the size and placement of a room it is necessary to decide how you intend to use it. You may want to consider certain rooms as a group. For instance, if you plan on entertaining a lot, giving cocktail parties where people stand and move around, you should probably consider a relatively open arrangement between your living room, dining room and family room. In this case the family room might tend to be more a den or TV room rather than a playroom. If the budget permits a billiard room, this is the perfect adjunct for an entertainment flow.

THE LIVING ROOM

Over the last fifty years living rooms have become more and more formal, and are used less and less. The advent and development of television changed the living habits of most people. Before that time it was not unusual to find a piano in most living rooms. Entertainment was self generated, and reading was a much more popular recreation.

Gradually the use of the living room as a center of family gathering declined. As the standard of living increased, better furniture and decorations were possible, and once occupying the living room, they had to be carefully cared for and preserved. The living room became reserved for entertaining guests, and family activities tended to center around the TV in another room.

Over time the living room became used less and less. Although today we are not ready to eliminate the living room entirely, it's importance is much less, and it has tended to become smaller. Think carefully about your living room and the kind of space you want it to be. If you entertain a lot then you will want it to be larger and more impressive. However, most people today do not do much formal entertaining, and if that is the case for you, then consider a smaller living room which would allow more space to be devoted to other areas.

FAMILY ROOM

The family room has grown in importance as the function of the living room has declined. This is a room of more casual behavior. A lot of time is spent here watching television so the furniture takes much more of a beating. If you have young children it is a place for them to play and usually a good spot where Mom can keep her eye on them. Family rooms are frequently adjacent to the kitchen. Lots of food and snacks are consumed in the family room, and probably a few beers as well. It's a room where you don't always have to worry about being too neat.

THE DEN

When the children are older or out of the nest, the family room usually becomes a den. The furnishings are casual but perhaps, better. There may be a bar, and of course the TV which might now be incorporated into an entertainment center that also has music and sound equipment. The den can also be used as a library and be fitted with book shelves. If you collect things that can be displayed on the wall this may be the room for it.

When the family room gets the hard use of the kids, the pets, the food spills etc., the living room is usually kept for entertaining. However when there is an attractive and comfortable den, the entertaining is more likely to be done there, with the living room virtually abandoned except for cocktail parties.

THE KITCHEN

With the advent of all the modern appliances and labor saving devices we now have, the kitchen has become a very important room.

It is expected that the kitchen today, will be fitted out with beautiful cabinets and great looking appliances. If both adults in the household work, the emphasis in the kitchen may be on time saving devices such as a micro wave oven which enable meals to be prepared quickly and easily.

The kitchen can be a beautiful room, with greenhouse windows and plants. It should be roomy enough to permit a good set of table and chairs for casual eating. Only when cost is paramount should a galley type kitchen be considered. Of all the conveniences in a home, probably none is more important than the kitchen table and chairs with enough room around them to permit easy use.

When laying out the solar orientation of your house, try to situate the kitchen so that it will receive morning sunlight. Nothing is more pleasant than to start the day with a cup of coffee in a bright, cheerful and sunny kitchen. It's the perfect spot on Sunday mornings to relax with a good breakfast, and read the morning paper.

Over the years, no single thing has pleased and delighted my clients more than a well designed and sunny kitchen.

<u>RULE 20</u>

NOTHING LIFTS THE SPIRITS MORE THAN A KITCHEN WITH MORNING SUNLIGHT

This is so important that it should bear heavily on your choice of a site, and the orientation of your home.

A lot of kitchen cabinet companies show ads picturing an island in the kitchen containing either a sink or a stove. Beware this set up. Besides using up a lot of extra space, it is also inconvenient. Food taken out of the refrigerator for preparation usually must be taken to the sink for washing. If the sink is in the island the food has to be carried to the island, washed, and then carried back to the counter for further preparation. The same problem develops if the stove is in the island. There is rarely enough space on the island next to the stove to do the preparation, so in this case too, the food must be carried back and forth.

Stick to a traditional kitchen layout. If you are right handed, the refrigerator should be on the left of the sink with some counter top in between. The dishwasher should be to the right of the sink, providing more counter top. If you are left handed simply reverse the order. The stove can be set up on another wall with plenty of counter space on either side.

Beware wall ovens. They look good in the pictures, but besides requiring an additional costly cabinet housing, they are really inconvenient for a normal flow of work.

If you are planning a gourmet kitchen, and will need extra space, consider using a butcher block table on rollers as your additional preparation space. This can be used as an island, and help out as a serving table, but still be rolled out of the way when not needed.

A popular variation on the kitchen is the "Country Kitchen". These are usually done in early American style with hewn plank type tables and chairs. Lots of country kitchens have a wood stove. This provides an excellent family gathering place.

Another variation is to have the kitchen and the family room as a single space. Frequently a breakfast bar is used as a divider. This provides a nice set up where Mom can relate the affairs of the day to Dad while she cooks dinner, and he has the obligatory beer on the couch.

If you are going to have a micro wave, there are so called space saver units that mount above the stove. These are pretty good but they are on the small side. Most appliance manufacturers offer a one piece unit with a stove top, an oven below, a micro wave oven above, and a recirculating exhaust hood on top of that. These are excellent units, especially the one offered by GE.

<u>THE DINING ROOM</u>

The Dining Room is usually a neglected room. It generally is used only a few time a year on important holidays. However, most people do not want to give it up. The dining room often winds up in an "el" off the living room where it can barely be seen. This has always struck me as a mistake. The dining room furniture is usually the best furniture in the house, and the best preserved as well. The dining room is the one room in the house that is always neat with flowers on the table and a nice display of china.

ROOMS AND THEIR ARRANGEMENT

I have always been in favor of opening the dining room to the living room so that it can be more easily seen. Especially with the trend toward smaller living rooms, the openness to the dining room creates a feel of much greater space. However it is nice to define the boundary between the rooms. I am partial to doing this with open archways and railings. Depending on the style of the home, the arches can be done in stucco for a Mediterranean look, or angular timbers and brackets for a Tudor style. In contemporary designs you can do interesting treatments with half walls of glass brick.

If the dining room does not get used much for eating, at least this way, you get more for your money by using it decoratively.

THE MASTER BEDROOM

Most people prefer a spacious master bedroom but occasionally I run into a client who says "what for? After all I am only going to sleep there." Most women however, seem to like to use the master bedroom as their personal place and retreat. Today, it is common to have a TV in the bedroom for watching while in bed. A master bedroom is very nice when there is room for an occasional chair or two, and perhaps a little draped table. These things will vary greatly according to your personal taste. However, there is one thing that is very important for a master bedroom.

RULE 21

NO MATTER WHAT SACRIFICE IS INVOLVED, A GOOD SIZED WALK IN CLOSET IS SOMETHING YOU WILL BE GRATEFUL FOR EVERY SINGLE DAY.

A final word of caution about the master bed room. Be very careful about window placement. Headboards, highboys, and dressers with large mirrors all require a lot of wall space. Plan your furniture arrangement when planning the room so that you will not wind up with windows that conflict with furniture.

THE HOME OFFICE

The home office is a relatively new room to consider in a home, but I believe it is a room that will become more and more necessary as time goes on. Lots of people today already have a home computer, and more and more people are getting them all the time. A trend is beginning where people will be able to do their work from home through computer links. Education is moving more and more toward the use of the computer. Today you can shop, manage your investments, consult an encyclopedia, send electronic mail, fax, and have your phone answered by computer.

A quiet room, with a closable door is needed to create a comfortable space to use the computer, and perform the myriad paper work tasks that modern living thrusts upon us. Such a room can also double as a sewing or hobby room.

CHAPTER 9

GETTING THE PLANS

We have arrived at the point where you want to get a set of plans for your dream home. You've accumulated your notes and clippings, and had some time to consider the style and content of your new home.

Before you can really describe the home you want it is necessary to set your priorities. Sit down and list the rooms you would like to have and their approximate sizes. Then indicate where you would be willing to cut if cost and budget restraints require it. Would you cut an entire room, make some rooms smaller, or all rooms smaller.

Go through your clippings and decide what style you would like, what kind of windows you want, what special features you want. If you have some ideas that on second thought you don't like or want, then discard them. Keep the rest and try to put them in order of importance. Unless cost is no object, you are going to have to make some choices. Talk it over and decide what you would eliminate if you have to. This is not an easy process, and it requires some discipline and maturity. Very few of us are fortunate enough to be able to have every thing we want. You are going to have to be realistic, and realize that you will have to give up some desires in order to have some other more important ones.

A client once came to me and asked if I could help him find a building lot. He explained that he and his wife had been looking for several years but just could not find a piece of land that satisfied them. I asked them to describe the kind of lot they wanted and this is what they said: "It should be nicely wooded with some mature trees and also have a stream or pond. It also must have a good view." I told them that God had not yet created that lot, at least not in the North East. If they wanted a view, the land would have to have high elevation, and streams don't run up hill. If you expect to have a good view, you can't have a lot of trees.

To my astonishment, they didn't seem to grasp what I was trying to tell them. They indicated that they would just keep on looking until they found what they really want. There are people like that who can't seem to come to grips with reality, and they just look, and look, and look. I think they don't really want to find what they are looking for, because then they will have to make decisions and take actions which they are incapable of doing. They would rather continue living in their fantasy, where no decisions are required.

The point of the story is that you can't have everything. You have to be realistic and decide what you want most, and what you are willing to give up. Try making a list, and writing down what you absolutely must have as a minimum, and what you would like to have if you can. If you do this conscientiously, you may be surprised at the end to discover how many of the really important things you can have.

PLAN BOOKS

This is something that we have already discussed so I will not devote a lot of additional space. If you have found a plan in a plan book that suits you, then by all means buy the plans. Most localities in which you build will require that the plans be sealed by an Architect or Professional Engineer who is licensed in the State where you intend to build, and who will certify the plans comply with the State and local Building Codes. Often, if there are changes required, they can be made by plan notation and amendment.

THE ARCHITECT

An architect of course, is trained in the business of designing buildings and drawing their plans. Most architects tend to specialize in a particular area of design, such as commercial and industrial, public and institutional, and residential.

A good way to choose an architect is to look around for a home whose design or style you admire, and find out who the architect was who designed it. This can easily be done at the local Building Department where the plans are on file bearing the Architects name and professional stamp.

If you go to an architect that has been recommended, or who you found in the yellow pages, don't be afraid to ask to see samples of his work. Above all don't be embarrassed to ask his fee schedule.

On a number of occasions I have had clients bring me a set of plans for which they have paid an architect a substantial fee, asking me for a bid on the construction. In every case the construction costs were greater, and even double, the clients budget. This resulted in a waste of a lot of time and a considerable sum of money.

RULE 22

A SET OF PLANS YOU CAN'T AFFORD TO BUILD, IS WORTHLESS.

It is not necessarily fair to blame the architect for this. In most cases the Architect will ask you what you have in mind and take notes as you describe all the things you want. He then sets about drawing a set of plans that embodies all of the things you asked for. Most people have no idea of construction costs, and so invariably describe a home much more expensive than they can afford.

In dealing with an architect you must be very emphatic about your budget and what you can afford to spend. You must make it very clear that plans for a home that costs more than you can afford, will be worthless to you. He should be able to make a rough estimate based on a cost per square foot at the outset. That way, a maximum size can be determined as a working basis for the design. As the design progresses he must consult with you on priorities and their cost so that a usable result will ensue.

You will have to do your part. You must spend the time, be realistic, and make the tough choices.

An Architect can offer you many additional services. He can obtain bids on the job from builders or from the individual trades. He can supervise the job, and prepare the payment requisitions for the contractors, deal with the Building Department, and obtain all the necessary approvals and Certificate of Occupancy. However, these services are not cheap. If you are building a home of more than a half million dollars, it probably contains a lot of specialized and custom treatments that have been drawn and specified by the Architect. In this price range, you should have the architect be responsible to see to the proper carrying out of his design.

BUILDERS

If you are going to work with a builder it is important that you find one with the appropriate qualifications to build a true custom house. There are several classifications of builders.

DEVELOPMENT OR TRACT BUILDER

The development or tract builder is a builder who works on specific subdivisions which offer a selection of set models. He builds the same models over and over and will not build anything other than the models he offers. This is usually a high volume operation which gains it's efficiency from repetition.

OFF SITE BUILDER

There are off site builders who will build on any lot, but usually restrict operations to a selection of designs which they offer. If you ask them to build your design, they will try to talk you into one of their designs. These builders will usually advertise themselves as "Custom Builders", however they are not custom builders at all. They offer you a choice of colors, a choice of kitchen cabinets and plumbing fixtures, and then call it custom building.

THE GENERAL BUILDER

The General Builder or General Contractor is a builder who will undertake a fixed contract to build a proposed set of plans. He usually is capable of doing a variety of projects and limits his operations to jobs not exceeding a certain size rather than type. In this kind of arrangement the plans and specifications of the job are predominant. Any change or departure you request from the plans will result in an additional charge. If an error or omission is discovered in the plans, and they must be revised to correct the problem, there will be additional charges for the changed work.

THE DESIGNER BUILDER

The designer builder is a true custom builder. He will undertake the design of the home you want, and it's construction. He will work with you every step of the way on the design. Because of his exact knowledge of costs he is able to monitor the cost of the design as it proceeds. He is able to offer alternatives and compromises in the design so as to be able to achieve the home you want at a price you can afford without loosing the character of the home.

A designer builder will usually ask a fixed fee for doing the design. It was always my policy, that if the job went forward and I received the contract to build, I would credit the design fee against the contract price.

A designer builder is a special kind of a person. He must have lots and lots of patience in working with you, making revisions and changes, and completing the job to your satisfaction.

Most builders wouldn't touch this kind of a job with a ten foot pole. They simply do not know how to work closely with a client. They find it frustrating and nerve racking, and lack the patience to explain everything, and answer all your questions.

If you are considering a designer builder, ask for references, and speak to clients he has worked for. See if they were satisfied and pleased with the work, and above all if they feel they were dealt with fairly.

CHAPTER 10

CHOOSING THE BUILDING PROCESS

BEING YOUR OUR OWN BUILDER

Many people, having acquired a set of plans, whether from an architect or a plan service, want to act as their own builder.

Residential construction is very visible. People who have observed the process of construction believe that it is not very difficult, and that they can do it themselves. "After all," they say, "why pay a builder all that markup he adds to the cost? I can hire the subcontractors just as easily as a builder, and I will save all that money!"

This attitude has ended in disaster for many wannabe builders who embarked blindly on a task about which they knew nothing. It's like the old saying "Ignorance is bliss."

A number of years ago, I entered into a contract with a fellow who asked me to design a home for him and quote him a price for building it. When I submitted my proposal he was very satisfied, and signed the contract. He then told me that only two years before, when he was working in another area, he had contracted to build his own house. He said, "Never again! I thought I knew what I was doing, but I made every mistake in the book. The mark up you add on the cost of the job you certainly earn, and you are entitled to every penny of it. I never want to go through those hassles again. I would have saved money if I had hired a builder, rather than trying to do it myself". BUT... HE DIDN'T HAVE THIS BOOK!

On another occasion I designed and built a house for a school teacher. The job was during the summer time and as there was no school, he was on the job every day, watching, asking questions, and sometimes interfering. Everything received his detailed scrutiny. I asked him for only one thing, and that was if he thought something was being done wrong, not to question or give instructions to the workers, but to bring it to my attention instead. In a typical instance, one night he called me and said he was very concerned about the floors in the house. He said he had climbed the ladder up to the second floor and found that in some places the floors seemed to bounce up and down when he walked on them. I had to explain to him that he was walking on the subflooring, and that later on, another layer of thicker plywood would be installed over the sub flooring.

What was interesting was, that by the time the house was completed, I had educated him so thoroughly that he said to me, "Ya know I've watched this job every step of the way and it really isn't very difficult. I think I could build a house better than you can, because I learned from your mistakes". All I said to him was that I thought he would find that it's harder than it looks.

Sure enough, the next summer when school was out, he took his savings, and borrowed some money from his brother, and undertook the construction of a speculative house, expecting to reap a handsome profit from his summers work.

What actually happened, is that he built the wrong kind of house in the wrong location. Because he did not control his costs, he had to ask a price much higher than the house was worth, and which nobody would pay in that location. In the end when he could not keep up the construction mortgage payments, the bank foreclosed, and he lost all of his and his brothers money. I can still hear his words... "I can do it better than you." BUT HE DIDN'T HAVE THIS BOOK!.

RULE 23

NO MATTER HOW EASY IT LOOKS, IT TAKES TIME, KNOWLEDGE, PATIENCE, AND DETERMINATION.

Would you try to remove an appendix. or argue a case in court without knowing what you were doing? Nor should you attempt to build a house without the necessary knowledge.

This book is not intended to teach you how to perform any specific trade. It is intended to teach you in detail, the nature of the work to be done at each step in the building process, from buying the lot to planting the lawn. It will tell you how to plan and how to avoid mistakes. Each part of the work will be described in sufficient detail so that you will know what you want your subcontractors to do, and whether or not they do it right. In Chapter 12 you will learn how to hire and deal with sub contractors. This book will guide you through the labyrinth of building.

THE ONE SHOT DEAL

When you call in subcontractors to bid on your job, they will see that you are an owner builder. To them you are a "one shot deal." They cannot look forward to getting further work from you if they do a good job, so they will automatically give you a higher bid. They reason that it only involves one job, and that if they don't get it they have plenty of work, but that if they do get it they will make a killing, and you will never know. All the bidders will do the same thing, and "high ball" the job. They know the others are doing it too. It's an unwritten rule. Chapter 12 on Subcontractors will give you the strategy to beat their game.

BUYING THE MATERIAL

A lot of amateur builders want to contract with a subcontractor for both the labor and the material he will install. It would seem that this relieves the builder of the problem of figuring out what materials are needed, ordering them for timely delivery, receiving them and supervising their placement on the job site, and being responsible for them. However, what seems to be an advantage will expose you to the possibility of serious financial loss.

Many small subcontractors, are financially marginal, and operate out of their home, their pick up truck, or their hat. Because they probably won't have the money, they are going to ask you for regular and frequent payment advances on the work, so that they can pay for the material. If you make the advances you will assume that the money will be used to pay for the materials, but this may not be the case. If the subcontractor is in financial difficulty he may very well use the money you advance him to pay some older and more urgent debt from another job. He may also try to inflate the amount of the advance to more than the value of the work he has completed, in order to get some money ahead, or to meet an urgent bill. Often these people are behind on their car or truck payments, their mortgage payments or their credit card payments. They are constantly juggling money in an effort to catch up. If a supplier doesn't get paid by the subcontractor he can and may, file a lien on your property without letting you know. If you pay the sub contractor in full after the lien has been filed you may still be responsible to pay the lien. When a lien is filed in the County Clerk's office it is considered notice to the world including you. If you pay the contractor after the lien was filed it will be held that legal notice was given, and you will still be obligated to pay the lien as you had a duty not to pay the contractor until the debt was satisfied. If you pay the sub contractor in full before the lien is filed, you will not be responsible for the lien, as no timely notice was given that the materials were not paid for.

When you are building you have enough to worry about without having to worry about liens and law suits. A professional builder will purchase the materials himself whenever it is possible, so that he can pay for them himself, and thus avoid liens.

Usually the mechanical trades furnish their own material because there are too many small items and fittings to keep track of. However, if you are unsure, you might want to buy the major plumbing fixtures and lighting fixtures yourself.

Buying the materials leads to other responsibilities. If you don't have the right materials on the job at the right time, the subcontractor will leave the job, thus causing delay, or he will try to charge you for waiting time.

Most lumber yards and masonry supply yards have outside salesmen who will be glad to call on you, and help you work out your material order. They will know what you need. Before doing this however, you should have the suppliers bid on the major material requirements, which they can do from a set of plans. Make them itemize prices in the bid. Do not accept a lump sum bid unless they guarantee it to be complete for all needs. You should get at least three bids, and let each bidder know that he is bidding against his competitors.

During the work, ask your sub to give you a list of material that he will need for the next several days.

When you receive your bills it is essential to compare the prices charged, against the prices that were quoted. Frequently prices quoted by a salesman do not get to the billing department. If you find an error, call the salesman and have him get it corrected. That way he will make sure it doesn't happen again.

RULE 24

DELAY IN THE PROGRESS OF THE JOB ALWAYS COSTS MONEY.

If you have obtained a construction loan, the longer the job takes, the more interest you'll pay. If you already own the lot which is most likely, the longer the job takes the more taxes you will pay. Some localities tax the construction based on the percentage completed as well as the land.

Most suppliers charge, 1 1/2% interest on unpaid balances more than thirty days due. If delay in the work delays your receiving a construction advance from the bank, you may also be hit with finance charges from your suppliers.

INSURANCE

If you are acting as your own builder it is important that you insure the new house during the course of construction against fire and casualty loss. Discuss this with your insurance agent. Usually if you buy your home owners policy at the beginning of the work you will be able to obtain a rider covering the home during the course of construction.

Construction insurance usually does not cover the materials which are delivered to the site until they are actually incorporated in the construction and become part of the building.

It is important not to deliver materials to the site more than a day or two from the time they will be used. Large piles of lumber invite theft. Unfortunately, there are people who cruise around in pick up trucks, looking for construction materials that can be stolen during the night. Sometimes the workers on the job may take materials home in their pick ups.

Another scam works like this: You ask your carpenters for example, to figure out a list of materials they will need for the next three days, so that you can avoid over stocking the job. The carpenters may need sixty sheets of plywood for the roof sheathing but tell you they need seventy. The extra ten disappear, and you never know the difference unless you are astute enough to count the number of sheets installed, and estimate the waste. Be guided accordingly.

RULE 25, THE RULE OF RULES

THE FORGOING IS A TASTE OF WHAT YOU ARE IN FOR IF YOU WANT TO BE THE BUILDER. YOU HAVE TO BE TOUGH, DILIGENT AND ABOVE ALL YOU MUST VISIT AND INSPECT THE JOB SITE EVERY DAY. IF YOU DON'T HAVE THE TIME AND THE DETERMINATION, AND BE ASSURED IT TAKES A LOT OF TIME AND EFFORT, YOU WILL BE BETTER OFF, AND YOU WILL SAVE MONEY IF YOU HIRE A GOOD DESIGNER BUILDER. IF THE WORKERS YOU DEAL WITH SEE THAT YOU ARE UNCERTAIN OR UNKNOWLEDGEABLE THEY WILL TRY TO TAKE ADVANTAGE OF YOU. YOU WILL BE DEALING WITH SOME OF THE WORLD'S BEST EXCUSE MAKERS. WHATEVER IS WRONG THEY WILL CONVINCE YOU IT'S NOT THEIR FAULT.

The biggest pitfall that you must avoid is undertaking something for which you are not emotionally prepared. Think about this carefully. You are going to have to be firm with bureaucrats and contractors. There will be mistakes and frustrations. People will not keep their promises and things won't arrive when they are supposed to. Weather may hamper you. For instance, you can't pour concrete if the heavy concrete truck sinks in the mud. You will have to be flexible and innovative. If this is not your cup of tea don't get involved because you will just wind up hating your new home. Leave it to a professional.

I have made the forgoing deliberately pessimistic because I owe you absolute honesty. BUT! if you want one of the most exciting and fulfilling challenges there is, and believe you can handle it, then go for it. There are few things more satisfying than creating and building your own home, and saving big money in the process.

In the next section I am going to take you through the construction of your home step by step. I will explain how it is done and what to watch out for. I will give you the knowledge to keep them all honest.

If you have decided to use a builder, this knowledge will afford you the ability to work closely with your builder in deciding options and details. You will understand what is going on and be able to alert him if something seems to be going wrong.

If you take up the challenge of being your own builder, you will learn step by step how to do it.

PART THREE

BUILDING THE HOUSE

CHAPTER 11

THE CONSTRUCTION MORTGAGE

Unless you have saved the money to build your house, and will be able to pay from funds you have, you will need to borrow money.

The usual vehicle to do this is called a construction mortgage. In a construction mortgage the lender will advance funds to you as the work progresses, in accordance with a schedule adopted by the lender. The total construction loan is usually limited to 75% of the total cost. When the construction is completed, usually at the time the final advance is to be made, you will close the final mortgage with the lender and the construction loan will be rolled over into your permanent mortgage in accordance with the amount and terms originally agreed in the mortgage commitment. During the construction phase, the lender will bill you monthly for the interest on the amount they have advanced. In this period you make no repayment of principal. After the permanent mortgage is closed your regular amortization payments will begin.

In order to obtain a construction mortgage you will have to provide certain information, but above all you will have to convince the bank that you know what you are doing. Lenders are very hesitant to lend money to home owners who intend to do their own building. Experience has demonstrated that in most cases the job takes very long to be completed. It is also common that the owner overspends his budget and has to come back to the lender for an increase in the mortgage in order to complete the job.

The greater the equity you are investing in the job, the more comfortable the lender will be. They will want you to put in at least 20% of the costs. A good start is to own the building site free and clear, which can count as your contribution.

In addition to the usual financial information the lender will want a complete set of approved plans, and a reasonable cost estimate. If you own the lot they will want to see a copy of the deed. They will inspect the site, and have their in-house appraiser evaluate the plans to see if your estimates are realistic.

RULE 26

DO NOT TRY TO ESTIMATE THE JOB YOURSELF.

Unless you are very experienced it is suicidal to try to estimate the job yourself. You may think that you can get bids on all the trades, and costs on all the materials from the suppliers to make your own cost projection. Don't do it! There are too many things that you will not think of or know about, and therefor leave out. You will not be able to estimate the unforeseen events and costs. Be assured MURPHY'S law is applicable.

The best course is to invite bids on the entire job from a few reliable building contractors. This will give you some figures to take to the bank that they will accept. If you know a builder, architect or engineer who can help you prepare the cost estimate, that would be acceptable.

After the bank has processed all of the information, and is willing to make you a loan, they will send you a loan and mortgage commitment. This is a document that sets forth the exact amount they are willing to loan you, and all of the conditions and terms they will require you to abide by. When you sign and return the mortgage commitment to the bank within the prescribed time the deal is set, and the loan is committed to you.

FINANCIAL DISCIPLINE

Once you are committed to a loan and a specific budget for your construction, it is of the utmost importance that you stick to it. As you go along in the construction you will be tempted over and over to do a little more, and upgrade the original plan.

RULE 27

THE MOST DANGEROUS WORDS AN OWNER BUILDER CAN SAY OR THINK ARE, "AS LONG AS I'M AT IT I MIGHT AS WELL DO IT. IT'LL ONLY COST A LITTLE MORE".

There is an almost irresistible temptation to overspend. As you review each part of the work you will think of ways to improve it. Then you will start to rationalize. This is the only chance I'm going to get, and I really like those better windows. It'll only cost a little more. This is a situation that will arise over and over. "As long as I'm doing it why not get those cabinets I really like", you will say, and while you are saying it you will completely forget about the other additions you already made. Unless you really have the additional funds available for the changes and upgrades, you must have the utmost discipline.

I have had clients almost have a heart attack when they saw the final total of all the extras they asked for. "Oh my God, I had no idea it would add up to so much, where am I going to get the extra money?" Sometimes there is no alternative but to go back to the bank and ask to increase the mortgage.

I once built a house for a young couple that kept adding on extras. Each time I quoted them the additional cost, and assumed that they had the money to pay for them. At the end of the job the last six hundred dollars of extras had to be charged to their Master Card.

There may be some legitimate changes that you should make after you see the construction, and realize that you may have overlooked something important. It is essential, that in your budgeting, you allow some additional funds for the necessary and legitimate changes. But above all you must resist getting carried away in the excitement of it all.

RULE 28

DON'T BECOME OVER FOCUSED ON THE DETAILS.

While you are looking at some detail, it can seem that it is the most important thing in the entire job. This can lead to stomach aches, fights with the sub contractors, and the waste of money. Don't let details get out of perspective.

Once I was building a house for a young couple and they had not chosen the Formica pattern for the vanity top in the half bath. (Not a highly critical item, right?) They spent two and a half hours in my office one night, looking at samples and trying to make up their minds. They just went around and around and around and couldn't decide. Finally I got them to agree to let me decide, and they would see it when it was installed.

It was obvious to me that they were in detail shock, and over focused. The fear of making a wrong decision kept them from making any decision. The samples they had narrowed the choice down to, were pretty much the same, and I was sure that later on, in a normal mood, they would like any one of them, which turned out to be the case. I am a paragon of patience, but that night I came close to throwing my clients out of my office.

On another occasion, I was building a large contemporary home for a client on top of a rather rocky knoll. The view was good and the knoll was surrounded by some beautiful mature oak and maple trees. Because the house was several hundred feet back from the road the utility company had installed a pole up on the knoll about eighty feet off one corner of the house, in order to bring their power cables up to the building.

Every time I came on the job site, my client would complain about how ugly the utility pole and the wires were. He wanted to have the power lines installed underground. I pointed out that the knoll was all rock, and that to bury the power lines would require blasting and some expensive excavation work. "I know", he would say, and then proceed to complain again about how ugly the pole was. I finally said to him, "you are suffering from a classic case of over focus syndrome. You can't get your mind off this pole. It is not that important. I am sure that after you live here a while, that pole will blend in with the trees behind it and you won't notice it any more".

A few months later when I visited the client, I asked him if he still was upset about the pole. "No", he said, "I've gotten used to it and I don't even notice it any more. I'm sure glad you talked me out of wasting a lot of money putting the power lines underground".

CHAPTER 12

SUBCONTRACTORS

WORKING YOURSELF

Unless you are really skilled in a trade, don't plan on doing any of the work yourself. Some people think that if they undertake some of the work they will save money. In order for this to be true you must have the necessary skill and the time. Otherwise, you will merely delay the job and it will wind up costing you more.

If you have time, and want to work, there will be many small tasks that need to be done that don't fall into the work of any particular subcontractor. Most of this will be moving materials and cleaning up. There is lots of cleaning to be done at the end of the job, such as vacuuming carpet, cleaning bathrooms, washing vinyl floors, cleaning counter tops, putting in screens and washing windows.

CUTTING DOWN THE MESS

Construction workers and working men in general, are the biggest slobs in the world. They think nothing of leaving greasy hand prints on freshly painted walls, or dropping snips of wire into newly laid carpet. They will leave their debris and waste wherever it falls, and expect someone else to clean it up. They will throw scraps of sheet rock out the windows and pieces of shingles onto the ground. They will amaze you in the ways that they can make a mess. Unless you want to be the full time clean up laborer, you have to make some arrangements, because once you pick up a shovel and a broom, and they see that you are going to clean up, then any slight effort at neatness that they might have exercised will be totally abandoned.

SUBCONTRACTORS

You will have to determine at the outset how you intend to dispose of the construction debris. Many communities allow the debris from the construction of a private home to be buried on the site. Check with the Zoning Administrator or the local environmental agency.

If you intend to bury the waste on the site, the place should be prepared when the land is being cleared or readied for the first work. Chose a location on the property that will be out of the way but not too far from the construction. The best way is to have a bulldozer dig a long deep trench a minimum of fifty feet long and eight feet deep if the ground permits. Don't underestimate the size of your burial hole. The job will produce more garbage, waste and debris than you can imagine.

If you don't intend to bury the debris, the alternative is to have a waste removal company place a trash container on the site. It should be at least thirty yards capacity. Make sure the container is placed near the construction but not where it will interfere with the movement of concrete trucks and delivery trucks.

When you hire each subcontractor make it clear that you expect them to clean up after themselves, and place all the dirt and debris they create in the trench or the container. If it is made clear at the beginning they will agree to it, although during the work you may have to remind them occasionally. If you wait until they are working on the job to tell them you expect them to clean up after themselves, they will claim that their price didn't include clean up.

It is also a good idea to provide four or five rubbish barrels on the job, in which the sweepings can be put, and carried to the trench or the container.

FINDING SUBS

Before you go out looking for subs it's a good idea to list all of the subs that you will require. Here is a typical list. Bear in mind that some of the subs may do more than one of the requirements listed.

TREE SURGEONS AND LAND CLEARING SPECIALISTS
EXCAVATOR
MASONRY AND/OR CONCRETE CONTRACTOR
FRAMER
SIDING INSTALLER
ROOFER
PLUMBER
ELECTRICIAN
HEATING, VENTILATING AND AIR CONDITIONING CONTRACTOR (HVAC)
INSULATION CONTRACTOR
SHEET ROCKERS (DRY WALL CONTRACTOR)
TAPERS (PLASTERERS)
TILE INSTALLER
TRIMMER (CARPENTER)
KITCHEN INSTALLER
PAINTER
HARDWOOD FLOORING INSTALLER AND FINISHER
FLOOR COVERING CONTRACTOR (CARPET & VINYL)

71

SUBCONTRACTORS

SEPTIC INSTALLER
WELL DRILLER
PUMP CONTRACTOR
PAVER (BLACK TOP)
LANDSCAPE CONTRACTOR
GUTTER & LEADER INSTALLER
GARAGE DOOR CONTRACTOR

There are several ways to find good subcontractors. If you have chosen a lumber yard where you intend to buy your lumber, it is a good place to ask for recommendations concerning framers and carpenters. The people who work in the lumber yard usually know who are the good and reliable contractors that are in demand. They are usually reluctant to recommend someone they are not sure about. Most lumber yards sell concrete block and masonry supplies and can advise you about masons as well.

Another good way is to ride around where there is new construction going on, and inquire who is doing the work. Development builders only hire subcontractors that experience has shown to be reliable and reasonable in price.

Another very good way is to ask the subs you have already hired. They work on many jobs, and know the people in the other trades. They know who does good work and who does not.

Above all they know all the gossip. They know who is in financial trouble, who are the drinkers etc. If you establish a good rapport with your subs they can be of great help.

Use the yellow pages with caution. Contractors who do good work and are in demand usually have plenty of work and don't spend the money for a big ad in the yellow pages. Subcontractors in general who do new work, don't advertise much. The plumbers and electricians who have big ads in the yellow pages, usually specialize in trouble calls and home owners work even though they may say in their ad that they do "new work". That is not to say that they don't know how to do new work or that their work will not be good. It is, that their price is likely to be higher.

The yellow pages can be helpful in finding people who do the quick jobs, like paving the driveway, or putting up gutters and leaders. These jobs are so short that these contractors cannot depend solely on new work, and must also advertise for home owners work. Another good example of this would be a garage door contractor.

HIRING SUBS

First of all, appearances can be very deceiving. A sub may show up with a smart looking pick up truck with a custom paint job and you think, here is a guy who looks reliable. You look in the back of his truck and all his equipment is neat and clean and you are impressed. Usually these contractors do their work in a neat, clean and beautiful manner, but they rarely have the lowest price.

The guy with the messy truck is not looking to impress anybody. He may be so busy that he doesn't have time to clean out his truck. On the other hand he may just be a slob.

No matter how they look, these subcontractors are all good talkers. They will tell you what great work they do and how they do it better than their competitors. I've met contractors who couldn't read or write, but they could sell refrigerators to Eskimos.

What you must do, is get at least three bids on the work. You may be surprised that the fellow you were leaning toward, and who sounded good, comes in with the high price. You must also ask for references, and check them out. Ask the people whether the contractor was reliable, and did good work Ask if he showed up when he promised, and if he stayed on the job or kept disappearing. Ask them how much they paid and what work they had done.

BEATING THE ONE SHOT DEAL

A lot of strategies have been tried in this regard, and chances are the subs have heard all the stories. For instance, if you tell the sub that your brother is going to build a house soon and that if he does a good job for you, you will recommend him, he is not going to believe it or any variation on that story. Never mind telling him about your connections and how much work you can help him get. He will know it's a story.

Here is one that works. Let's say you are taking a bid on the plumbing work. You say, my brother is a plumber and he wanted to do the work for me, but he works down in the city and he just doesn't have the time to come up here, but he said he would go over the bids for me and he will get the plumbing fixtures for me so don't include them in your bid. The fact that you are not asking the plumber to furnish the fixtures makes the story believable. The plumber may balk at this. He will say that if he has to be responsible for the fixtures he has to furnish them. Tell him that you won't hold him responsible for any defective fixtures. If he still argues, tell him to give you a separate price on the fixtures and that if his total price is in line you will let him furnish the fixtures.

As you go along you will develop your way of dealing with the subs. However, the incentive that I have found to be of the greatest value is in prompt payment. Most builders that these subs work for, do not pay very promptly. They are always waiting for an advance from the bank and juggling their finances. The subs usually have to wait thirty to sixty days to get paid, so they in turn are always scrambling for money.

Have them break down their bid into the phases of the job. For instance the plumbing would be, the underslab drainage and cast iron work, the roughing in of the piping after the house is framed up, and the finishing installation of the fixtures. Have him break down the price for each phase. Tell him that as soon as he has finished each section of the work, and had it approved by the plumbing or building inspector, that you will immediately write him a check. No waiting for the bank advances. This is where your having a little working capital comes in handy.

RULE 29

SUBCONTRACTORS WILL GO FIRST TO THE JOB WHERE THEY WILL GET PAID THE FASTEST.

Subcontractors are always scrambling for money to pay their help and their bills. They will come fastest and work the hardest on the job where they know they can pick up their money quickly.

Prompt payment is your strongest lever in negotiating the price to begin with, and assuring performance as you go along. Pay promptly but never pay for something that has not been done. For instance, the agreed amount for the cast iron plumbing work is $1000.00. The plumber comes to you and says he is done, and asks for his payment. First, you must inspect the work. But, don't put him off, do it at once, and together with him. Let him show you what he has completed. If there is some small item not finished he will usually tell you before you catch it. Like, "I ran out of rubber fittings for the lead elbow but I'll put it in tomorrow." Then you ask him for the inspection report. "Oh", he'll say, "I am going to call the inspector tomorrow morning to make the inspection, I guarantee you it will be all right. "Then you say, "well I'll give you the check tomorrow after you have put in the rubber fitting and the inspector has approved the work." "Look" he will say, "I really need the money now so I can make my payroll tomorrow." Now, don't turn him down, but don't pay for what is not done either. Write him a check for $800.00 and hand it to him. Tell him you will give him the other $200.00 tomorrow when everything is finished and the work has passed inspection.

RULE 30

YOU MUST MAKE IT CLEAR TO EVERY SUBCONTRACTOR YOU HIRE, THAT YOU WILL NOT PERMIT ANY BEER WHATSOEVER ON THE JOB.

Many a job has had unnecessary problems because of beer drinking. You must make it clear that you will not tolerate this, and anyone found drinking on the job will be immediately dismissed. If any worker cannot wait until after work for a beer, you will be well rid of him.

FORM OF THE AGREEMENT

It is not necessary to use complicated legal contract forms when hiring sub contractors. Most subcontractors will offer you their bid on a typewritten sheet or written on a pre-printed form called "PROPOSAL". Make sure the location of the work is properly stated. Make sure your name, as the customer, is properly shown with your address. Make sure that the proposal states that the work will be done as called for by the plans. If there is a cost breakdown and/or payment schedule, make sure it is shown. Any special stipulation about the work should be stated in the proposal. Make sure that whatever the contractor has promised is stated in the proposal.

RULE 31

HE WHO HOLDS THE MONEY, HOLDS THE KEY TO THE CONTRACT.

This is stronger than any contract you could write. The subcontractors cannot afford law suits. They need their money. If the work is not complete, always hold back some money to insure it's completion. If you pay in full. leaving some details incomplete, you may wait a long time for your sub to come back because he will be interested in staying on the next job where he is going to be able to collect more money. A sub is very slow to return to a job to finish some work when he knows that he is not going to get any further payment. As you will not have the lure of future work, your strength is in holding back money. Don't be unfair, but don't be an easy mark either. Always hold back more than the unfinished work is worth so your sub will be well motivated to finish quickly.

SUPERVISING SUBS

Supervising subs is truly an art. Your objective is to get them to perform their work promptly, efficiently and with good craftsmanship. In order to elicit this, you have to know how the work should be performed. If you don't know, and you ask why a certain thing looks wrong, you will get every excuse imaginable.

As we go through the course of construction I will try to alert you to all the tricks they like to pull. What you must do is watch the work very closely and inspect everything carefully. When the subs see you doing this, they will not try to get away with some of the stunts they usually pull. You should also look for opportunities to give praise. If something looks particularly good, tell them so, and praise the work.

When workers feel that their efforts are appreciated, it is human nature that they will be more careful, and try harder to please you to earn more praise. When you see something that you don't think looks right you cannot come out directly and find fault. You must always be oblique. "Oh" you must say, "I really thought the trim on that window would be more impressive than it turned out. I was hoping it would look fancier. Is there any way we could make it look better?" "Well I could round the corners on the window sill, that would make it look better", the sub might say." Oh. that's a great idea" you say, "could you do one so we can see how it looks?" "Sure", he says, "let me get my router from the truck and I'll show you how good it can look." "No kidding", you say, can you really make it look like molding?" "No problem" he replies and gets his router, and does one window sill with a nice edging and rounded corners. "Wow" you say, "I had no idea such a little change could make such a huge difference. That looks really great. Can we do that on all of them?" "Well I guess so" he says. "That's fantastic" You say, and before he can say that it involves extra work, and he would appreciate getting paid a little extra, you say, "lunch is on me. Let's all go up to the diner and have something good to eat." You may drop twenty or thirty bucks in the diner but it'll come back to you many times over.

If they think you appreciate their work, they will try harder. However, if you're critical, cranky and fault finding, they will not try as hard, and the work will suffer. "The hell with you", they will say to themselves. This is a game you cannot win and must avoid at all costs.

Be pleasant, tell a joke, bring coffee once in a while, and look for things to praise, but do not lower your standards or accept poor work because you don't have the heart to ask them to do it over.

Once I came onto a job site while my trim carpenters were working. They apparently hadn't heard me come in, and just as I was about to enter the room they were working in, I stopped short because of something I heard, and I listened. One carpenter was saying to the other, "are you going to leave that like that?" "Yeah" said the other guy, "it's good enough." "When the boss sees that", said the first guy, "he's going to make you change it." I turned around quietly and walked out. I was pleased to know that my workers were beginning to understand that I would not accept improper work. Seeing the way to drive the point home, I entered the building again, making sure I made enough noise so that the men would hear me coming. After a minute or two I pretended to notice the work they had been discussing. What happened here?" I asked, "this joint looks like it separated." "Naw", said the second carpenter, "I cut the miter a little short, I have to make a new piece." "That's great" I said, "I really appreciate your not letting something like that slip by". Out of the corner of my eye I could see the first carpenter grinning and nodding his head.

In a word, it's **diplomacy.**

I had a painter, who did very good work. Whenever I had occasion to introduce him to a client, I would say, "I'd like you to meet Pete. I call him "Rembrandt" because he is so artistic, and paints with such perfection. He is the only subcontractor that has done every home I have built in the last twenty years because he is the only one who can consistently live up to my high standards".

Blarney! you say? Of course it is. I know it, and Pete knows it, but he loves it anyway because he is proud to have his good work acknowledged and appreciated even though he knows I'm laying it on.

RULE 32

APPRECIATION AND PRAISE OF GOOD WORK IS THE BEST WAY TO ASSURE IT'S CONTINUATION.

CHAPTER 13

CLEARING THE LAND

THE BUILDING PERMIT

Before starting any work it is a good idea to apply for your building permit. Most communities don't require a building permit for you to start clearing the land, however some do. Rather than run afoul of the Building inspector at the outset, apply for the permit and ask if it is OK to start land clearing while you are waiting for it to be issued. Nothing angers a bureaucrat more, than when he thinks his authority is being ignored. If you are not sure whether something you intend to do is in accordance with the rules, rather than say the hell with it, go and ask. If an inspector feels that his authority has been flouted, and you have done something that he thinks required his OK, he will make you miserable for the rest of the job.

The better policy is to be humble. Go and ask permission. Tell the inspector you want to make sure it is OK with him before you proceed. Usually the inspector will be so pleased that you recognize his authority, that even if what you want to do is iffy, he will give you the benefit of the doubt, and tell you it's OK to go ahead.

RULE 33

KOWTOW TO AUTHORITY, NEVER FLOUT IT.

Even if you think the inspector is being picky, don't argue, just do it. You can't win a dispute with someone who has the last word. Apologize for the mistake, even if you don't think you made one, and thank him for bringing it to your attention. Tell him you want the house you are going to live in to be as perfect as you can make it. Even ask for suggestions. When he sees that you are going to be compliant, his ego will be soothed and he will think it won't be much fun to pick on someone like you.

STAKING OUT

The very first thing that is necessary, is to have a surveyor stake out the building lot. If the lot is very deep it may not be necessary to identify the rear corners, but the side lines should be flagged at least every hundred feet up to a hundred feet behind the location you have chosen for the house. The minimum set back from the front property line should be flagged. Most surveyors mark property lines temporarily with wood lath or little flags on wire. These markers are easily dislodged and fall over in the slightest breeze. The first thing I always do is drive a good substantial wooden stake next to the lath and tape the lath to the stake. Do the same with the little flags. If there is going to be a septic system and/or a well, have the surveyor mark out these locations as well. If you don't build your septic system at the location shown on your approved site plan, it may not be approved.

ROUGHING OUT THE LOCATIONS

You are going to need at least a hundred foot tape and a couple of rolls of surveyors marking tape in different colors. Both of these items can be purchased at a hardware store. The house location should be sited on your plan. Scale off from the side lines to the house on the plans, and then tape off the same distance on the ground. If there are trees and brush, it is sufficient to tie pieces of ribbon on the trees and brush to mark the approximate location for the house. We are going to assume for this discussion that your building lot is wooded. If it is not, just skip over the parts that have to do with clearing the trees.

You should allow about twenty feet all around the house location as the area to be cleared so that there will be enough room for the construction. If there are any particularly nice trees within this area that you would like to save, identify them with another color ribbon. If it turns out they are in the way, they can always be taken down later. At the outset be conservative in removing trees. It should also be remembered however, that big old trees near a house can also be a danger. They may die and fall, or they could be blown over by a hurricane or powerful wind. A big tree is not difficult to take down before the house is built, but afterwards it can be a very expensive proposition to remove without falling on the house.

The next thing to do is to roughly mark out the driveway. Tie ribbons in the low branches of the trees along both side of the driveway so that the machine operator can clearly see the path to be cleared.

The third thing is to determine the location of your tree and stump disposal area. If the land allows, a large trench must be dug similar to the one described for rubbish burial. Brush, stumps and logs, take a lot of room to bury so don't under estimate the amount of trench that will be required. Make sure that there is enough accessible area to dig a second trench if necessary. If the ground is rocky and difficult to dig, it may be possible to dispose of the brush, logs and stumps, on the side of a down sloping hill, where earth fill may be placed over the material and blended into the side of the slope. The worst case is to have the material trucked off the site. This may be necessary on a small lot where there is just no disposal area. However this should be regarded as the last resort because it is expensive.

CLEARING

The first step is to hire an excavating contractor and have him bring a bulldozer to the site. Bear in mind that you have spent some time on your site and are very familiar with it. You know what trees to remove and which ones to save. You know where the markers are, and where the disposal areas are. The bulldozer operator is seeing your lot for the first time, and does not have your familiarity. You cannot just tell him what you want and leave. He will forget, and become unsure about certain instructions. As a result the job will not be done as you wanted. This will just cost you more money. When you come to the job the next day and discover the errors and omissions, it will take more machine time to complete the work which probably could have been completed the day before.

When you have a bulldozer working on the site I strongly recommend that you stay there to answer questions or make judgements about individual trees that may have been overlooked. When the machine operator knows that you are on the site to give him guidance, he will be more confident and work faster.

Running a bulldozer is hard physical work. The machine is very noisy, and having no springs it is quite punishing. From time to time your operator may shut down the machine and get off to stretch his legs and/or have a smoke. He needs these breaks, and if you wait for them you can take advantage of the time by discussing the job and reviewing with him what you want him to do.

The first thing is to get him in to the location where the brush, stumps and logs will be buried, and have him start digging the trench. This will take a couple of hours. After the trench is prepared, have the operator start taking down the trees, starting with the ones closest to the trench. You will need to have arranged with your excavating contractor to supply an extra man on the job with a chain saw.

It is usually easier to push a tree over without cutting it down. If the tree is not too big, the dozer can push it over and the weight of it falling will pry the stump right out of the ground. If you fell the tree first, it will be much harder, take longer, and therefor cost more, to remove the stump. The dozer will have to dig around the stump cutting through the main roots, and undermine it until it can be pried out of the ground. This takes a lot longer than taking the tree down without cutting. If the tree is too big for the dozer to push over, the operator will work around the roots, severing the main members on one side until he is able to push the tree over. If the trees are close together the first tree may not have enough room to fall and wind up leaning into another tree. This is a dangerous situation and you should be a good distance away when the operator starts to push the tree. Sometimes when the machine first hits against the tree, dead branches in the tree may break off and fall. These are referred to as "widow makers" for obvious reasons. Be aware of this danger and stay back. If the tree is leaning into another tree, the operator will probably be able to push the tree and the stump, drawing it away from the tree it is leaning on. Sometimes there is not sufficient maneuvering room and if the dozer pushes the stump the tree might fall on the machine. Although most machines have a strong roof covering to protect against this danger, there are a lot of small dozers around that do not have this protection. The alternative is to rig a heavy chain around the base of the tree and have the dozer pull the tree free of the other tree.

Under no circumstances let the operator get carried away, and start knocking down a lot of trees. The resulting tangle of trees and brush can be very difficult to deal with, and also dangerous for the man with the saw who has to climb into the mess and start to cut it up. Sometimes a limb on a felled tree may be holding the trunk off the ground. If this is not noticed and the limb is cut, the heavy trunk could shift or fall and injure the man with the saw.

When the first tree is felled, make the operator wait until the man with the saw can cut off the brush, cut loose the stump, and section the trunk. Then let the dozer operator push the cut up material into the trench. It is important to cut up the trees before pushing them into the trench.

Otherwise they require so much space, and are so difficult to compact, that you will require too many trenches. After the first tree is cut up, and in the trench, there will be a little more room to take down the second tree. The same procedure should be repeated until there is a substantial clearing in which to work. The dozer operator can then take down the trees and push them into the clearing, aligning them parallel to each other with sufficient space in between for the chain saw man to be able to work. After a few trees have been stripped and cut up, they can be pushed into the trench. If the dozer operator is experienced, he will know how to pack the trench.

RULE 34

DON'T BECOME AN INSTANT WOODSMAN!

To some people a chain saw exerts a certain lure. It is one of those things that gives the user a sense of power and control. It cuts through the trunks of giant trees like they were butter, with the motor screaming and saw dust flying. Don't think that this is one of the jobs you can do, unless you are very, very, experienced with the use of a chain saw in the woods. Just as the saw races through a tree trunk it is equally effective on human flesh and bone. The slightest touch can rip a gouge you wouldn't believe. There are endless ways to get hurt with a chain saw. For instance, you are holding a running saw in your hand at your side, and you turn your body. Unknowingly you bring the flat of the blade against your leg. The projecting knives on the blade will slice your jeans and your flesh underneath in a blink of an eye. There are a lot of horror stories I could tell you about chain saw accidents. Suffice it to say, a chain saw deserves a very great amount of respect. It is a killer and it is not for amateurs.

RULE 35

FORGET THE FIRE WOOD, JUST BURY IT!

Even if you had a use for it, cutting and handling sections of a tree trunk is a lot of physical work. Green wood with it's high moisture content is quite heavy. You have to carry it piece by piece and stack it a good distance away, where it will not interfere with the clearing and the construction. It simply isn't worth it to do it yourself, or pay someone else to do it. If you want fire wood it will be a lot cheaper to have a cord of wood that is already cut, split and dried, delivered and stacked where it will be convenient to use, after the house is finished. Don't let friends or others come on your lot to cut and/or take the wood. It's too dangerous. If they get hurt, you can be liable. Only allow a bona fide contractor, who provides you first with a certificate of insurance, to enter on the job, and do any work of any kind.

We'll talk more about wood later on when we get to the subject of fireplaces.

STABILIZING THE ACCESS

After the house site is cleared, the driveway should be cleared next. If stumps are removed from the driveway there can be craters. All the soft top soil should be scraped off the driveway and the house site using the bulldozer. Stack the top soil out of the way where it can be saved for future use. Imported top soil is expensive, so it pays to save the native material.

Chances are the driveway drops off from the road and will need fill. If the driveway is fairly level it will hold water and can become a mire. Sometimes you can get fooled. If you clear the ground in the summer time the soil is usually dry and hard, but when the rain comes it can turn very soft. If you are clearing in the spring the chances are that the ground is going to be soft.

A lot of heavy trucks are going to have to come in and out of the site, and it is essential that the access is hard and stable. If the driveway area is soft, and wheels sink down, the best bet is to have some tailings delivered and placed on the driveway. Tailings are stones that vary in size from an apple to a grapefruit. They are screened out of bank run gravel. A good layer from six inches to a foot will press down into the ground and provide a good bearing surface. Another layer of screened gravel, called "Item 4", should be placed and compacted on top. This initially can be done with the bulldozer. During the course of construction, the heavy trucks will compact the driveway to a good solid base.

If there is a drainage ditch along the edge of the road it will be necessary to place a culvert pipe in the ditch before covering with the tailings and gravel. You should use a piece of corrugated, galvanized iron pipe, or heavy duty flexible plastic pipe, which is now available, at least 25 feet long and 12 inches in diameter. If you have purchased a lot in an approved sub division, the subdivision map will show what is required for the culvert. The lumber yard should be able to supply the necessary pipe.

PREPARING THE HOUSE SITE

If it hasn't already been done, the top soil should be removed from the construction area and the building platform prepared, as was discussed earlier. A reasonably level and smooth building site will make things a lot easier, so it pays to take the extra dozer time to do it.

Before moving on to the next step these are the things that should be completed:

TREES AND STUMPS ARE REMOVED FROM THE HOUSE SITE.
TREES AND STUMPS ARE REMOVED FROM THE DRIVEWAY.
TREES AND STUMPS ARE REMOVED FROM THE SEPTIC AREA.
TOP SOIL HAS BEEN REMOVED FROM THE ABOVE AREAS AND STACKED OUT OF THE WAY.
ALL TREES HAVE BEEN CUT UP AND PACKED INTO THE BURIAL TRENCH(S).
THE TREE BURIAL TRENCHES HAVE BEEN BACK FILLED AND SMOOTHED.
THE GARBAGE TRENCH HAS BEEN DUG.
THE DRIVEWAY HAS BEEN STABILIZED AND A BASE INSTALLED.
IF THERE IS TO BE A WELL, A PATH TO THE WELL LOCATION HAS BEEN CLEARED AND STABILIZED TO SUPPORT THE WELL DRILLING RIG.
IF THE CONSTRUCTION OF THE HOUSE WILL PREVENT ACCESS TO THE WELL AND/OR SEPTIC LOCATIONS AFTERWARDS, THOSE THINGS SHOULD BE INSTALLED NEXT. IF ACCESS WILL BE AVAILABLE, THEY MAY BE LEFT FOR LATER.
A CULVERT HAS BEEN INSTALLED IF NECESSARY.
THE BUILDING PLATFORM (AREA) HAS BEEN LEVELED AND SMOOTHED.

CHAPTER 14

LAYING OUT THE FOOTINGS

DIAGRAMS

Laying out the footings is a task that you can do yourself, but it is much easier to have someone helping, who can also double check against mistakes. I usually ask my masonry contractor to assist me. As he is going to pour the footings, and build the foundation walls, having him help in the layout, gets him involved in the responsibility for the layout to be square and accurate.

To layout the footings, you will need two fiber glass surveyors tapes 100 feet long. They should have feet divided into 12 inches on one side, and feet divided into tenths on the other side. Because frequently the ground is too hard or stony to drive wooden stakes easily, I prefer to use 12 inch spikes instead. You will also need a spool of mason's line and a hand calculator that does square roots.

The first step is to make a diagram of the house foundation. Mark in the length of the front, rear and sides, and then compute and mark in the diagonals. For illustration we will assume that the house is a rectangle 42 feet long and 26 feet wide

COMPUTATIONS

Figure 1

Shows a typical diagram of a rectangle. It is not necessary to draw these diagrams to scale as long as you draw reasonably straight lines. Distance AB is marked as 42 feet. Distance CD is marked 42 feet. Distance AC is marked 26 feet and distance BD is marked 26 feet. Now we want to find out the exact distance from A to D. We will do this by using the Pathagorian theorem which we all learned in high school.

In case you have forgotten, Pathagorus was a Greek mathematician who discovered that the combined squares of the smaller sides of a right triangle, equal the square of the hypotenuse, or the longest side.

Figure 2

Shows a typical right triangle. The angle between side A and side B is 90 degrees or a right angle. Side C1 opposite the right angle, is the hypotenuse.

Pathagorus discovered that $A^2 + B^2 = C^2$ which is therefor called the Pathagorian theorem.

A simple example is the three, four, five, right triangle.

$$Side\ A = 3$$
$$Side\ B = 4$$
$$Side\ C = 5$$

Thus:

$$A^2\ is\ 3x3 = 9$$
$$B^2\ is\ 4x4 = 16$$
$$C^2\ is\ 5x5 = 25$$

Therefor

$$9+16 = 25$$

Or:

$$A^2+B^2 = C^2$$

Returning to Figure 1, we want to find the length of the line AD. Applying the theorem we have:

$$Side\ a^2\ is\ AC^2 = 26x26 = 676$$
$$Side\ b^2\ is\ CD^2 = 4^2x4^2 = 1764$$

Thus:

$$676 + 1764 = Side\ c^2\ is\ AD^2 = 2440$$

There for:

$$AD = square\ root\ of\ 2440$$

Is:

$$49.396$$

Figure 3

Our original rectangle with the diagonal dimension, AD, shown as 49.4 feet.

There are a number of ways to construct a rectangle on the ground without using calculation. They depend on a trial and error approach. Not only are these methods time consuming, but they are more susceptible to error.

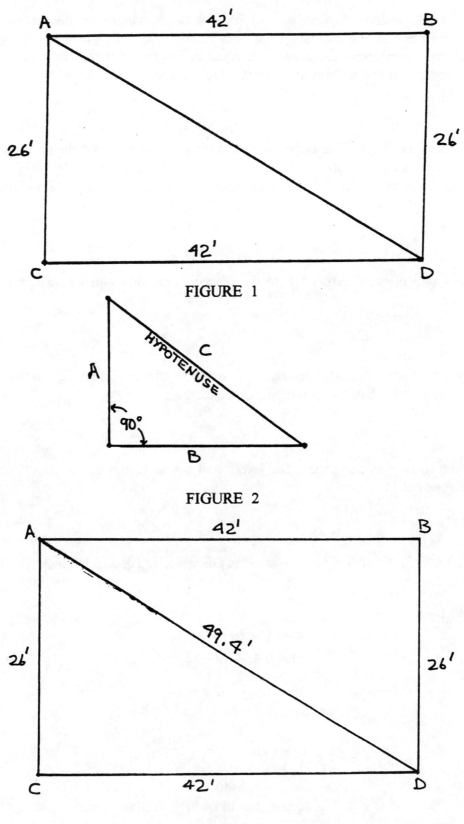

A — 42' — B

26'   26'

42'
C   D

FIGURE 1

HYPOTENUSE
A
90°
B

FIGURE 2

A — 42' — B

26'   26'

49.4'

42'
C   D

FIGURE 3

A popular old fashioned way, was to lay out the rectangle on the ground using the dimensions of the sides and approximating the right angles by eye. In a proper rectangle the two diagonals which run from opposite corners are equal in length. Thus the method is to measure both diagonals, and adjust the angles until both the diagonals are equal in length.

Figure 4

Shows a basic rectangle. The opposite sides are equal in length and the diagonals are equal in length when the corner angles are right angles. However, if an error is made in the dimension of one of the sides, the diagonals will still be equal and the error may go undetected until it is too late.

Figure 5 & 6

Illustrates two possible errors where the diagonals are still equal although the opposite sides are not equal.

Figure 7

Illustrates a more complicated layout. Note however that no matter how complex the plan becomes it is nothing more than a group of attached rectangles.

Figure 8

Shows the rectangles comprising the layout and the diagonals to be calculated Solve the rectangles as follows:

Rectangle 1

distance BC is 3, distance CF is the same as DE which is 20, and FG is 3. The total length of BG therefor is 26.

Using our theorem:

$$\text{Side a} = BG = 26$$
$$\text{Side b} = AB = 42$$

Thus:

$$a^2 = 26 \times 26 = 676$$
$$b^2 = 42 \times 42 = 1764$$

Thus:

$$a^2 + b^2 = 676 + 1764 = 2440$$

Therefor

$$c^2 = 2440$$

And:

$$C = \text{square root of } 2440 = 49.396$$

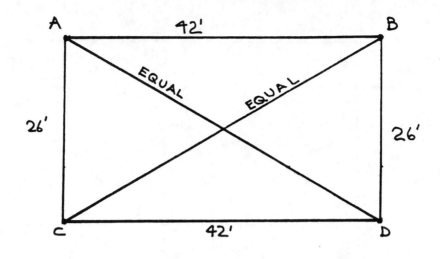

FIGURE 4

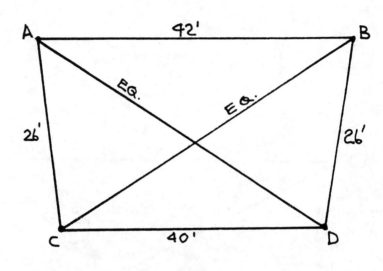

FIGURE 5

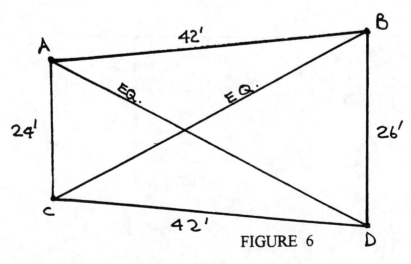

FIGURE 6

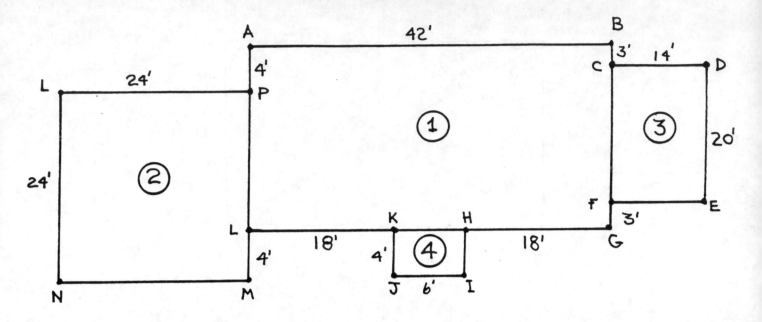

FIGURE 7

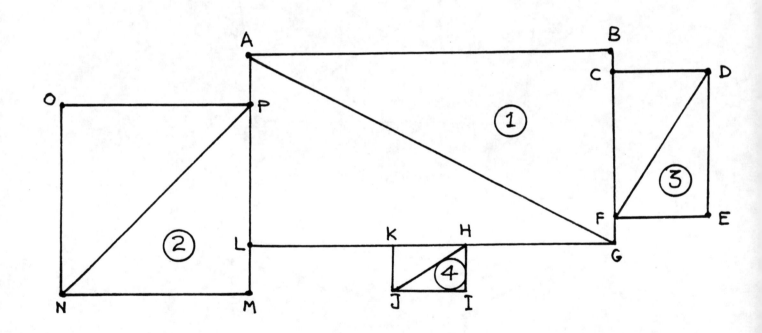

FIGURE 8

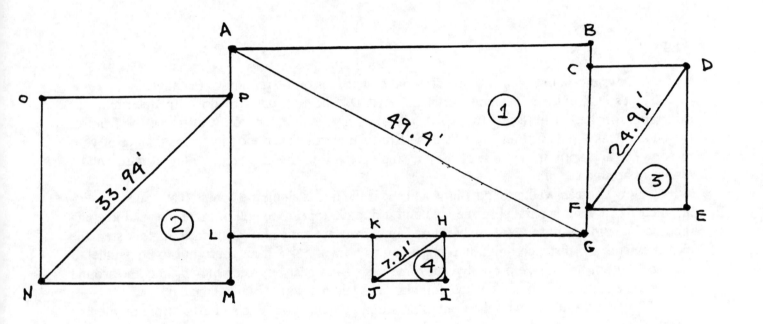

FIGURE 9

Rectangle 2

$$24x24 + 24x24 = c^2$$
$$576 + 576 = c^2$$
$$1152 = c^2$$
$$c^2 = \text{sq. root of } 1152$$
$$C = 33.94$$

Rectangle 3

$$14x14 + 20x20 = c^2$$
$$196 + 400 = c^2$$
$$596 = c^2$$
$$c = 24.41$$

Rectangle 4

$$4x4 + 6x6 = C^2$$
$$16 + 36 = C^2$$
$$52 = C^2$$
$$C = 7.21$$

Figure 9

Shows our house plan with the diagonal dimensions of the respective rectangles.

Let's start with our simple rectangle, ABCD. The first thing to do is to determine the orientation of the house. Drive two pins (spikes) along the line that you want to be the front of the house. Make them further apart than the front dimension. Tie a loop in the beginning of your mason's line and hook it over one of the pins and extend it to the other pin. Pulling it taut, wind a few turns around the pin.

Now you can walk around a little and see if the line is along the course that you want. For instance if you want it parallel to the road and it doesn't appear so, pull out one pin, and keeping the line taut, move it forward or backward until you are satisfied. Remember in this step the measurements and distances are not as important as how it looks. It may turn out to be parallel to the road but not harmonize properly with some large trees near by. Keep moving the line around until you are satisfied. When the whole foundation is laid out you can still change it.

If you are satisfied with the front orientation, go along your line and drive a pin on the line where you think a corner ought to be. Take your tape and measure from that pin, along the line the exact length of the front, which in our example is 42 feet, and drive another pin which will then represent the opposite front corner. Step back again and see if you like your side to side positioning. Move your pins left or right until you are satisfied.

Take one of your tapes and hook it on one of the corner pins and extend it back in an approximate right angle for the length of the end, which is 26 feet. You may need a hand here because sometimes the tapes slip off the pins. Now hook your other tape on the opposite front corner and extend it out along the approximate diagonal for the required distance which is 49.4 feet. You will need to use the scale on the tape that is in tenths. Now holding that tape in one hand pick up the other tape and bring them together so that the 49.4 foot mark on the one tape is exactly at the 26 foot mark on the other tape. Now you can hold both tapes in one hand and pull them taut, but not so hard that they slip off the pins or pull them out. With your free hand you can now place a pin at the exact juncture of the two dimensions on the tapes. After you have hammered the pin into the ground, you can hold the tapes on the top of the pin and make sure the intersection of the measurements is on the head of the pin. If it is slightly off adjust the pin accordingly. With a little practice you can become adept at this maneuver.

You can now repeat the process with the other diagonal and set the opposite rear corner. After it is set, measure between your two rear pins. If you have done it accurately the dimension should be within a half an inch which is accurate enough for this step. If you find there is an error, there is another way to find the last corner which is less prone to inaccuracy.

Hook a tape on the back corner you have first laid out, and extend it approximately parallel to the front line for the called for, 42 feet. Hook your other tape on the front corner now nearest to you, and extend it backwards the 26 foot distance until it intersects with the first tape. Bring the two dimensions on the tapes together. They should be intersecting at right angles, and you will feel that it is easier to hold them in one hand with equal tautness. Drive your final pin at the point of intersection. You know that your front and rear are equal, and that your ends are equal. To check the layout, measure the diagonals. If they are equal within a half an inch, you've got it. If not, repeat the steps from the beginning more carefully.

After your four corners are established run your mason's line around the entire perimeter and make it fast. You can now see the exact rectangle which will be the house.

RULE 36

DON'T PANIC WHEN YOU SEE THE SIZE OF THE FOUNDATION.

You didn't make a mistake. When foundations are laid out on the ground they always look too small because your eyes have nothing to compare them to. Have confidence in your plan.

Many a client called me in a panic after seeing the foundation, and was sure that some grievous error had been made.

Let's now add to our rectangle to create the layout as shown in figures 7, 8 and 9. Your basic rectangle is now, ABGL. Take another piece of line and attach it at point A. Bring it forward directly across the top of the pin at L and extend about six feet. Place a pin and tie the line to it. Make sure your line is straight, and passes directly over pin L. If the pin interferes with the string, hammer it deeper into the ground. Now starting from point A, measure along the line with your tape, a distance of exactly four feet and place pin P. Measure from pin L along your line exactly four feet and place pin M. Recheck, and make sure that pins APL and M are in a perfectly straight line. This is important, as it assures that the second rectangle you lay out will be square to the first rectangle. Now you have points P and M, which are two corners of rectangle No. 2. Proceed to lay out the rest of rectangle No. 2 in the same way that you did the firsts rectangle. Extend your tape from point M toward the location of point N for the required 24 feet. Extend your tape with the scale in tenths, from point P toward point N. Grasp your two tapes in one hand with the exact dimensions intersecting, and set pin N at the intersection. After the pin is set, hold the tapes on the head of the pin with equal tension, and make sure the intersection of the dimensions falls on the head of the pin. If not, adjust the pin location. Now run your tapes from N to O and from P to O, having them intersect at right angles. In this case both dimensions are 24 feet. With equal tension set pin O at the point of intersection, and you have completed rectangle No. 2.

LAYING OUT THE FOOTINGS

On line BG, measure the appropriate dimensions along the line and set pins C and F. Complete rectangle No. 3 as you did rectangle No. 2.

Measure along line LG and set pins K and H. Complete rectangle No. 4. Remove the string from the original rectangle and run it around the entire perimeter of the completed house layout, winding it a turn or two on the pins, as you go.

You can now see the layout of the entire house. Assuming this is the layout for your house, you would next check the positioning. Make sure there is room for at least a thirty foot apron in front of the garage, so cars can be maneuvered easily. Check for conflicts with trees or other natural features. If you find there is a tree or two, too close to the foundation, remove them now before any further work is done. If the pins and string are disturbed by this, reset them after the area is cleared of all brush.

In case you don't have the diagonals calculated, or you don't have a tape in tenths, or the paper with the diagonals on it blew away, there is another way to lay out a rectangle on the ground. It depends on the use of what is called a 3,4,5 triangle. In a triangle which has one side 3, and a second side 4, and the hypotenuse 5, you will see that $a^2 + b^2 = c^2$. Therefor, the triangle is a right triangle, and the angle between the two smaller sides is 90 degrees.

Going back to your original rectangle, you establish your front line and set your points C and D. We are now going to lay out a 3,4,5 triangle, but to be more accurate we will use the squares of the sides so that the triangle will be larger.

From point C, measure along your front line toward point D and set a pin exactly 16 feet from point C. Now take your two tapes and run one from point C at an approximate right angle for a distance of 9 feet. Run the other tape from the pin you just set 16 feet from C, on the approximate diagonal for a distance of 25 feet. At the intersection of the 9 and 25 on the tapes, set another pin. You now have constructed a right angle on the ground.

Remove the pin 16 feet from C as it is no longer needed. now extend a line from C up across the pin you set at 9 feet, and run the string for a distance of more than 26 feet, set a pin and secure the line. Make sure the line runs directly over the pin at 9 feet. Now measure from point C, up this line for exactly 26 feet and set a pin which will be point A.

You now have established points A,C and D, and can establish the last corner as done previously. Recheck all dimensions, making sure opposite sides are equal. If all dimensions check you have laid out the initial rectangle. Remove the pin at 9 feet, and run your string around the perimeter. For additional rectangles repeat the same process. For practice, draw out the above instructions on a piece of paper.

CHAPTER 15

BUILDING THE FOOTINGS

WIDTH OF TRENCH

Assuming that the foundation of your house is now laid out on the ground with a string around the perimeter, the next step is digging the trench for the footings. for this example we are going to describe the construction of a modified slab foundation.

The trenching is going to be done with a machine called a "Backhoe". This machine has an extended, articulating arm, on the end of which is attached a digging "Bucket" equipped with large steel teeth. The width of the trench is determined by the width of the bucket. Building codes usually require a normal footing to be 16 inches wide, therefor it is only necessary to use a 16 inch wide bucket. However, most backhoe owners have equipped their backhoe with a 24 inch wide bucket, to use for digging septic system trenches. If your trench is dug 24 inches wide instead of 16 inches wide, it will be 50% wider than necessary and therefor use 50% more concrete than needed. The mason will base his labor charge on the amount of concrete he pours so the labor charge will be 50% higher than necessary.

Using our foundation example from figure 7, you measure around the perimeter you will see that there are 230 lineal feet of footing to construct. A standard footing is 16 inches wide by 8 inches high or thick. The cross section of the footing is therefor:

$$8" \times 16" = 128 \text{ Square Inches}$$

As there are 144 square inches in a square foot we have:

$$128 \div 144 = .88 \text{ Square Feet. (Round to .9)}$$

By the same ratio every lineal foot of footing will require .9 cubic feet of concrete. Thus:

$$230 \times .9 = 207 \text{ Cu. Ft.}$$

A cubic yard contains 27 cubic feet. Thus:

$$207 \div 27 = 7.666 \text{ Cu. Yds. of concrete.}$$

We convert the quantity to cubic yards as concrete is sold by the cubic yard.

Following the same process for a footing 8" x 24" we have:

$$8 \times 24 = 192 \text{ Sq. In.}$$
$$192 \div 144 = 1.333 \text{ Sq. Ft.}$$
$$230 \text{ Lin. Ft.} \times 1.333 = 306.666 \text{ Cu. Ft.}$$
$$306.666 \div 27 = 11.358 \text{ Cu. Yds.}$$

Thus

$$11.358 - 7.666 = 3.69 \text{ additional Yds. for the 24" footing.}$$

If the concrete costs $80.00 a yd. and the labor to pour it is $60.00 a yd., that is an additional cost of $ 516.60. This is wasted money. It is also one of the things that nobody wants to tell you. If you ask why a 24" bucket is used you will be told,"That's the way we always do it! When you hire your excavator you can save this wasted money if you can find one with a 16" bucket. However, that may be difficult because they have been digging footings 24" wide for so long that they think that's the width they are supposed to be.

SETTING THE ELEVATION

FIGURE 10

This is a cross section view of the foundation for a modified slab, and how it relates to the initial ground elevation and the final elevation.

The first thing to determine is how deep to dig the trench. In order to figure this out you need to know the depth required by your local building department, that the footing is required to be, below the final grade. This depth is set to be certain that the bottom of the footing will be below the lowest level the frost will go into the ground. In the example shown, the required depth below the final grade was 42 inches. An extra 2 inches was allowed for error. This depth is shown as No. 1 on the diagram. If the requirement in your area is more or less, just adjust the total height of the foundation accordingly. The total height is shown as No. 2.

The ground level you are starting with is shown as No. 3. Note that initially, the foundation will be above the starting ground level by about two feet. See No. 4. This allows enough height to fill and grade around the foundation allowing for ups and downs in the starting ground level and providing enough height to slope the final grade away from the foundation, assuring that drainage will flow away. No. 5 shows the final grade which is 8 inches below the floor level. See No. 6 and 7. The floor level is the level at which the wood framing will begin. Codes require that the final grade be at least 8 inches lower than the lowest wood member. This is to help prevent insect intrusion.

If the top of our foundation (7) is 2 feet (4) above the starting ground level (3), then we merely need to subtract 2 feet from the total height of the foundation (2) and the difference will be the depth of the trench required (8). If your required frost depth is less than the example, the trench will be shallower, and conversely if the frost depth is greater, the trench depth will be deeper. However, even if no frost depth is required, the trench should be at least 8 inches

BUILDING THE FOOTINGS

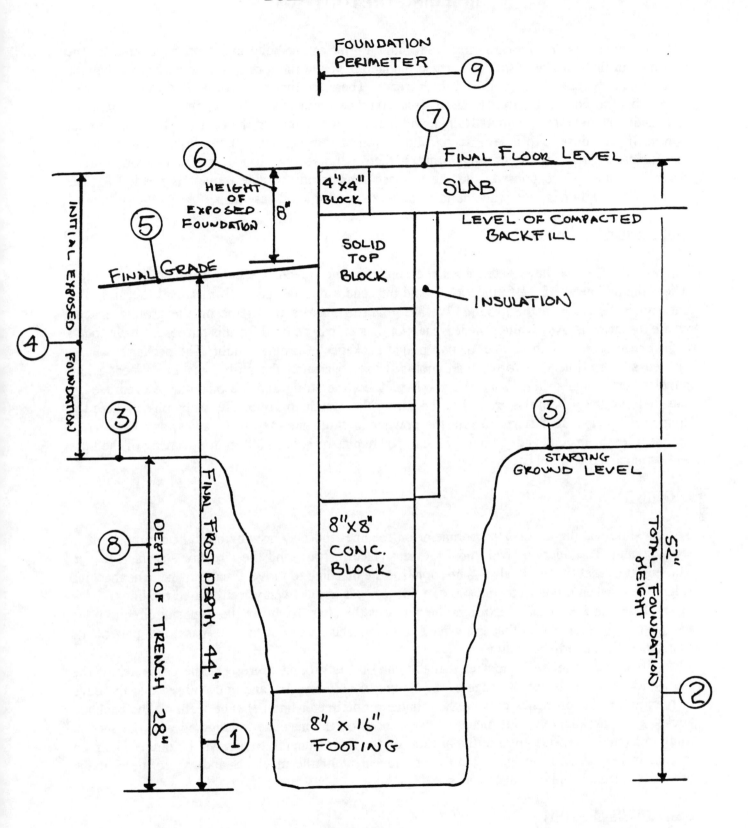

FIGURE 10

94

deep to provide the form for pouring the footing. Forms can be built on top of the ground for the footing, but the expense of the lumber and the labor to build the forms, and later remove them, is greater than the cost of digging an 8 inch trench. There are times when the ground is so soft or sandy, that the sides of the trench fall in. This would be a time to dig the trench wider so that even if the sides slope in, the required 16 inch width can be maintained at the bottom. There is another option. If the house is to have a second floor, you can buy enough of the floor joists ahead of time, and use them for the footing forms. If there is no second floor then use the roof rafters. After the footings are poured, pile the stripped lumber on the side until it is needed for the framing. This option is used when building a foundation for a full basement.

MARKING THE LAYOUT

Now that we have determined the depth for the trench, we can return to our example where the perimeter of the foundation is laid out, and a mason's line is run around the pins. The line should be close to the ground. We are going to make a white line on the ground exactly where the string is. Any white powder, chalk or plaster, can be used for this purpose. I have found it the cheapest, to buy three or four two pound packages of ordinary flour. The packages can be opened at the corners to form small spouts. Proceed around the string, making a neat white powder line on the string. When the line is finished, the string and the pins may be removed. I usually leave the pins in the ground at the end of the foundation opposite to the place where the digging will begin. If it starts to rain the powder or flour line may wash away, and have to be redone after the ground is dry again. If the opposite pins have been left in, the relaying of the lines will be much easier and faster.

DIGGING

The backhoe will dig around the perimeter on the line, and may now be brought into position to start digging. The operator will know the best place to start, and the direction in which to dig. The object is, that there will always be room for the machine to move along the line. The machine is large, and when it comes to the end of a line it needs about twenty feet beyond the line to back up. If there is a tree or obstruction in the way it is then best to dig in the opposite direction. He will also dig in such a way that the wheels of the machine will not have to pass over part of the trench that has already been dug.

It is important to remember that the line on the ground represents the perimeter of the foundation wall and is not the edge of the footing. See Figure 10, and you will see that the edge of the footing is four inches outside the foundation perimeter line (9). The teeth on the backhoe bucket are approximately four inches apart, so position the machine for digging with the second tooth in from the outside edge of the bucket, on the line. Thus the trench will be dug a minimum of four inches outside the line. Due to the movement of the machine, and the softness of the ground the trench will be a little wider.

USING THE TRANSIT

The excavator must now set up his transit or builders level, for the purposes of digging the trench. The best location for the transit is in the middle of the foundation. In this position it can rotate 360 degrees and follow the machine as it trenches around the perimeter line. Later on we will position it outside the perimeter, but for now, inside is the easiest.

Figure 11.

This is a simple diagram to remind you of the way in which a transit is used. The transit (2) is set upon the tripod (1). It is equipped with leveling screws and bubbles so that the telescope may be made exactly level. When you look through the level telescope (2), the line of sight is a precisely level line. With the telescope focused on the measuring stick, you can read the exact height above the ground, of the line of sight. The measuring stick is calibrated in feet and inches. The telescope lens has cross hairs at the exact center. The precise point on the measuring stick intersected by the cross hairs can be read to the fraction of the inch. Because the transit is a telescope, the stick can be read clearly up to several hundred feet away. Always make sure that the zero end of the stick is on the ground. In the diagram, the line of sight is at 3 feet two inches above the ground. We want the bottom of the trench to be 28 inches below the ground. If we add that amount to the 3 feet 2 inches, we get a total of 5 feet 6 inches.

When the stick is positioned on the bottom of the trench, and the cross hairs intersect the 5 foot 6 inch mark, then we know that the trench is exactly 28 inches deep. Once the desired reading on the stick is determined, it may be marked with a sliding target that fits on the stick, or if you are using an ordinary ruler, a piece of tape may be placed at the mark. This will help avoid mistakes or forgetting the desired reading.

As the backhoe digs around the perimeter, every few feet, the depth of the trench is checked with the assistance of the operator's helper. According to the reading, the operator will adjust the depth of his digging. A good operator can stay within ± 2 inches. The helper follows in the trench, leveling the bottom and removing the loosened soil. Remember we want to pour the concrete for the footing on top of good, solid, undisturbed, virgin soil, so that no compaction will occur. If it rains between the time the trench is dug and the concrete is to be poured, it will be necessary to shovel out any washed in material. When the trenching is complete, it may be necessary to do a little hand digging where the machine cannot make a perfectly square corner.

During the digging of the footing trenches, the earth that is removed should be piled outside the trench. If it is put inside it will interfere with later steps in the construction. When the trenches are finished, the backhoe operator should level out the piles of earth, back from the trench. He does this by "back blading" with his front bucket.

SETTING GRADE STAKES

With the trench completed we are almost ready to pour the concrete footings, but there are a few more things to do.

When we pour the concrete into the trench, we need a way to spread out the concrete to a perfect level. Obviously if the footings are not level then the block wall on top of the footings will not be level, and the final slab will not be level.

There are several methods for doing this, but the one that I feel is the simplest and most reliable is to set grade stakes. The grade stakes will preferably be wooden stakes an inch or an inch and a half square, and at least a foot long with a wedge point on one end. These stakes are driven into the bottom of the trench every four or five feet, around the entire trench. We want to

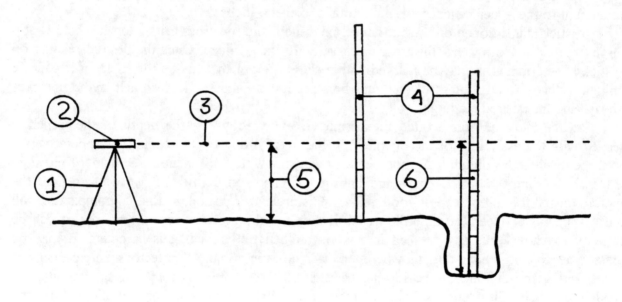

FIGURE 11

drive these stakes into the ground so that the tops of all the stakes will be at the same precise level. To do this we need to set up the transit again, but this time instead of setting it in the center of the foundation, we will set it up back from the foundation about fifty feet. The reason for this, is that it gives greater accuracy. When we set the transit in the center of the foundation, we did it so that we would always be able to see the measuring stick and it would not be blocked by the machine, which would happen if it were` outside the foundation. However, when the transit is inside the foundation there is a greater possibility for error. If for instance, the transit is slightly out of level so that in a distance of forty or fifty feet the elevation would read a half inch too low, then when we rotated the transit 180 degrees to the opposite direction, the elevation would read a half inch too high, thus doubling the error, and resulting in a one inch difference from one end to the other. Because the trench can only be dug within a tolerance of a couple of inches anyway, this possible error is not significant. But now that we want to set the grade stakes with absolute precision, such a possible error is not acceptable. So, we set the transit back from the trench, far enough that the traverse of the telescope would not exceed more than 60 degrees. Thus if there is an error, the error will be almost the same for all readings and therefor will not materially affect the final result.

Readings are taken around the trench until the highest spot is found. This is where the first stake is placed. Because the footing are required to be a minimum of 8 inches high we start at the highest point. Therefor, at points where the bottom of the trench is lower, the footing will be more than 8 inches high. You should find the lowest point in the trench and work out the average depth. Use this average as the height dimension when calculating the amount of concrete needed.

The first stake is driven into the bottom of the trench until, by the ruler, it is 8 inches from the bottom of the trench to the top of the stake. The measuring stick is now placed on the top of the stake and the exact reading taken, and marked on the stick. Each successive stake is driven into the bottom of the trench until it's top is at exactly the same height as the first stake. As the stake is driven in, after each few taps, the measuring stick is placed on the top of the stake, and a reading is taken through the transit. The stake is tapped in, until the reading is exactly on the mark of the initial reading taken for the first stake. This process is continued until all the stakes around the trench have been set at the same elevation. It is a good idea to check opposite ends a second time, to make sure no error has occurred.

FOOTING INSPECTION

At this point, most building departments require a "Footing Inspection". The Building Inspector wants to ascertain that the bottom of the trench is firm and virgin soil. He makes sure that there is no ground water seepage into the trench, there are no tree roots in or under the trench, no mud holes or other conditions which would indicate that the ground could not support the weight which will be put upon it. The Inspector will measure the height of the grade stakes to make sure that the footing will be at least 8 inches high.

ORDERING CONCRETE

Once the inspector has given his approval you are ready to pour the concrete. We already covered the mathematics of determining how much concrete to order for a given footing. However in practice, the trench will have come out wider than 16 inches. As we have already noted the average depth will be greater than 8 inches. It is important to use the full dimensions for the calculation. Use 18 inches for the width of the trench and 9 inches for the average depth of the footing.

It always seems that when poring concrete, it takes more material than the calculations indicate. To be safe, I always order a half a yard extra. If you pour, and come up half a yard short, the concrete company will make a large penalty charge for delivering such a small amount of additional concrete, and every one will be waiting around until it comes. It's a lot cheaper to possibly waste $35.00 or $40.00 worth of concrete than pay a $150.00 penalty, and wait around another hour or two.

POURING THE FOOTING

In pouring the footing it is very helpful if the clearing around the trench allows the concrete truck to reach all of the trench with it's dispatch chute. If not, it will be necessary to move some of the concrete by wheelbarrow. If the ground is soft or muddy after a rain, this will be difficult. It's a good idea to have some planks on hand in case a ramp for the wheel barrows is needed. It is true that it is basically your mason contractor's problem to place the concrete. However, the easier you can make his job, the more he will appreciate it, and you will have a happy and cooperative contractor to work with.

The concrete driver will mix some water with the concrete in the mixer, and let some of it down the chute for the contractor's OK as to it's degree of firmness. When the concrete is too firm, it's very hard work moving it in the trench. When it is too wet it runs away and is hard to control as well as the fact that concrete with too much water will not cure as strong as it should. When ready to go, the truck driver will allow concrete to flow down the chute into the trench. Experienced drivers know just how much this flow should be. At the same time he will gradually move the truck forward or backward, allowing the chute to move along the trench. The masons will level the concrete with rakes or a special concrete hoe, so that the concrete is level with the top of the stakes. Any leftover concrete can be dumped inside the foundation and spread out so it will become part of the final fill.

CHAPTER 16

STARTING THE FOUNDATION

ORDERING BLOCK

The next step is to figure out the number of concrete block and other masonry materials that will be needed, and have them delivered to the site.

The first four courses around the foundation will be regular 8 inch concrete block. Years ago concrete block were made 18 inches long and had three holes in them. Then they were shortened to 16 inches. Now with the development of lighter and stronger concrete, the block have two holes and are 16 inches long. Three 16 inch blocks end to end are 4 feet long. Therefor, the easy way to compute the block is for every 4 feet of foundation perimeter, you will need three blocks. If the perimeter of the foundation is 320 feet you have:

$$320 \div 4 = 80$$
$$80 \times 3 = 240$$

It will take 240 blocks to make one course. Therefor if we have 4 courses of regular 8 inch block you must order 960 regular 8 inch block.

For the fifth course you will use an 8 inch FHA block. An FHA block has a solid top so the holes do not go all the way through the block. In different areas these blocks may be known by a different name. They are used for the top course so there will be a good solid base on which to lay the final course of 4 inch by 4 inch block. The 4 inch by 4 inch blocks are sometimes called 4 inch splits because they are made by splitting a 4 inch by 8 inch block All the block are 16 inches long.

Your block order will look like this:

$$8 \times 8 \times 16 \text{ regular} = 960$$
$$8 \times 8 \times 16 \text{ FHA} = 240$$
$$4 \times 4 \times 16 \text{ splits} = 240$$
$$\text{Total Blocks} = 1440$$

You will need a bag of mortar for every thirty blocks so you need 48 bags of mortar. You will also need about 5 yards of masonry sand.

The block will be delivered piled in cubes on pallets, which are wooden platforms, or in cubes secured with plastic wrap. The truck delivering the block will have a crane capable of lifting the cubes off the truck and placing them on the ground. Most masons prefer that the cubes be placed inside the foundation, which will minimize the distance they have to be carried.

You will probably wind up with a few extra blocks because outside corners use only a half block per course. A few extra blocks on the job will come in handy for a variety of purposes.

LAYING OUT FOR THE BLOCK

The first thing the mason will do is measure the footings from front to rear and end to end. If the trenches were not dug perfectly straight, it may be necessary for the block to be set a little to the outside or a little to the inside of the footing. After determining this he will set up his front line by driving a nail in the corner of the footing. If the concrete is only a day or two old the nails will drive into the concrete easily. If the footing concrete is harder, it may be necessary to use special masonry nails. From the first nail he placed, he will tape the precise distance, and set a second nail at the opposite corner. He will then set the other points using the same procedures that we used when laying out for the footings. Because the points are below the level of the ground, when measuring the diagonals he will use masons levels set upright and perpendicular at the points. With the levels extended above the ground the diagonals can be measured.

He next will set up his transit and shoot elevations around the footings until he has found the highest point. He will then find the lowest corner and determine the difference between it and the highest point. Let's assume the difference is a half inch. He will start with the corner and set the first blocks in thicker mortar, a half inch higher than usual so that when the blocks are laid successively level, when they come to the high point in the footing, they will pass over.

All the corners will be laid first. Using the transit, the elevation of each course will be made exactly the same, so that when the FHA course is laid all of the corners will be precisely level to each other.

When the level of the block gets above the ground level, it will be possible to check the diagonals again, very carefully. Slight adjustments to the position of the blocks may be made so that the diagonals are exactly equal.

After the corners are done, a mason's line is stretched between them, and the in between blocks are laid in, with their tops always made level to the string. If due to bumps in the footings, some blocks in the first course stick above the string, at that place, the joints will be made thinner for the next course. This process is continued until all the blocks are completed and exactly level.

SUB GRADE INSULATION

The next step is to install insulation inside the foundation wall. In warm climates where the ground never freezes, this insulation is not necessary. In cold climates it prevents the cold outside that portion of the foundation which is above the ground, and the cold of frozen ground, from penetrating into the foundation.

I prefer to use rigid styrofoam insulating boards that are 2 feet wide, 8 feet long and 2 inches thick. The R value should be about 10. These are placed against the inside of the block foundation wall with the 2 foot width in the vertical plane even with the top edge of the FHA blocks. To hold this insulation in position until the back filling is done, use a few masonry nails in each sheet. The nails can be easily driven into the joints between the block. The styrofoam material can be cut easily with a razor knife and should be installed neatly without spaces or voids.

In most of the country, the temperature of the ground, 4 or 5 feet below the surface, is relatively constant all year round. It will usually be somewhere between 50 and 60 degrees Fahrenheit When the house is finished this heat in the ground will rise to the slab and provide substantial heat inside the building even if there is no heating system in operation. Think of the perimeter insulation as a means of keeping this heat inside the foundation. If an internal temperature of 70 degrees is maintained, and the ground temperature is 57 degrees as it is in the Northeast, there is only a 13 degree temperature differential, and very little heat will be lost into the floor. In a heated house the slab temperature will stabilize above 60 degrees. Carpet installed over styrofoam padding provides additional insulation keeping floors warm and comfortable. In the summer time the slab will have a very noticeable cooling effect.

THE WATER SERVICE LINE

Before backfilling the foundation the water service line should be installed. Make a hole through the block just above the footing in the location where the water service will be brought to the house. Install the water line through this hole and bend it upward close to the foundation. Have enough line coiled up at this point so that when it is extended it will reach the point inside the foundation where the water line will come up through the slab. If you try to bring the water line to that point before the backfilling, it will surely get damaged and knocked out of place. The line should be a minimum of 3/4 inch and be of soft copper or 200 pound test, PVC flexible waterline. I prefer to use copper inside the foundation. It is easier to bend and work with. The plastic line is stiff and difficult to shape to come out of the floor at a precise point.

Leave 4 or 5 feet of line turned up outside the foundation for future connection to the water service line.

BACKFILLING

We are now ready to backfill the foundation inside and out. We want to use a material that is readily compactable. Do not use the excavated earth, or any soil containing significant amounts of clay or organic substances as they cannot be properly compacted, and will settle, later on. The best material to use is "Run of Bank" gravel with low clay content and no stones larger than a grapefruit. Course sand is also good. These materials only compact about 5%. in volume.

There are several different ways to put the gravel into the foundation. I prefer to use a small bulldozer as it's constant movement does a good job of compaction.

The material should be delivered and dumped in piles near one end of the foundation where there is good maneuvering room. The dozer will slowly push material toward the foundation starting a pile about six feet away. Each blade of material should be pushed up the incline of the pile until it slides down the far side by itself. This technique is very important if disaster is to be avoided. When a bulldozer pushes material forward, even though it may be higher than the foundation wall, the pressure moves outward in front of the blade in the form of a cone, similar to a beam of light. If an attempt is made to push material over the top of the foundation in a horizontal plane, the downward pressure into the material will press it against the foundation wall and topple it over.

RULE 37

WHEN BRIDGING A WALL ALWAYS PUSH MATERIAL UP HILL.

The secret is to always move the material up hill and allow it to trickle down to the foundation and eventually over it.

When there is a good amount of material inside the foundation wall, the dozer may level off the pile, but at least two feet above the top of the wall. It can then drive down the gravel inside the wall, thus compacting it against the inside of the wall as has already been done on the outside. It is always important to fill both sides of a wall at the same time so that the pressure of the material is not all on one side, which could shift the wall or cause it to tilt.

Once a good hill is established over the wall, the length of the slope inside and outside can be increased to reduce the steepness of the incline, making it easier to push material into the foundation. The gravel should be placed in front of the base of the inside ramp gradually extending forward and outward, in a layer of about 8 inches thick. Each blade full of material should be pushed over the one before so that the dozer is continually compacting the material already in place. When approaching the foundation walls from the inside, care should be taken that there is no large boulder in front of the blade that cannot be seen by the operator. Such a hidden boulder, when the machine approaches closely to a foundation wall, could be driven right through the wall.

After the first 8 inch layer, which is called a "Lift", has been placed inside, a mechanical compactor should be run around the inside of the wall to compact the area where the dozer did not go. Usually this is about 2 feet inside the walls.

While this is going on the dozer should carefully fill in the trench around the outside of the wall, and place a layer of material, up 8 inches on the outside, so as to be at the same level as the material inside. The compactor is then run around outside while the dozer begins to place the second lift inside the foundation.

This process is continued inside and outside, always maintaining equal pressure on both sides of the block walls, until the gravel is up to the level of the FHA block. A good dozer operator can back blade and level the material to within an inch. The ramp can be cut down in the final stages leaving just enough material for the dozer to get out from inside. If some of the 4 inch block are dislodged they can easily be reset. It is a good idea to leave the four inch block off for about 10 feet, where the gravel will be pushed in.
This makes the leveling easier.

The compactor should be run over the entire interior area and if the material is low anywhere, more material should be brought in by the dozer.

RULE 38

AT THIS STAGE IT IS BETTER IF THE GRAVEL LEVEL IS AN INCH TOO HIGH RATHER THAN AN INCH TOO LOW.

When preparing to pour the slab, a string is stretched across the foundation on top of the four inch block. The string will represent the final top level of the concrete floor. Measuring down from the string, and advancing the string from one end to the other, the final hand grading is done. It is easier to shovel out a little excess material, than to fill in all the low spots. When the gravel is low, rarely will the men doing the final grading put in enough additional material.

The result is that you may pour a slab 5 inches thick when you intended it to be only 4 inches thick. This can increase your concrete cost, and your labor cost for the slab, a substantial amount. Hundreds of dollars can be wasted. And probably because the concrete order comes up short, you'll get a penalty charge for an additional small yardage delivery. The best point to prevent this is when the dozer is finishing the grading. Check with a string and make sure the gravel is not too low. It is very simple for the dozer to bring it up a little. Good supervision here, saves hundred of dollars later.

THE FULL BASEMENT FOUNDATION

Building a full basement foundation is similar, and in some respects easier, than the modified slab foundation we have been describing. Where before we laid out the foundation on our surface platform, we now want to build our foundation in the ground so we have to dig a hole to put it in. Usually an 8 inch block foundation is not buried in the ground more than 4 feet as required by most codes. If this is the case don't dig your hole more than 3 feet 4 inches deep so you can slope the final grade up toward the foundation for drainage purposes. The top of the foundation will be 8 inches higher due to the thickness of the footing, and we want the final grade to be 8 inches lower than the top of the foundation. Using this elevation allows enough height to install some high basement windows. If you want the house close to ground level, with one or two steps up to the entry, you should go about 7 feet into the ground.

You also have to decide how high the basement ceiling is going to be. A conventional foundation is usually 11 courses high. This would give a seven foot four inch height, but the slab will come up 4 inches on the first course of block so you will have a 7 foot high basement. In almost all designs there will be some sort of girder beam for floor support which can stick down as much as 12 inches. That would leave only a six foot clearance under the beam. If you are planning to use the basement as a family room or some other purpose besides storage, you may find that low a clearance inconvenient. You can raise the basement height another 8 inches simply by adding another course of block around the top of the foundation. This does not cost very much more, and I assure you, you will be grateful for the additional ceiling height.

FIGURE 12

This is a cross section through a full basement foundation. No. 1. is the starting ground level, and No. 2. is the excavation in the ground. In this case we are showing the house low to the ground with two 8 inch steps at the entrance. No. 3 is a concrete or brick step supported by block and footings constructed perpendicular to the foundation. The back filled earth can never be sufficiently stabilized to support a free floating step without it eventually settling. Even were we to do that, we would still need to build footings into the ground below the frost line. It is less trouble to extend the footing forward and lay two, cheek walls of block, to support either end of the step.

In this example the excavation is 7 feet 4 inches deep. The bottom is leveled as close as possible. We use the transit as before, to control our depth and level.

If you want the house to sit higher you just need to add 8 inch steps in front. For each step added, the excavation will be 8 inches shallower. No. 4. shows the final grade. To raise the house, lower levels No. 1. and No. 4. shown on the diagram and add steps (No. 3.) accordingly.

It is best to dig the excavation with a bulldozer as a ramp down into the hole will be useful. The excavation should not be any larger than necessary to stabilize the banks so that a minimum of backfilling will be required outside the foundation. See No. 2.

THE FOOTINGS

The hole isn't wide enough to allow a backhoe at the bottom, to trench the footings, so in this case we will form the footings, (5). We want the footings to be higher than the ground so that we will have a means of leveling for the slab. It is easier to add some good bank run material (6), than to try to level the compacted virgin material in the bottom of the hole. The bank run under the slab will also promote good drainage.

Because the bottom of the hole is not perfectly level the footing forms will not be perfectly level either. The footings must be level, so we will perform a step very similar to the setting of the grade stakes we did before.

We find the high point of the ground inside the footing, but this time instead of driving a grade stake, we will drive a nail slightly into the inside of the form exactly 8 inches above the bottom. Then with our transit set up in the bottom of the hole, we determine the exact elevation of the nail and proceed around the forms setting a nail at the same elevation every four or five feet. Sometimes the mason may set a nail at each corner, and then using a chalk line, snap a line on the inside of the forms at that level. Additional nails can then be placed at the height of the chalk line. This is faster than setting each nail with the transit. When the concrete is poured into the forms, it will be leveled to the nails just as we previously leveled it to the top of the grade stakes. Don't forget your footing inspection before you pour. Your plans probably call for lally columns in the basement which require their individual footings. 24" square is desirable.

Just a word here about setting the nails inside the footing. All the people I've seen do it try to hold the measuring stick against the inside of the footing form and move it up or down as the man on the transit says. Then they make a pencil mark at the bottom of the stick where the nail will be set. This is very difficult to do. Kneeling down it is very hard to hold the stick correctly upright without something to lean it against. Then, once the height is determined, you have to continue to hold the stick in one hand and without moving it, make the pencil mark with the other hand. It is almost impossible to do this without the stick slipping. Time and again I have seen that these nails have to be reset over and over again because of error.

My little trick for this problem is to use a knife. Holding the flat of the blade horizontal, stick the point of the knife into the side of the form and it will support the weight of the stick set on top of the blade. Move the knife up or down as the transit man commands, and when he gives you the OK, drive the nail where the point of the knife is in the wood.

After you strip the forms from the footings, save the lumber on the side until it can be used for the first floor joists (7).

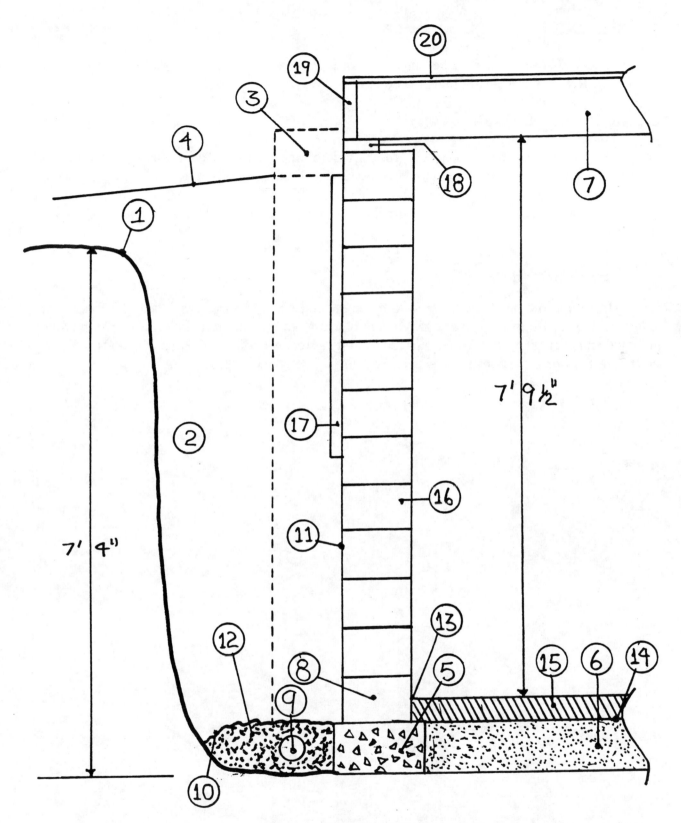

FIGURE 12

BACKFILLING

The gravel (6), can now be pushed down the slope to the footings, and spread with the bull dozer. Remember Rule 38, higher is better than lower.

LAYOUT FOR THE BLOCK

You layout for the block just as we did before. Set the corner nails, and square up using your diagonal measurements. This should be easier than before because now the footing are not in the bottom of a trench.

We have already covered how to figure out the number of block and bags of mortar required.

SETTING THE BLOCK

In setting the block I am going to recommend a departure from the usual process which will save a lot of trouble. Deliver only enough block down into the foundation excavation to lay just one course around the perimeter of the footing. After this course of block is laid (No. 8), we must consider our provisions for drainage and sub surface water control.

CHAPTER 17

DEALING WITH DRAINAGE AND GROUND WATER

We have been following the logical progression of construction, and have come to a subject that should be considered at this point. This subject may be the most important, and most misunderstood aspect of building a house. It is routinely mishandled by the biggest and the best builders, as well as the little guys, and self builders. But unlike them, you are going to know the pitfalls in handling drainage and ground water, and how to avoid them.

Earlier in this book we talked about understanding the drainage patterns of a piece of land when in the selection process. Now we will deal more specifically with the control of water on a specific site.

There are a multitude of stories about poorly engineered subdivisions that were built in the dry season and became disasters in the spring. Inadequate provisions to handle rain water, result in erosion and wash out that can easily carry away substantial parts of lawns and driveways. Ponds form in front yards, and basements are flooded.

In the late 70s there was a great deal of development on Staten Island, which is the Borough of Richmond, and part of New York City. This relatively rural area began to sprout housing development after housing development. Homes were built on small lots in attached rows or semi-attached groups. The land was quite level and no major drainage system had yet been installed in the streets as do exist in the more populous Boroughs of the City.

The largely mythical belief in the value of basements was followed. People wanted that extra space, envisioning it as a future family room or shop. Builders catered to the myth and built the basements. After all, a basement is cheap extra space.

A few years later disaster struck. Unknown to the people who bought the houses, they had been built during a seven year long drought. A couple of years after the houses were built the rainfall began to increase and the level of the underground water rose. Finally it happened. There was a heavy rain and the water table rose. Basements filled up with water. Streets became flooded. Every time it rained the same thing happened again.

The home owners sued the builders, and demonstrated against the City. The politicians as usual, sought to pass the buck. Why were subdivisions approved? Why were permits issued etc., etc? Every body pointed at the other guy.
RULE 39

WHEN YOU BUILD A HOUSE ON LEVEL GROUND AND PUT A HOLE UNDER IT, SOONER OR LATER THAT HOLE WILL FILL UP WITH WATER.

It is really as simple as that. Where can the water go after the ground becomes water logged and can absorb no more? Can you put a pump in the basement to pump the water out? Pump it where? Up on the street? Add it to the rain? It will just circulate back to the basement.

Well, said one fellow, I'll build my basement like a swimming pool. I'll build a reinforced concrete shell without any joints. That will keep the water out. You couldn't make a bigger mistake.

One time they were building a large motel. It was in a U shape and had a very big swimming pool in the center of the U. One night, a month or so before the motel was finished, there was a terribly severe and prolonged rain storm. The night watchman in making his rounds, noticed an open drain in the bottom of the swimming pool, and water was coming up through it. The watchman went down into the pool, found the cover for the drain, and screwed it into the opening so no more water could come in.

The next morning when the workmen arrived they were astounded at what they saw. There in the middle of the motel was this huge concrete boat with it's top six feet above the ground level.

The drain that the watchman closed was a pressure relief valve, and was particularly left open, so that if the ground water rose, it would rise inside the empty pool and keep the pressure equalized with the outside. The gutters had not yet been installed on the roof eaves, so the entire run off of the roofs fell into the U where the pool was. The ground became quickly water logged, and the pool, with it's relief drain closed, floated up just like a boat. What if it had been the fellows basement, and his house was sitting on top?

Rule 39 cannot be overcome. Even though the ground water may not rise high enough to flood your basement except once in a hundred years, who knows if that time will not be tomorrow, or next week? If you need a basement for a storm cellar, then fine, it has a purpose. But otherwise it will be of very questionable value.

Assuming then that we are working with a lot that has enough slope to enable us to direct drainage flow, let's consider the first line of defense against a wet basement.

FOOTING DRAINS

A footing drain consists of a perforated pipe which is run around the outside of the footings at a level not higher than the top of the footing. See Fig. 12, No. 9. The pipe is installed in a bed of stone, No. 10., which is under and over the pipe. The common problem is water which seeps down through the earth outside the foundation. If the soil is not very porous, this water will build up at the footings, seeping under the footings and rising. It can easily enter the basement through the joint between the basement floor and the foundation wall, No.13. Water of course, will seek it's own level. If the level builds up outside the foundation, it will rise inside to the same level.

To prevent any of this seeping water from soaking through the blocks of the foundation, the outside of the foundation must be carefully water proofed by coating it with tar No. 11., or other waterproofing materials. Great care should be taken in the application of this waterproofing.

There are spraying methods which are effective. However, when the material is applied by brush it does not work into every nook and cranny of the block surface. I prefer a good heavy application of roofing tar applied with a trowel in a good layer at least a quarter of an inch thick.

Did you ever wonder why we install gutters and down spouts at the edge of the roof? The primary purpose is to keep the water that runs off the roof, from falling on the ground next to the foundation, so that it will not seep down and enter the basement. Many people do not really comprehend this purpose, including the people who install the gutters and leaders. How often have you seen down spouts discharging water right next to the foundation? This does not carry out the purpose of the gutters, yet you see it done time and time again. The down spout should conduct the water at least ten feet away from the foundation. Occasionally you see down spouts installed this way, but not often. It is not a very attractive arrangement. I prefer to install a "T" fitting in the footing drain pipe at each corner of the building where a down spout will be located, and extending a piece of pipe up vertically to just above the final grade level. The down spout can be run directly into this pipe, and the run off water will be carried away by the footing drain system.

Before the earth is backfilled against the foundation, the stone of the footing drain must be covered with a material that will keep the earth from settling into the spaces between the stones and thus clogging the water flow. A layer of red rosin paper over the stone or a layer of hay is usually used for this purpose, No. 12.

There is one more critical thing to be done if the footing drain is to work. That is, a connection must be made to the perforated pipe, to carry away the water which seeps into the pipe or which has come from the roof gutters. If the water collected in the footing drain has nowhere to go the drain system is worthless. This would seem obvious, yet over and over, footing drains are installed without a proper and functioning outlet. Many times I have seen an outlet pipe run from the footing drains about ten feet, and then buried. This will hardly be adequate to get rid of the water from the footing drain, and illustrates that the installer or builder who did such a job did not really understand the purpose and function of the footing drain to begin with.

RULE 40

FOOTING DRAINS THAT DO NOT HAVE AN OUTLET PIPE PITCHED DOWNWARD, AND RUN TO DAYLIGHT, ARE WORTHLESS.

The outlet pipe must be run away from the drain with a slight downward pitch, and be extended until it comes out of the ground to daylight. Therefor. it must be run in the direction of the downward slope of the land. It might be necessary to run this pipe a hundred or two hundred feet to reach daylight, but no matter how far, it is absolutely essential.

If the land being built upon has more slope, it is not unusual for ground water to run beneath the surface of the slope, following its declining course. If this course runs into an inground foundation, a considerable amount of water can be accumulated. If you do your foundation excavation in the early spring when the ground water is running, you may see this water seeping out of the sides of the hole. If the flow is substantial, or you suspect it might be, install a second perforated pipe along that side of the foundation with a second outlet pipe run together with the first one. This is really very little extra trouble, so better safe than sorry.

It is better that these ground flows are not allowed to accumulate against the foundation wall while seeping downward to the footing drain. A flaw in the waterproofing might allow water intrusion through the block. The best job is to backfill this side of the foundation with one inch stone the same as was used for the footing drain. This would create a "French Drain", which we discussed earlier, against the foundation. Ground water would percolate down through the stone to the footing drain without reaching the foundation wall.

UNDER SLAB DRAINS

If when you excavate for the foundation, you find water coming up out of the bottom of the hole, further provisions must be made.

When forming for the footings, install some short lengths of the four inch plastic pipe through the footings to connect the outside with the inside. After the footings are poured and stripped, connect lengths of perforated pipe to these outlets, and extend the lengths of pipe into the center of the foundation area. Instead of backfilling with bank run gravel, backfill inside the footings with one inch stone. This will permit any ground water under the slab, to drain out to the footing drains. In this case the outlet pipe to daylight should be doubled.

Every foundation and drainage situation is different. Always use common sense. The object is to give the water a place to go before it enters the basement area. The use of perforated pipe and stone is the means to create the pathways that are needed. Remember, you cannot dispose of extra water underground, you must conduct it, with pitch to assure the flow, to daylight.

Where your conduits come out into daylight it is a good idea to cover the ends with wire screening to prevent any small animals from nesting in the pipes, which could clog them.

SURFACE DRAINAGE

We have covered the first requirement, and that is getting rid of the roof run off without letting it seep into the ground around the foundation.

The second most important thing is to final grade around the foundation so that all water will drain away from the house for a distance of thirty feet. If the slope of the land is so great that this cannot be done, then grade a sufficient swale at the bottom of the slope to conduct the water away. Be careful that you don't build swales that will direct the run off onto your driveway. Some people have done this in the belief that the driveway provided a good means of conducting the water to a lower road, and getting rid of it that way. Much to their dismay, they found that in the winter time the driveway was frequently covered with a glaze of ice, when sun melted snow ran down and froze.

Consider reversing the pitch of the swale to the non driveway end of the house. If this appears that it will still result in an excessive flow which will erode the grass and shrubbery, install a precast concrete catch basin to receive the water at the end of the swale. Run plastic pipe under ground to carry the water from the catch basin to an appropriate discharge point at daylight.

CHAPTER 18

FINISHING THE FOUNDATION

PLUMBING WASTE LINES

We have laid the first course of block for the full foundation, and installed our footing drains. See Fig.12, No's 8,9,10. This installation was made much easier by being able to work from the inside of the foundation. Had we waited until the foundation walls, No.16, were completed, it would have been necessary to use ladders to get down into the space between the foundation wall and the side of the excavation, No.2.

Working in this confining area presents the increased hazard of being harmed, should the side bank of the excavation collapse and pin a worker against the wall.

If we are planning to have plumbing facilities for a kitchen or bathroom in the basement, the next step would be to install the drain lines in the backfilled gravel. This is only feasible, however, if the land has sufficient slope, that the drain line under the basement floor can be run out at a downward pitch, and still have a high enough elevation to meet the inlet of the septic tank, or the sewer connection. Obviously the connection for a toilet must come from underneath, but if only a sink is planned, or a washing machine drain, the drain line may exit the foundation through the wall several feet higher than the slab. If just a washing machine discharge is desired, the drain line may be even higher because the, washing machine pumps out the waste water which can be discharged at a higher level than the machine itself.

There are sewage pumps and pump up toilets that can be used to raise the sewage discharge. More on this when we discuss plumbing.

Assuming that we will have a toilet, a sink and a washing machine in the basement, the drain lines for these facilities must now be installed in the backfilled gravel by the plumber. Connections must also be provided out of the floor, to receive the drain line or lines, coming down from the floor above.

112

If drain connections are intended to come up inside a wall, and the toilet is to be properly positioned, very careful measurements must be made to insure that the connections are precisely located. Errors in through the floor plumbing layout are very common, and happen more often than not. Great care should be taken in the layout. The pipes must be laid in trenches and pitched downward at a quarter inch to the foot to obtain proper sewage flow. In this regard, too much pitch is just as bad as too little. When there is too much pitch, the liquid tends to run away from the solid material which can be left in the pipe to form a clog. The drain will be low enough to run under the footing and should be extended beyond, at least a foot or two. This outlet location should be carefully marked and noted so that a trench can be dug to it after the foundation is backfilled.

All of the connections up through the floor should extend high enough to be above the floor level after the concrete slab is poured. These connections should also be sealed so no concrete can get into them during the pour.

There is also a problem with plumbing connections being moved or tipped over during the concrete pour and finishing. It is a good idea to drive some lengths of steel bar into the ground next to the connections and fasten them securely with wire. Pieces of half inch reinforcing rod are good for this purpose.

Many building departments require inspection of footing drains and under slab plumbing. This is the point when both inspections can be done at the same time. Check with you building inspector for the requirements, and schedule your inspection if necessary.

PREPARING FOR THE SLAB

We are still at the stage where only one course of block has been laid. It is much easier to pour the slab at this point, than to do it after the foundation walls have been built up. It is obviously much easier to deliver the concrete down the discharge chute, without the obstruction of the foundation walls.

Your mason contractor will make the preparations for the pour. The plumbing lines if any must be covered over and the area raked out for a final level. The final level is not as critical in pouring a basement floor as it is when a slab foundation is being built. You are going to pour a 4 inch thick slab on top of the gravel grade. If the gravel is higher or lower the finished height from the floor to the ceiling will vary up or down accordingly, which should present no problem.

THE BASEMENT FLOOR DRAIN

This is a determination you should make according to the way in which you intend to use the basement. If you are going to use the basement for a shop or work area where water may be spilled on the floor or the ability to wash the floor is important, then it is a good idea to install a floor drain. A standard cast iron body with a perforated lid is made for this purpose and can be purchased from your masonry supplier. The drain body can be centrally located and then connected with plastic pipe to the footing drain system. For the drain to work properly it should be centrally located and depressed below the final floor elevation. The concrete should be pitched toward the drain.

If you are planning to finish the basement area, the pitched floor may be objectionable. In that case eliminate the drain. For a basement, the entire floor is not usually pitched to the drain.

Generally an area of about 6 feet in diameter around the drain is pitched inward. Spills and water can be swept into this area. If we were doing a garage floor, where car washing or melting snow and ice could create a larger volume of run off, then it would be better to pitch the entire floor to the drain.

THE VAPOR BARRIER

After all the piping under the slab is complete, and the base raked level, the next step is to put down a vapor barrier. Fig. 12, No.14, This will consist of a large sheet of poly plastic material 6 mils thick. It is best if this is a single piece. If more than one piece is used, it should be overlapped, and the joint should be sealed with reinforced plastic tape, such as package sealing tape. Where any drain line, or anything which pierces the floor is located, the vapor barrier should be carefully cut with an x and slipped over the pipe. The vapor barrier should then be taped around the base of the pipe so no gases from underneath the plastic barrier can escape where the barrier is penetrated by the pipe.

At the perimeter, the plastic material should lay on top of the footing, and be carefully cut about 1 1/2" inches back from the block. The edge of the plastic sheet should be taped down to the footing and pressed firmly to make a good seal. The footing should be carefully swept before the tape is applied. The object here is that the vapor barrier, as well as preventing the passage of moisture, will also prevent the entrance of low pressure gas.

After the plastic membrane has been placed, it should be walked on as little as possible, and care taken not to tear it. If a tear occurs, repair it with the adhesive tape.

The procedures I have been describing about sealing the vapor barrier will probably be unfamiliar to your mason and he may question the reason. The reason is, to prevent the entrance of a gas called Radon. You probably have heard of it. The next chapter will be devoted to a detailed discussion of the Radon myth.

REINFORCING WIRE MESH

The next step is to place the reinforcing wire. This is a wire mesh made from wire of varied thicknesses, and meshed in different sized squares. The commonly used mesh for residential slabs is made of #10 wire arranged in 6 inch squares. The wire is spot welded together to form a strong web. This material comes in 6 foot wide rolls with about 500 square feet to a roll.

The mesh rolls are stiff and difficult to unroll. It is best to have three men for this operation. Two to unroll the mesh, and the third to hold the end down. After the desired length is unrolled, which would be either the length or the width of the slab to be poured, it is cut with heavy duty wire cutters. The wire has a strong tendency to curl. In order to counteract this, the cut piece is lifted up and turned over. Then it is walked upon, and the bends taken out. Once made reasonably flat the length of mesh is carried into the foundation area and set in place. You can see that if the mesh were unrolled, and stomped on top of the vapor barrier, it would most certainly damage the plastic, which we want to avoid.

The lengths of mesh should be placed with the edges butting, and tied together with wire at least every two feet. No gaps should be left in the mesh layout. Pieces can be cut and tied together with wire to fill in. Masons generally, do not do a conscientious job here, so you must be on top of it. These requirements should be made clear to them when you award the job, so that they cannot later claim that what you are asking is extra work, which they don't usually do.

CONCRETE SHRINKAGE

When concrete is poured, a process of drying and setting begins. The drying is the result of a certain amount of water coming to the surface and evaporating. The setting is a process of hardening which is the result of chemical reaction in the concrete. Usually, a few hours after the concrete is placed and leveled it will have hardened enough that it can be walked on and finished by troweling with steel trowels. Today there are troweling machines available which greatly reduce the labor of finishing.

The rate of setting is related to the temperature. The chemical reaction in the concrete generates heat which promotes the setting. However, if the weather is hot there will be too much heat and the concrete will set too rapidly. Conversely, in the winter time, the heat will be dissipated, and it will take much longer for the concrete to set.

Concrete which is poured in the summer time under a hot sun, will dry much too quickly. This results in excessive shrinkage and extensive cracking. Additionally, concrete which sets too fast will have much less strength. If you have to pour under these conditions it is essential that a supply of water be available to keep the concrete wet. The concrete should be kept moist until it is no longer in the direct sun.

The slower the concrete sets, the stronger it will be, and the less shrinkage will occur. In severe heat the concrete should be wet down regularly for three days. Additionally there are drying inhibitors which will slow the drying process. These are liquids and can be easily spread over the finished concrete with a large squeegee. The fact that the concrete is poured over the vapor barrier helps hold the moisture in the concrete, and prevents the dry gravel underneath, from sucking it out.

The shrinkage of the concrete will cause so called drying cracks, which may vary in width from a hairline to as much as a quarter inch. The wetting of the concrete as it sets, the reinforcing wire, and the mix of the concrete, all help to minimize the cracking. The stronger the concrete mix is, the less shrinkage and the less cracking. At least a 3000 lb. mix should be used for slabs. Usually the drying cracks cause no problem. If you find them unsightly in your basement floor, they may be filled in with special mixes made for that purpose. A good coat of rubber based paint over the floor will be very attractive and make the floor very easy to sweep. When you sweep a concrete, floor a light dust always comes off. This is prevented by the sealer or paint.

If you are poring a slab on grade that will be the floor of a living area, it will most likely be covered with carpet. Prefinished wood flooring in squares may be glued directly to the concrete. Vinyl may also be applied but the preparation of the concrete must be more careful in filling cracks and eliminating bumps and bits of dirt which will show through the vinyl.

If you are planning to apply tile to the concrete floor, care should be taken to prevent the formation of drying cracks in the area to be tiled. Drying cracks are pretty well formed after a few weeks, but sometimes, depending on the chemistry of the concrete they will keep widening for up to a year. If tile is cemented over such cracks, and they keep widening, the tiles themselves will crack. Cracks as wide as an eighth of an inch can appear in a tiled floor six months after the tile has been laid.

The shrinking may be controlled by installing joints in the concrete around the area to be tiled. Joint material made of vinyl may be obtained from a masonry supplier. The shrinkage will occur at the joints which may separate slightly, so make sure they will be in an area to be covered with another flooring. The vinyl separators will stay flush with the concrete so that no groove can be felt through the carpet later.

RULE 41

THE SLOWER CONCRETE DRIES, THE BETTER THE RESULT.

In a few days, concrete will achieve about half of it's strength. In thirty days it will reach about 80 to 90%. It takes a full year for concrete to completely harden. Chemicals such as salt should never be put on concrete that is less than a year old or serious damage can occur to the surface.

Retaining the heat of the chemical reaction of the concrete is important for the concrete to cure and harden properly. If the freshly poured concrete is exposed to freezing temperatures, the surface of the concrete will be damaged. The freezing expands the moisture in the surface, and it will flake and spall. You particularly don't want this to happen to outside walkways and patios because there is not any really good way to repair the damage, and the surface will always be pitted and unsightly. Not only will the cold damage the surface of the concrete, but by taking away the internal heat of curing it will stop the concrete from achieving it's proper strength.

If freezing is expected, the concrete must be covered. Don't let the mason talk you out of it. Insulating blankets are made for the purpose but small contractors rarely own any. The next best way to protect the concrete is to cover it with plastic sheeting, the same as was used for the vapor barrier, and then shake out a good layer of hay on top, at least six to eight inches thick.

If the slab is going to be exposed for a while, or if you are going to wait for warmer weather to continue, cover over the top of the hay with another layer of plastic sheeting. This will prevent rain, snow and ice from matting down the hay and destroying it's insulating ability. If a slab is left exposed, so that frost goes deep in the ground under the concrete, the soil underneath will expand, and heave the floor upward. This can cause a lot of cracking and damage. If the slab is well insulated the frost will not penetrate because the hay insulation will retain that rising ground heat that we discussed earlier.

SCREEDS AND SCREEDING

With, our vapor barrier down, and our reinforcing wire in place, we have taken care not to tear or penetrate the plastic barrier which is also going to function as our Radon shield.

When the concrete is poured, it is necessary to have a means to level it. To accomplish this a process known as screeding is employed. A screed is a long beam which is pulled forward as the concrete is poured. Excess concrete above the level of the bottom of the screed is pulled ahead. The screed is usually oscillated from side to side to help level the concrete. Because wood warps, and is not always straight, screeds are now made of aluminum, similar to a 2x4 and about 12 feet long. In order to keep the screed level, as the screeding is performed, screed guides are set before the concrete is poured These guides are usually 1 inch diameter pipes which are set longitudinally to the direction of the pour, in parallel, about ten feet apart. The guides are set up on blocks of wood. With the careful use of the transit, they are set to the exact level desired for the finished floor. The screed is held across the guides, resting on them as it is pulled forward to level the concrete.

Many masons like to set the screeds on wooden stakes driven into the ground. This makes the leveling process easier but means that the stakes are driven through the vapor barrier. Because we are concerned with maintaining the integrity of the plastic as a Radon barrier, do not let the mason drive stakes through it. The screed guides can be leveled with wooden blocks although it is a little more trouble.

If the concrete is to be pitched in any way, the screed guides are set to the desired slope. As the screed is moved forward, any voids that appear in the concrete should be filled in and rescreeded. When the screed guides are removed the groove that is left must be filled in with concrete.

HOOKING THE MESH

When the concrete is being poured, the reinforcing mesh that was installed, tends to be flattened down to the bottom of the slab. For it to perform it's purpose, the mesh must be in the middle of the concrete. This is accomplished by using steel hooks which are usually bent from pieces of reinforcing rod. As the screed is advancing, the concrete is being raked and roughly leveled in front, so the screed will not have too much concrete to push. While the raking is being done, the mesh should be engaged with the hooks, and lifted upward so that it is in the center of the thickness of the concrete. This is a very important step. If it is not done, the reinforcing mesh is largely wasted. Many masons don't bother to lift the mesh, or if they do, they do it half heartedly with the rake. Once again, when you award the job, you should make it clear to the mason that you expect the mesh to be properly lifted with hooks, not rakes.

FLOATING THE CONCRETE

After all of the concrete is put in place, Fig.12, No.15, a procedure known as floating, is performed. This is usually done with a "Bull Float" which is like a trowel about three feet long attached to a long pole. If we had already built up our basement walls, the use of the bull float would be impossible, but because our wall is only one block high the mason can stand outside the block, and move the float back and forth over the concrete.

The float tends to level out any ridges in the concrete, such as where the screed guide grooves were filled in, but more importantly, it brings some of the finer mix of the concrete to the surface with some excess water. "Floating" this so called "Cream" to the surface, insures that no stones will be visible, and provides a good smooth concrete layer at the top which can be troweled and finished to a smooth hard surface.

TROWELING AND FINISHING

After the floating is finished, a layer of water will be on top of the floor. If it is in the hot sun this layer should be kept from evaporating too quickly by adding water as necessary. The water will disappear by chemically reacting with the concrete. If the water evaporates away the cure will not be proper, and the concrete will be weak, and tend to crack quite a lot.

You now must wait until the concrete becomes firm enough to walk on, and do the finishing troweling. If the weather is cold the wait may be a long one. In cold weather, some temporary lighting should be provided, as the finishing will probably go well into the hours of darkness.

When the mason judges that the concrete has set enough, he will do his first troweling. This used to be done by hand while on hands and knees, but today everyone uses a power trowel machine which has four trowels that are continuously rotated. The first troweling will help to dispel the remaining cream and level out any undulations.

In finishing concrete, timing is all important. When the concrete has set to the point that the troweling creates a very smooth surface which begins to shine, the final finish can be done. To get a really good job, the consistency must be just right. If the weather is too hot, the concrete may dry too fast for the final finishing, and care should be taken to keep it sprinkled with water to slow the process until all surfaces can be troweled.

In cold weather this will not happen. It is a matter of waiting until the "Set" is advanced enough. Cold weather pours, make for a long day, lasting into darkness. Frequently masons become impatient and leave too soon. Often it is necessary to return in the middle of the night, or very early in the morning, to perform the final troweling.

If you are working into a long cold night, it will pay off if you keep your masons supplied with pizza, hot coffee, donuts, etc.

COMPLETING THE BLOCK WORK

Now that the basement floor is finished, the rest of the block can be delivered right down into the basement. The mason can lay the rest of the block Fig. 12, No.16, from the inside, which makes things a lot easier for him. When the wall gets to about five feet high, the mason will have to put up some scaffolding to finish the top courses. Remember the top course of block should be a solid top FHA block.

Make sure to have the mason shovel up the mortar which has dropped on the floor in front of the block. If this is allowed to harden it will have to be laboriously chipped away with a hammer, and you very well may be stuck with the job.

RULE 42

NEVER BACKFILL A BASEMENT BEFORE THE WEIGHT OF THE HOUSE IS ON THE FOUNDATION.

Leaving the matter of the full foundation, let's pick up the modified slab foundation where we left off.

UNDER SLAB PLUMBING

The plumbing drain lines will be trenched into the backfill as we discussed for the basement floor. However, in this case there will be more connections, as we are sure to have a kitchen and at least a half bath on the ground floor. We are also going to extend the copper water line which we left rolled up, to the point where it will come out of the floor. This will usually be in a laundry room or utility room. The copper line should be sleeved with a foam insulation where it exits the floor, to prevent it from abrading against the concrete. The water line will have a tendency to slight movement resulting from the pressure changes constantly occurring when in use.

The layout of the plumbing connections is very critical. Drain lines will be positioned to come up inside walls, which permits virtually no margin for error due to the size of the fittings. Positioning must be exact. It is also very important to make sure the lead bend for the toilet is accurately placed. So often the toilet connection turns out to be too close to the back wall, or too far, so that the toilet cannot be properly set. Or it may be too close to a side wall for comfortable use. Usually the toilet is to be centered between a vanity and a wall. If this is not done accurately, not only will it be difficult to use, but the error will stand out like a sore thumb.

Measurements should be taken from one end of the foundation, which is easy to do by hooking the tape over the outside edge of the block. Measure all points from the same end, and later on when the carpenters layout the walls, make sure they measure from the same end. Because there were so often, errors with the plumbing layout, I set up strings on pins to represent the edge of the future wall where a plumbing connection was to come up. I would set some four inch blocks on the side of the string where the wall was to be, leaving a gap for the fitting.

Sometimes an error in a toilet connection is not discovered until the toilet is set in place and it becomes noticeable. That usually means the tile work and the concrete floor have to be broken up to correct the mistake. This can be very difficult if a move of only a few inches is necessary. There's lots of mess to clean. The freshly painted walls will probably be dirtied or worse. Then there is the cost, inconvenience and delay in repairing the floor, and trying to get the tile man to come back for such a small job. Check and double check, and after the floor is poured, check again. If a correction has to be made, make it then while the concrete is still green and easy to break up.

THE VAPOR BARRIER

The vapor barrier should be installed in one piece and/or taped at the seams and sealed around all of the emerging pipes. Let the plastic fold over the perimeter course of four inch block.

THE REINFORCING MESH

This should be handled and installed in the same manner as outlined for the basement floor. Take care not to damage the integrity of the barrier.

PERIMETER INSULATION

In this foundation, the concrete slab is going to come up against the outside course of four inch block which will be above final grade and therefor able to conduct a certain amount of cold into the edge of the slab. To prevent this, a thermal break is installed which consists of half inch thick joint insulation. This usually comes in ten foot lengths by three inches wide. If this is not available, it is easy to cut some strips from half inch "Homasote" board. These strips should be laid flat on top of the four inches of the FHA block that is exposed, and standing vertically against the inside of the four inch perimeter block. This creates an effective thermal break insuring that the slab will remain warmed by the rising ground heat.

SCREEDING

The screed guides should be set up in the same way as previously described, taking care not to penetrate the barrier.

POURING THE SLAB

This will be done exactly the same as described before, except the outside screed guide should be the top of the four inch perimeter block, insuring that the final floor level will be the same elevation. If you have been able to maintain a clear area around the outside of the foundation, and graded out the soil removed by the trenching, the concrete truck should be able to move around the perimeter of the foundation. This makes the placing of the concrete much simpler and faster. You mason will be grateful if you have taken the trouble to make this possible.

FINISHING

This is executed in the same way as previously noted, except that I recommend you ask the mason to take special care in the hand troweling around the plumbing connections and especially the lead bend for the toilet. If, for instance, the concrete around the toilet connection is rough, the tile cannot be properly set and will be out of level. That of course means that when the toilet is set, it too, will be out of level. Nobody likes a rocking toilet. This is one of those nasty little problems which can so easily be avoided by an extra minute of care at the right time.

GETTING ALONG

In the last several chapters, I have mentioned a lot of little things that you should insure are done correctly by the contractors. If you feel reluctant to be so frequently on top of them, as I have suggested, take the time to explain to them the reason for what you are asking. You will be surprised to discover how few of the reasons why things should or should not be done, are known by the contractors. Chances are, when they learned the trade they were told, "This is the way you do it". If they asked why, they were told, "Because that's the way we always do it." I always found that when I took the trouble to explain, the men were grateful for the knowledge. How often I heard, "Oh yeah, I always wondered about that".

You can bet that the point will be included in their sales talk to their next prospective customer.

CHAPTER 19

THE RADON MYTH

POLITICIZING SCIENCE

The 1980s were a time of rising environmental concern. In earlier times it seemed that scientists conducting investigation and experimentation to unlock the secrets of nature, were motivated by their curiosity and dedication. They struggled to find the funding to carry on their work. They were not motivated by the desire for fame and wealth but only by the desire to know.

Today the field of science is quite different. Scientists are mostly employees of large organizations. They strive not only for knowledge, but also for advancement up the economic ladder. To succeed they know that they must garner attention and publicity. They have learned that science today, is inextricably involved with politics. Society rewards certain scientific achievements and demands others.

Interest in the environment and it's protection is a political matter. Many scientists perceive environmental discoveries as the road to advancement and financial success. Some are so anxious to proclaim some new finding, that they fail to adhere to established scientific principles of proof and repeatable experimentation.

Remember the men who published their discovery of how to create nuclear fusion in a jar? They were extolled as geniuses. However when the dust settled nobody else could confirm their findings. They were over anxious for glory.

DOOM AND GLOOM

It has become fashionable in the scientific community to predict environmental chaos and doom. Most of the dire predictions are based on questionable evidence, incomplete data, faulty computer models, unsupported hypothesis, outrageous mathematical extrapolation, and last but

121

certainly not least, a political agenda. Completely unsupported findings are quickly repeated by the media as fact and established dogma.

THE ICE AGE AND GLOBAL WARMING

Fifteen thousand years ago, a blink of an eye, compared to the billions of years the earth is believed to have existed, much of the northeastern part of the United States was covered by a giant ice cap that had moved down from the polar regions. The geological evidence for this is pretty solid, yet no scientists can explain why the weather obviously got colder to allow the ice to expand, or why the weather got warmer again and melted back the ice. Never the less, the concept of "Global Warming" is heralded as absolute scientific fact. Could it not be that the earth is still in the warming trend that melted the ice cap? Is it reasonable to assume that the evolution of the earth and it's species is frozen in time because so called intelligent man has arrived? Are we not part of the evolutionary process? Scientific knowledge is a mere speck on the thread of time the earth has existed.

THE CANALS ON MARS

Many years ago when I went to school, in the good old days when you could receive a fine education in a public institution, we were taught in science class about the sun, the stars, the planets, and man's striving to learn about our solar system. One of the things we learned, and which was confirmed by the Mount Palomar telescope, which by then had been built, was that there were structures on Mars which were canals. Because these canals were straight and geometrical, it was believed that they must have been created by intelligent life. The existence of the canals was taught as absolute scientific knowledge, as they could be clearly seen through telescopes.

Many years later, NASA began to send out space probes. These were satellites equipped with sophisticated cameras and transmitting equipment. One of the first such probes was a fly by of Mars. It was hoped that signs of intelligent life would be discovered. How exciting that would be. Yet when the satellite came close to Mars, and the cameras began to send back their pictures, the scientists were astonished to find that there was absolutely no sign of any canals on Mars or discernible signs of intelligent life either.

Probably if you are under forty, you never heard of the canals on Mars, even though it was once taught as absolute fact.

RADON DANGER?

Most of the scientific findings which are disseminated as fact about the environment today, are based on supposition, not proof. One of the most notorious of these myths is the danger of contracting cancer as the result of Radon gas entering your home.

Prestigious publications have run articles on the dangers of Radon and how to avoid them. It is always presented as absolute fact that Radon in your home can cause cancer. Yet there are no studies that bear out that assumption. To the contrary, a study done at the University of Pennsylvania concerning Radon, concluded that there was no correlation between the incidence of cancer and a higher level of Radon in the home. The media ignored this study, and continues to this day, to publish articles about the dangers of Radon.

ENVIRONMENTAL EXTREMISTS

Unfortunately the media, either knowingly or unknowingly promote the politics of environmental extremists and their agenda. Too many scientists willingly lend themselves to this cause because they have not been able to keep politics and their personal beliefs out of their science. Their desire for advancement and notoriety influences their conclusions.

THE BEGINNING OF THE MYTH

Many years ago when the mining of Uranium became important for the production of atomic bombs, many people engaged in that pursuit, and striking Uranium was akin to finding gold. After a number of years, doctors began to notice that the incidence of cancer among uranium miners was greater than in the general population. As time went on, and the miners exposure lengthened, and the cases increased. Investigation was conducted, and as a result, the incidence of cancer was linked to the miners exposure to very high levels of an invisible and odorless gas called Radon. This gas is the result of the decay of radioactive materials found naturally in the earth.

Scientists had known for some time that Radon occurs naturally almost everywhere, however no ill effects had ever been linked to Radon, so it was considered harmless. However, with the findings of a higher incidence of cancer among uranium miners, the extremists pounced.

THE HYPOTHESIS

The assumption was made, that if exposure to Radon in a uranium mine increased the chances of getting cancer, then anyone, who is exposed to a lesser amount of Radon, but for a longer time, would then also have a greater likelihood of contracting cancer.

Instead of testing this theory, for after all that is all it was, it was taken as fact. After that it was only necessary to determine the maximum safe exposure to Radon, above which a person would be at risk.

THE FALLACY

The hypothesis which these scientific extremist so anxiously clutched to their breasts, assumes that the effect of exposure to Radon is cumulative. This we know is true of a toxic substance like lead, which once taken in, cannot be eliminated by the body. In such a case the concentration of the poison increases until it reaches a level at which it does damage to the body. We also know that most of us have some lesser level of lead in our systems without suffering ill effects. So it becomes a question of accumulated level.

However, the body does not absorb any substance from Radon. No physical material is ingested or absorbed by inhalation. There is only exposure to a minute amount of radiation, which is energy.

In most cases of the effect of undesirable materials we know that the body has systems to cope with these intrusions, and only when the unwanted substance exceeds the ability of the body to withstand it, or overcome it, does damage occur.

It is like saying, that if you drink a hundred glasses of water in one day you will doubtless die. Therefor, if you drink a single glass of water every day for a hundred days, you will also die.

If Radon was man made, and new in our environment, there might be more reason to assume an adverse condition as human evolvement did not acclimatize to the effect. However Radon has been around since the formation of the surface of the earth as we know it today, and since men lived in caves, containing Radon presumably.

THE FACTS

The so called danger of Radon exposure is nothing more than a mathematically derived assumption. There has never been a documented case of cancer caused by Radon exposure in a home. There are no studies or evidence to suggest that people who live in an area of higher Radon emanation have a higher incidence of cancer. In fact the study previously mentioned established that there was no increased incidence of cancer under those circumstances. Why then all the fuss about Radon?

THE LAWYERS GOT INTO THE ACT

Most people when they buy a house retain the services of a lawyer to protect their interests. The lawyers include in the contract of purchase, protection against all the adverse circumstances which might be discovered about the home. The previous favorite was termites. It was provided, that if termites or termite damage was discovered in the house being purchased, the seller would be responsible for their elimination, and the repair of any resulting damage.

When the Radon specter was raised, lawyers seized upon it as another proviso to put into a purchase contract. It is now pretty standard in such contracts to give the purchaser the right to have a Radon test made in the house, and reserves to them the right not to make the purchase if Radon is found. The contracts that I have seen all leave it that indefinite. Apparently the lawyers for the seller do not have the knowledge to specify the type of test to be used, the way the test is to be conducted, by whom, or any permissible level of Radon. As a result, any statement that purports to have found Radon, affords the purchaser the right to cancel the deal.

THE TEST

The instructions with a Radon test canister say that the open canister should be placed on something about two feet above the floor in the lowest level of the home. Windows and doors should be kept closed and the contents of the canister exposed for seventy two hours. The minimum allowable risk level is that if you live in the house continuously for about seventy years, your chances of contracting cancer will be increased by ten percent.

THE STING

No matter how foolish, the practical result of a so called unsatisfactory Radon test goes this way. The purchaser's lawyer calls the sellers lawyer and tells him that the Radon test was unsatisfactory. He further states that the house could be Radon proofed, but that it would be expensive, say about five thousand dollars. If the seller will agree to an allowance of that cost by lowering the price accordingly, the purchaser will not cancel the deal.

The seller of course is over the barrel. Doubtless he is anxious for a sale, and doesn't want to loose a willing and able buyer, so he has no choice but to agree.

The purchaser pockets the five thousand, and never spends a dime on Radon proofing.

THE REMEDIES

Unfortunately, the lawyers for the sellers, do not know how to protect their clients from this rip off.

I am not a lawyer and I am not offering you legal advice, but I will tell you what I did when I was confronted with a requirement for a Radon test in selling a new home.
I agreed to the test with the following provisos:

1. The test would have to be conducted by a licensed professional engineer who had been certified by the Local Board of Health as qualified in the performance of Radon tests.

2. The test canister used had to be obtained from a laboratory certified by the Board of Health as qualified for the analysis of the exposed canister.

3. In the event of an unsatisfactory test, the Board of Health would have to certify that the level of Radon is higher than the level that the Board of Health has adopted as a safe allowable standard.

4. If the Board of Health certified an unsafe level, the seller would have ten days in which to implement Radon control measures, and thereafter have the test repeated at the sellers expense.

Of course, the conditions of the test are not realistic. No one lives in a house for seventy years with the windows and doors shut. The simplest way to get rid of Radon is by adequate ventilation. The gas is not under pressure and rises only slowly into a confined space. A small exhaust fan, which changes the air in the home a few times a day is desirable in any event, and would insure the removal of any significant level of Radon. Had I needed to repeat the test I would have installed a small ventilating fan to change the air in the house.

PRACTICAL MEASURES

Given the fuss about Radon it would seem reasonable to take such precautions in the construction of a home, as are necessary to keep Radon out. The method of installation I have described for the under slab vapor barrier, will go a long way to prevent Radon entry.

After the slab has cured, the joint between the concrete and the block in the case of a basement slab, should be carefully sealed with a standard builders grade silicone caulking such as is made by General Electric. Do not use ordinary caulking compounds, because many of them shrink, and therefor cannot maintain the integrity of the seal against an entering gas.

In the case of the slab on grade foundation, the insulated joint between the slab and the outside four inch block, should be sealed in the same way. Thereafter, the plastic which was folded over that block, can be trimmed off to the sealed joint.

CHANGING THE AIR

I mentioned, using a small exhaust fan as a method of eliminating Radon accumulation. This is a matter which should be considered in any event. Our newer methods of construction, and better made windows, are making our houses more and more air tight. This is of course, very desirable for the purposes of heat conservation, because heretofore, up to half of the heat energy lost in a home was due to air infiltration. Consequently, the prevention of air infiltration makes a mechanical means of air changing desirable to eliminate stale air and cooking odors, as well as Radon.

It requires relatively little energy to heat the air that is expelled, because the amount of energy required to raise the temperature of a substance is in direct proportion to the weight of the substance. Air, because it is so light, therefor does not require much energy to raise it's temperature. However, if the conservation of that energy is a concern, there are exhaust fans with air to air heat exchangers, which can reclaim most of the heat.

CHAPTER 20

FRAMING

It is not the intent here, to school you in all the details of framing a house. There are many books available, that teach the particulars. Your point of view, is that of management and coordination.

Where I think there are pitfalls, I will go into enough technical detail, to enable you to appreciate the distinction being made. Especially, matters of energy conservation, will be carefully addressed, as they may involve decisions you will need to make.

Your need to oversee the framing work will be simplified by the fact that your framers will know the code requirements and the special requirements, of your building inspector. It is important that you specify in your agreement hiring the framers, that the work must meet the approval of the Building Inspector. Phrasing it in this fashion, will avoid a possible disagreement, as to what the code calls for. Most Building inspectors have certain pet requirements, which frequently, can be argued to be in excess of the code. Specifying that the Building Inspector must be satisfied, rather than saying "according to code", can save you an extra charge, where the carpenters feel that the inspector is asking for work, in excess of the code.

PLATFORM FRAMING

Platform framing is the method almost universally used today for framing a house. If, for instance, we began framing on a slab, the exterior walls and interior partitions, would be erected first. Then the floor joists for the floor above would be placed, spanning the partitions already built. The flooring plywood is then placed on the floor joists, resulting in a flat platform. The walls and partitions for the next floor, are then framed upon that platform, in the same manner as the first level.

This is a good and efficient method of construction. Working upon a flat platform makes the work simpler and faster, eliminating the need for scaffolding.

BALLOON FRAMING

This is an older method of framing, in which the walls are erected first, and then the floors suspended between them. It parallels the approach used in constructing stone walled buildings, and may have derived from that method.

In balloon framing a two story structure, the vertical elements of the outside walls are continuous in one piece. This is the way most old barns were built. Framing first to the roof, and then later, building the loft inside the structure, supporting it from the floor. It is apparent that building higher walls would be more difficult to do, requiring scaffolding and much bracing to keep them in place. Platform framing is simpler and provides a good rigid structure, except in one instance which arises in some modern designs.

If a house design has a two story atrium or sun space, contiguous to an outside wall, that outside wall should be balloon framed, for adequate rigidity. An exterior wall framed in two sections one upon the other, as in platform framing, without the lateral bracing of the intervening floor deck, lacks rigidity. Under stress, such as a high wind load, the wall would tend to fold in the middle. I have seen a house framed in this manner, with the entrance door in the high atrium wall. Every time the door was closed, the entire wall shook. Not a very reassuring situation.

POST AND BEAM CONSTRUCTION

This is a type of construction which still enjoys some popularity today. The frame of the house is built with vertical posts and horizontal beams forming the frame of the house as sort of a cage. Originally the posts and beams were fastened together with wooden pegs and this method is still used where authenticity is desired. The timbers of the frame are exposed to the inside, creating a solid, interesting look, valued in some contemporary designs. We would most recognize this style, in the old English Tudor construction. This was a development in building construction, which was easier and cheaper than making buildings solely from masonry. The Tudor frame was built as a cage, with the posts and beams pegged together. The walls were filled in between the timbers. Light branches were woven in the spaces as a kind of thatch work, which provided the support for a plaster coating, that was applied over the mesh of branches. This resulted in the typical English Tudor appearance which is so widely imitated today. The timbers of the frame were exposed and visible to the outside as well as the inside. The plaster walls were filled in the spaces. Later, in the development of the Tudor style, bricks were placed in the spaces, rather than the thatch work, resulting in a stronger wall.

The major difference between this type of construction and platform construction, is that in the post and beam method, the frame of the house must be totally constructed first to support the weight. The walls are some form of panels, placed in between the bearing members.

In platform framing, the walls themselves, are the bearing support for the platform forming the next level. Depending on the direction in which the floor joists are placed, some interior walls are "bearing", and some are "non-bearing".

PLACING THE SILL

The sill, also sometimes referred to as the shoe, is the first element of framing to be installed, as it's name might suggest. See Fig.13, item (1). This shows a 2 x 6 sill placed on the top course of block, even with the exterior edge. In some jurisdictions, the building codes require that

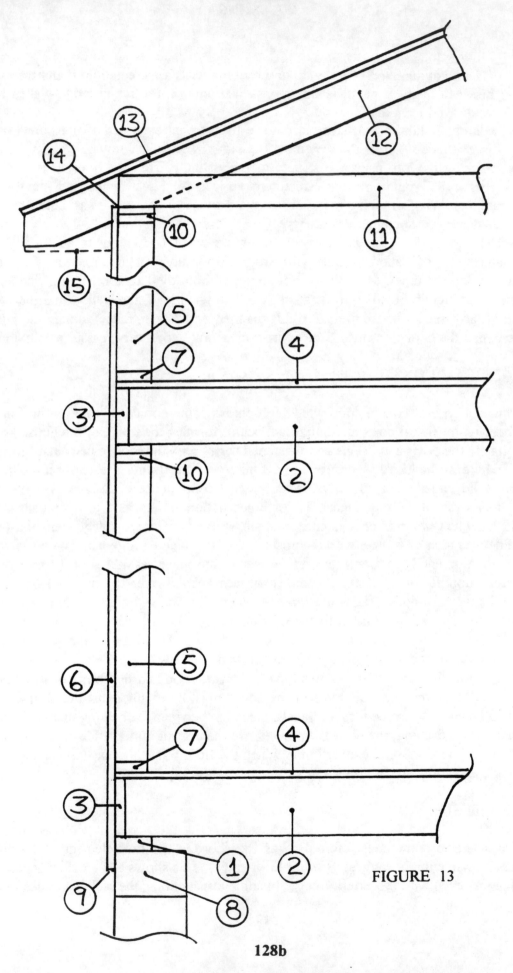

FIGURE 13

the sill be attached to the foundation by means of anchor bolts. In the case of a block foundation, these anchor bolts would be set and cemented into the block. The sill would have holes drilled in it so that it fit over the anchor bolts. The sill would then be held down by the use of washers and nuts on the upper, threaded ends of the anchor bolts. In certain hurricane and high wind areas, the requirements may be such that a block foundation is not adequate, and a concrete foundation might be required, with the anchor bolts imbedded in the poured concrete.

RULE 43

CHECK WITH THE LOCAL BUILDING DEPARTMENT FOR SILL ANCHORING REQUIREMENTS.

An oversight here could be very costly. Make sure!

AIR INFILTRATION

The area around and including the sill, is a major location for substantial air infiltration. Special care is needed to prevent this problem.

The sill rests on top of the concrete block. The surface of these blocks may not be perfectly even block to block, so that there may be spaces between the sill and the block through which unwanted air could enter. A sill placed on top of a poured concrete foundation would have even a rougher fit. A sill seal should be used. Fiber glass material is available in rolls for this purpose. It is 1" thick and 12" wide. A layer of this fiber glass is put down on the block with the sill being placed over it. The fiber glass will seal the voids under the sill.

The sill forms the nailer and support for the floor joists, Fig.13, No. 2. The band, No.3, is the same size as the joists. It is placed perpendicular to the ends of the joists serving to close the open spaces in between. The sub flooring, No.4, is nailed over the joists, thus completing the "platform" on which the first floor walls will be erected.

EXTERIOR SHEATHING

The exterior wall for the first level, No.5, is usually framed laying flat on the deck, and then raised to a vertical position after it is completed. The exterior wall will be covered with a sheathing, No.6, a single layer siding, or even a fiber board or rigid styrofoam. Frequently, the sheathing is nailed onto the studs while the wall is laying flat. It is positioned to extend below the wall, so that when the wall is erected to the vertical, the sheathing folds down over the band and at least an inch of the block. It is then nailed to the band.

A SERIOUS FLAW

This method of assembly, which is almost always used, is responsible for substantial air infiltration and resulting heat loss. It is so important that I will discuss it at some length.

If you examine Fig. 13, you will see that in order for the sheathing No.6, to fit tightly against the wall, six different elements must be in perfect alignment. The block, No.8, must align with the sill, No.1, which must align with the band, No.3, which must align with the sub flooring,

No.4, which must align with the partition shoe, No.7, which must align with the studs, No. 5, and so on. It is obvious that all these elements will not be perfectly aligned, and therefor substantial spaces will exist between the sheathing and the other structural members.

Now here's the problem. When the wind blows along the ground toward the house, it strikes the foundation, and much of it's force is directed upward. There is always a substantial space between the sheathing and the foundation No.9, as already mentioned. The wind blows up between the sheathing and the band. When it reaches the spaces between the wall studs, even though they will be filled with fiber glass insulation, a positive pressure is created within the wall. This pressure forces cold air into the house through every possible opening. Principal among these, are electrical outlet boxes containing wall switches and convenience outlets. Probably you have noticed on a windy day how cold air can be felt blowing out of the electrical wall switches. The space behind the baseboard, where the sheet rock does not meet the sub flooring, is another prominent space allowing significant leakage.

Experts tell us, that up to fifty percent of the heat loss of the average home, is due to air infiltration. Often, on a cold windy day, the temperature inside a home, may drop ten or fifteen degrees, no matter how hard the oil burner works.

PREVENTING SILL AREA INFILTRATION

There are several ways in which this infiltration can be eliminated. After having experimented with them, I have concluded that the simplest and most effective solution is to seal the space where the sheathing or siding overlaps the block.

Another situation that affects the width of this space, is the squaring of the sill. When the framers begin their work, the first thing they do, is check the square of the foundation. It is not unusual to find that the foundation is out of square. I have seen this vary from a quarter inch to as much as nine inches (Not on one of my jobs). The sill which forms the base for the framing must be absolutely square or the subsequent framing will not aline properly. If the carpenters find the foundation a little off, they will let the sill overlap the block to correct the squaring. This then, would obviously increase the width of the space between the sheathing and the block. Usually I would seal the space with silicone, using a caulking gun. However, if the space is too wide, the bead of silicone may not be large enough. In this case some backing is required as a stop, so that the silicone, when pumped in, will spread to fill the entire space. Stuffing the space tightly with fiberglass insulation will form such a suitable backing. Sometimes a second application of silicone must be made after the first has set, to completely fill the void. I always found it best to smooth out the silicone with my finger, to insure that it spread fully within the space, and adhered well to the inside of the sheathing and outside of the block. Although silicone is more expensive, use it. Avoid ordinary caulking compounds because they may shrink and crack in time. There are special caulkings available, which are regularly used on commercial buildings to seal marble and stone joints, which are very good. However, they may be difficult to come by, while every lumber yard carries builders silicone.

If the space is more than a half inch or so, it will have to be filled in with strips of wood to obtain a sufficient backing for the silicone.

At this point you can appreciate why I previously emphasized the need to square the foundation accurately. I like to use block for a foundation, not only because it is cheaper, but also because the foundation walls can be made straight and smooth. Poured foundations usually do not come out as well although they are considerably stronger, and may be advisable where earth pressure against the foundation is a consideration.

However, mistakes do happen. If there is a wide space between the foundation and the sheathing, because the foundation is not square, have the mason fur out the foundation as necessary, and then cover the furring with wire lath and cement parging. The parging, which is a coat of mortar, should be applied over all of the exposed foundation, for a neat and uniform appearance.

Where the framing is being erected on a slab on grade foundation, the overlap situation is the same, and should be sealed in the same manner. It is a little more difficult to do, because you may have to lay down on the ground to see under the edge of the sheathing.

RULE 44

SEAL THE SPACE WHERE THE SHEATHING OVERLAPS THE FOUNDATION.

Always overlooked, this saves energy costs year after year, and is well worth the effort.

FIGURE 14

This is a cutaway view of what is shown in the lower part of Fig. 13. The sill, No.1, rests on the block, No.2. The floor joists No.3, are supported on the sill, with the band, No.4, closing the openings to the outside. The sub flooring, No.5, completes the platform or deck upon which the walls are erected. No.6, shows a partition sill as it sits on the deck. No.7, represents the vertical studs forming the wall frame, and No.8, shows the sheathing applied to the stud wall projecting downward to cover the band and part of the block.

BRIDGING

Bridging is a means of stiffening a floor, and distributing the weight which is applied to a floor joist to the joists on either side. This spreads the load and reduces deflection. I am deliberately not using the word "bounce", because a properly constructed floor should never bounce.

Bridging is sometimes installed by using 1"x3" lumber as "X" braces between the joists. See Fig. 14A. There are also metal braces which are used in place of wood. These are rarely effective. They function rather than by compression, by forming hangers, whereby the bottom of a joist is suspended from the top of the joist to either side. The spacing between joists is not perfectly uniform, and frequently the metal cross bars are loose and without tension. It is rare to see these metal pieces properly installed so that they have any stiffening effect. When the joists are put in place, the tops of the braces are immediately nailed, because after the subflooring is laid, nailing will not be possible. The lower ends of the braces are left for nailing at a later date. I cannot tell you how many new, and even model homes, I have seen, where the bottom of the bridging was never nailed. Of course if it is not nailed, it is totally useless.

I prefer to use solid bridging, No.9, which when properly fitted and nailed, is far superior to the cross bracing. Each piece is individually cut and fitted tightly into place. It is a little more trouble, but the resulting solid floor justifies the effort. There are usually enough cut off pieces

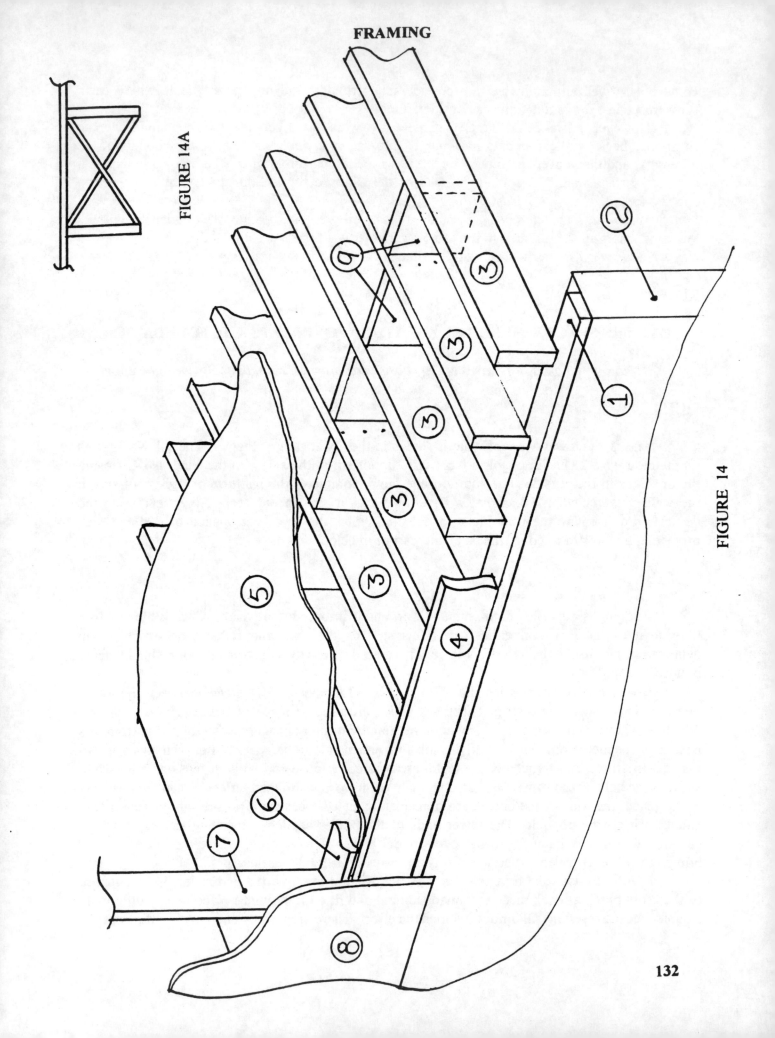

FIGURE 14A

FIGURE 14

from the joists, to make the solid blocking. The blocking pieces are slightly offset from each other to enable them to be end nailed through the joists.

CENTER GIRDERS

We have seen that the ends of the floor joists rest on the sill at the outside wall. However, the house will be too wide for a single joist to span the entire width, so an intermediate support will be required. If for example, the house we are building is 26 feet wide we would need a support at the approximate middle of that space. Usually floor joists are not used for spans of more than 14 feet. Dividing our space in half, we will have a span of 13 feet. At the center we will require a girder, running parallel to the outside walls, to form the support for the floor joists. Often, for this girder, a steel "I" beam is used. The beam will be supported by lally columns. A lally column is a steel pipe about three inches in diameter which has been filled with concrete, resulting in a post capable of supporting a great deal of weight. Sometimes this post is referred to as a lolly column rather than a lally column. The size of the steel beam, and therefor it's strength, will determine the spacing of the lally columns beneath it. If there is a particular reason that a long span of the girder is wanted without any columns, to achieve an open space under the girder, then the steel beam will have to be designed for the length of the span needed. Using a steel beam, can entail a few problems. If the beam has not been ordered sufficiently in advance, the framing may be delayed while waiting for it to arrive. The exact locations of the lally columns under the beam must be plotted so that the flange of the beam can be drilled at the fabricators yard to match the flanges of the lally columns which must be bolted to the beam. If the beam is not to be too long and heavy to handle, it must be made in two or more pieces which can be spliced together with a pre-drilled splicing plate. It is advisable that the joint between the beams be supported by a column. If the basement area is to be finished, the steel beam will have to be drilled in order to bolt nailers to it, which are needed to fasten the sheet rock. All of these requirements create the opportunity for error and delay.

Unless a specially long span was required, I always preferred to fabricate a wood girder right on the job. It's easier, faster, and less prone to error. You can use three 2x10s with half inch plywood laminated between them to make a very strong girder. The plywood creates substantial rigidity. The ends of several of these girders can easily be made to interlock. If there are to be any partition walls under the girder, it can be supported by a double stud concealed in the wall or the wall itself can be bearing if the proper haunch was provided in the floor. Otherwise, place a lally column every nine or ten feet, depending on the length of the open space. The girder may be supported temporarily on double 2x4 posts. This will enable precise height measurements to be taken under the girder for each lally column, which can be cut to the exact length by the supplier. This enables the length of the columns to accommodate the variations in the level of the concrete floor. If finishing is to be done, the wooden girder provides easy nailing. The position of the support columns must be determined before the slab is poured so that the proper footings can be provided under the column locations.

BASIC WALL LAYOUT

In framing an outside wall there is often a choice available for the spacing of the studs. For a one story ranch house, or the second story of a two story house, many building codes allow the wall studs to be spaced 24 inches on center rather than the usually required 16 inches on center. Using 24 inch centering, I have found, saves very few studs. The small savings which may be made are not worth the resultant lessening of rigidity of siding material and sheet rock due to the wider spacing. If you will be using fiber board, or styrofoam boards as sheathing, the closer stud spacing is essential to the rigidity of the exterior wall. There are many manufactured siding panels, which can be used as a single application siding without sheathing underneath. These materials sometimes have the tendency to warp and should only be used on studs spaced 16 inches on center.

The same condition applies to sheet rock, also known as dry wall, wall board, or gypsum board. Half inch thick material is fine on 16 inch centered studs but for 24 inch spacing it is necessary to go to 5/8 inch thick material to insure sufficient rigidity. This will increase the cost for material and labor for your wall finishing. If you opt for 24 inch spacing, don't expect your framers to take anything off their labor charge.

FIGURE 15

This figure shows typical wall framing including a window and a door opening. The sill, No.1, is set on the deck or slab as the case may be. The studs, No.2, are set vertically on the sill. In this illustration the studs are on 16 inch centers. There must be a stud every 16 inches regardless of the additional framing for a door or window. That is why the stud under the window is not centered in the space. It is, on the 16 inch spacing pattern. Plywood sheathing and siding comes in four foot wide sheets so it is important that there be a stud every four feet where a joint will fall. This facilitates the nailing of the siding or sheathing without regard to the window or door openings.

At the top of the studs is the double plate, No.3. This consists of two 2x4s or 2x6s whichever you are using. The 2x10 floor joists for the floor above, No.4, are shown positioned just above the studs which is the point of greatest strength. However, that is not always possible, and that is why the plate is a doubled member, so that it is strong enough to support a joist if it falls between the studs.

Above the openings for the door and the window are shown the headers, No.5. Because this is a bearing wall, supporting the floor joists above, No.4, solid headers are used to bridge the opening and support the weight. The headers are two 2x10s nailed together. A 2x4 or 2x6, No.6, is at the bottom of the header to create the proper opening height. Two shorter studs, called jack studs, No.7, are placed inside the opening under the ends of the header. As the name suggests they support the ends of the header. In the window a sill plate, No.8, is installed with two short jack studs underneath. In this case, the right hand jack stud coincides with the stud on the regular 16 inch center. Note that the side studs and jack studs for window and door openings are in addition to the normal studs on the 16 inch pattern, except of course, within the door way itself.

If the wall being framed is not a bearing wall, the solid headers may be omitted. In it's place are put short studs on the 16 inch pattern. These short studs would run vertically between the plate at the top of the door opening and the double plate at the top of the wall, and are called cripplers. Wall framing follows this basic pattern.

CORNERS

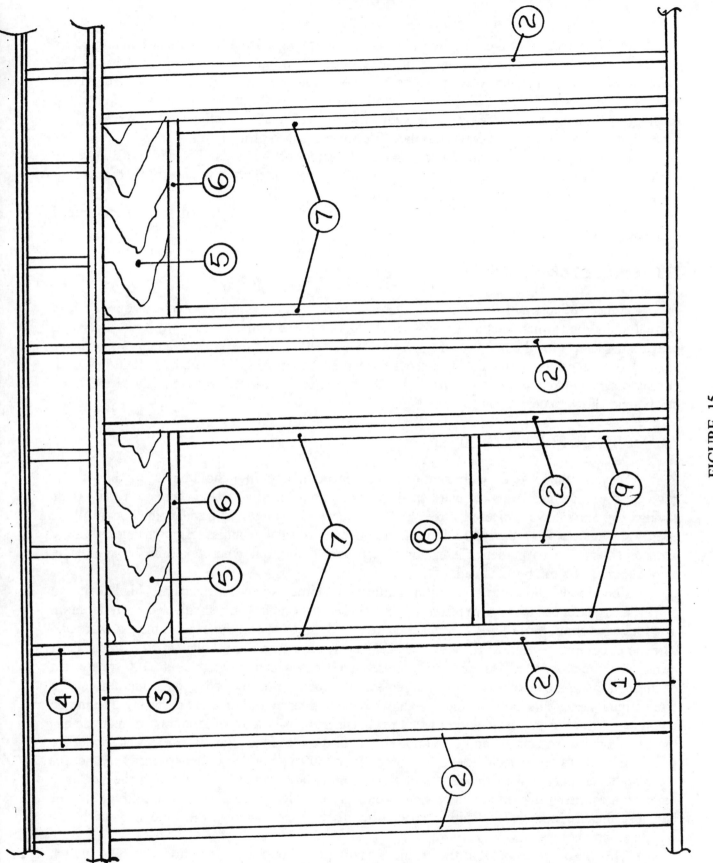

FIGURE 15

FRAMING

In the formation of a corner by the conjunction of two outside walls, most building codes require that the corner have a minimum of three studs. Figure 16 shows two joining walls. The usual studs on 16 inch centers are shown as No.1. An additional stud, No.2, is usually added and located to form a nailer for the sheet rock to be installed on the inside of the wall. When the sheathing or siding is in place, and the wall is to be insulated, the blind space, No.4, is not accessible and cannot be filled with fiberglass. The corner is also prone to air leakage.

Figure 17 illustrates a more preferable arrangement of the studs. The additional stud has been turned ninety degrees and placed to still form a nailer for the inside sheetrock, but to also allow access to the cavity, No.4, for proper insulation.

This is one of those small details that cost no more, but if followed, add to the energy efficiency of the structure.

PERPENDICULAR WALLS

Figure 18 illustrates the situation where an inside wall intersects with an outside wall. The normal studs on 16 inch centers are shown at No.1. Two additional studs, No.2, are added to provide the nailers for the inside corners. This is the usual manner of framing, and as you can see an inaccessible cavity, No.3, is formed which cannot be properly insulated. In Figure 19, an alternate arrangement for one of the added studs, No.2, is shown which eliminates the blind cavity, and allows access for insulation, No.3.

FRAMING FOR ENERGY SAVINGS

Making a house energy efficient does not depend on any single bold departure, but rather, rests on the implementation of many small changes, none of which alone, create a very large savings. So far I have indicated three areas where small changes in framing method result in energy savings. As we progress I will illustrate many more small changes. Each change may save a percent here or two percent there, none being astounding, but when taken in the aggregate, astounding results can be achieved.

I once built a house for a client in an interesting circumstance. It seems that his father who owned a large tract of land, gave he and his brother, each a building lot, subdivided from the farm. The lots were about three acres in size and were side by side, having the exact same exposure and climatic conditions. Both my client and his brother decided to build a house at the same time. I designed a two story Mediterranean style house on a full basement having about 2700 square feet of finished living area exclusive of the basement. My client's brother had a magazine design of a contemporary house he liked, and had already hired a builder by the time my client came to me on recommendation. In my presentation I told my client that I paid a lot of attention to many details that would conserve energy, and I described some of these changes to him just as I am doing for you. The brother's house incidentally, was only about 2000 square feet in living space. The houses were built and occupied in the fall. About six months later, after going through the winter, I received a call from my client. He was chuckling and sounded quite pleased. He told me that he had just finished comparing heating costs with his brother covering the time they both had occupied their homes.

The bottom line was that the brother's heating cost for the same period was 50% higher, even though his house was only three quarters as large.

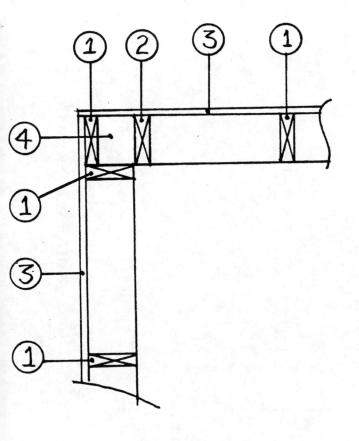

FIGURE 16

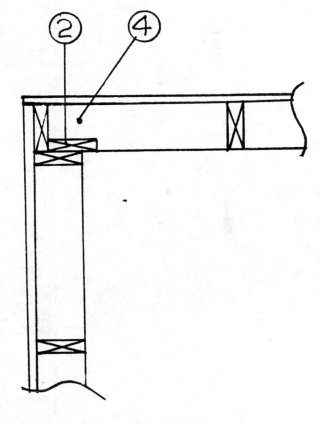

FIGURE 17

HORIZONTAL SECTIONS

137

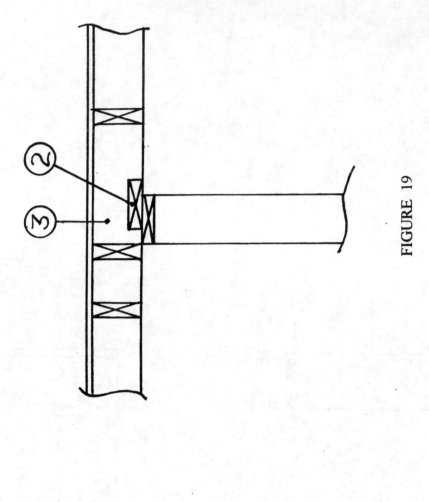

FIGURE 19

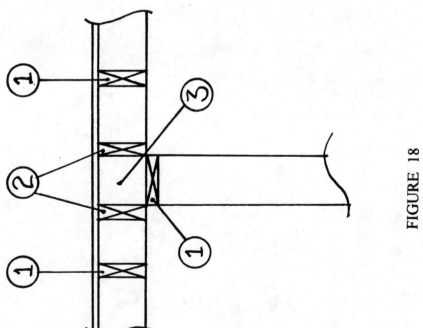

FIGURE 18

HORIZONTAL SECTIONS

FRAMING

Both houses were framed with 2x6s, both had windows with double glazing, and both had electric baseboard heating. Of course I was delighted to receive this confirmation of my belief that a lot of energy was wasted because of a number of small oversights or omissions in usual construction procedure.

CORNER BRACING

If you look at Figure 15, you will see that the skeleton of a wall has very little resistance to leaning sideways forming a parallelogram rather than a rectangle. This kind of lateral movement is called "Raking". If the outside of the wall is covered with plywood sheathing, the sheets of plywood nailed to the frame, create substantial stiffness and resistance to raking. However, if soft sheathing is used it will not be adequate to resist raking and prevent the collapse of the structure.

Diagonal braces may be installed, which are 1"x 3" strips, set into the framing so the outside remains flush for the siding. Another option is to use sheets of solid plywood at the corners.

THE SECOND FLOOR

Referring back to Figure 13, we see that after the walls of the first floor are erected to the vertical, the floor joists, No.21 are put in place just as the joists were placed for the first floor. The support of the inner ends of the joists will be provided by a bearing wall which should be positioned approximately over the girder in the basement.

The band, No.3, and the sub flooring, No.4, complete the deck which is then ready for the erection of the second floor upon the platform created. The second floor partitions are framed in the same manner as the first floor partitions. The studs, No.5, rest on the sill, No.7, and the double plate, No.10, rests atop the studs. The ceiling rafters are placed and supported in the same manner as the floor joists, using a bearing partition in the same axis as the bearing wall and basement girder below. Because the ceiling rafters will not be required to support a "live load" as the floor joists do, they are smaller in size In most cases 2x6s suffice. If the sheathing or siding is being fastened to the frame while laying on the floor, the sheathing should be brought even to the top of the plate, No.14. The sheathing will be made to extend beyond the sill so that when the wall is lifted into an upright position, the sheathing will rotate and cover the band, No.3.

If a single thickness siding, such as texture 1-11, which is a grooved plywood, or any one of the manufactured hard board sidings is used, it is essential that a small flashing be installed at the joint where the sheets of siding form a horizontal joint. This flashing, made from aluminum, is sometimes called a "Z strip", and is available pre shaped, from your lumber yard.

ROOF RAFTERS

The roof rafters, No.12, are positioned as shown in the diagram. A special triangular shaped notch is cut into each rafter so it will rest properly on the double plate. This notch is called a "Bird's mouth". See Figure 13B. The apex of the notch in Fig. 13, is at No.14. If the sheathing or siding has already been applied to the wall, the bird's mouth will fit over the siding. However, sometimes, especially when a single application siding is being used, it may not have been applied to the frame at this point, and will not be put on until the entire frame is completed. If this is the case, it is essential that you see to it, that the framers cut the bird's mouth large enough so that the siding can be slid up into position, flush with the top of the plate, inside the bird's mouth.

Very often when the siding is applied later, it cannot be installed to the top of the wall. If it does not reach at least to the bottom of the double plate, a slot will be left open into the wall. This will allow air from the overhang to enter the wall causing significant heat loss due to infiltration.

RULE 45

IT IS ESSENTIAL THAT THE SIDING OR SHEATHING ALWAYS COMPLETELY COVER THE FRAME.

This is important in order to combat our major enemy, air infiltration.

HOUSE WRAP, AN INFILTRATION BARRIER

There is a product now in general use, called "House wrap", sold under several trade names. One of the popular brands is "TYVEK" made by DuPont. This is a paper like material which is fibre reinforced for strength, and has the ability to block air transmission without preventing moisture transfer. The importance of moisture transfer, or the lack of it will be discussed further on.

The idea is to wrap the entire frame of the house in this material which comes in 9 foot long rolls. It is quite strong and resistant to tearing and is easy to install by stapling to the sheathing if it is already in place, or stapling to the frame if sheathing has not yet been installed. If a single application siding is to be used, it would be better not to install it in the course of framing, but to wait, and install it after the wrap has been put on. The idea-of the house wrap is to envelope the house in a sheath that prevents the infiltration of air into the house from the outside. It is best to install it continuously, without seams, around the whole structure. The second floor wrap will over lap the band, where it can be securely stapled.

Later, the siding may be installed over the wrap. It can be seen that the wrap will prevent air infiltration between the joints and/or laps of the siding.

Where the wrap covers door and window openings, it should be cut as a large X inside the openings, and the flaps so formed, folded back and around the framing of the opening and stapled in place. As was noted before, if the bird's mouth cut is too tight, the wrap cannot be properly installed to seal the framing of the upper wall. Cutting and patching around the rafters is not really desirable. Air, under wind pressure, can enter through the smallest crack.

Remember, for the house wrap to be effective it must be properly and carefully installed. Piecing it out will render it worthless.

CHAPTER 21

THE ROOF AND IT'S FORMS

Building the roof is part of the framing, however while the construction of walls follows a rather uniform pattern, the roof takes many forms and styles. The details of the framing, the angle cuts etc. will not be shown, rather the different styles will be represented schematically to convey a general understanding of the forms so you will recognize them when you look at building plans.

THE SLOPE OF THE ROOF

The slope of a roof is indicated by the vertical height in inches, attained in twelve inches of horizontal distance.

Figure 20 illustrates the slope of a roof which rises 3" vertically for each 12" horizontally. This is called a 3" pitch. The symbol on the left above the roof with the numbers 3 and 12 is the usual way the pitch of a roof is shown on architectural plans. This is a 3 on 12 pitch or simply a 3" pitch.

Figure 21 illustrates a 6" pitch and Figure 22 illustrates a 12" pitch or a "Full Pitch".

The indication of the pitch in inches makes it very easy for the carpenter to layout the rafters and determine the angle that must be cut on the upper end to meet the ridge rafter. He need only place his carpenter's steel square, which is calibrated in inches on each side, with the 3" mark and the 12" mark on the opposite side along the edge of a rafter, and the edge of the square will represent the angle of the cut. The angle to be cut is the complementary angle to the angle of the slope, so the square must be placed in inverted position on the rafter. At the bottom end of the rafter there are two cuts to be made. One is the angle of the slope and the other the complement of the angle, resulting in one horizontal cut and one vertical cut. Go back to figure 13, and you will see the cuts on the lower end of the rafter. Ask your framer to show you how this is done. It is really quite simple, and once

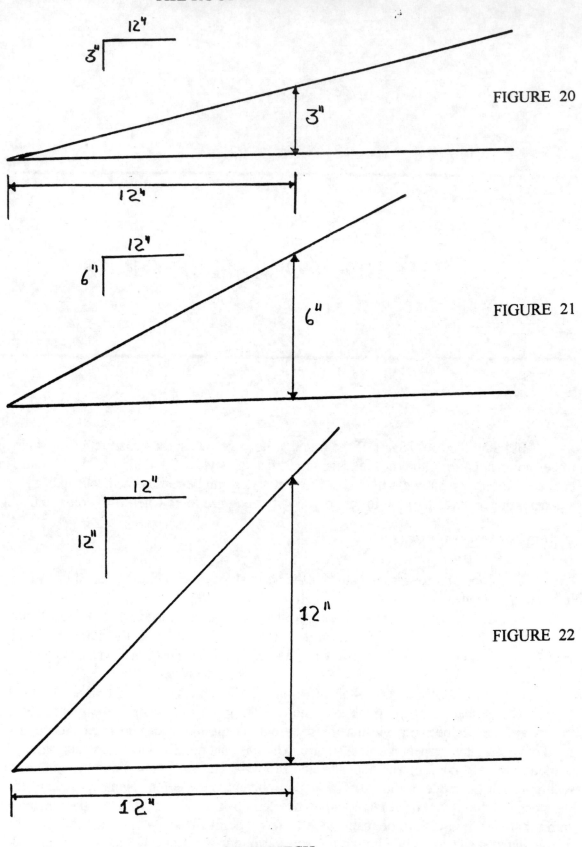

FIGURE 20

FIGURE 21

FIGURE 22

ROOF PITCH

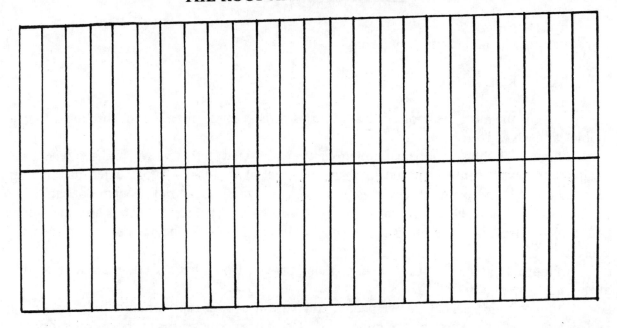

PLAN VIEW FIGURE 23

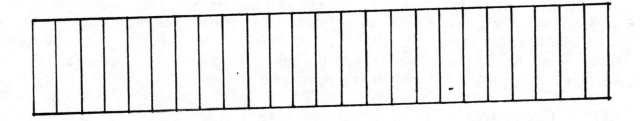

ELEVATION 4/12 FIGURE 24

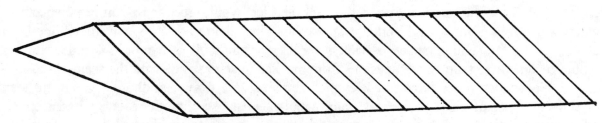

PERSPECTIVE FIGURE 25

GABLE ROOF

SCHEMATIC FRAMING

you see it you will understand immediately.

THE GABLE ROOF

This is the most common of all roof forms. It is a simple pitched roof forming a triangle or "gable" at each end.

Figure 23 shows a schematic plan view. A plan view is that view you have when looking straight downward. Schematic means that the actual lumber is not represented in scale for it's width and height but is just represented as a single line to illustrate the "Scheme" of arrangement of the rafters. A ridge beam runs horizontally in the center of the roof which is also the high point of the roof. The rafters are run perpendicular to the ridge beam. They are usually placed on 16" centers.

Figure 24 is the elevation view, or that view you would have if you were looking directly at the side of the house.

Figure 25 is a schematic perspective to give you a better representation of the actual shape and appearance. The rafters on the opposite side have been omitted for purposes of clarity.

Figure 26 is a section drawing showing the actual elements of the construction as they would appear in the architectural plans. The ridge beam, No.1, is at the top with the roof rafters, No.2 extending right and left. The 2x4, No.3, is called a collar tie, and is for the purpose of preventing the roof from flattening down when weight is applied, such as a snow load. The roof joists, No.4, would not usually be in a single span as shown here for the purposes of illustration. They would ordinarily be in two pieces, overlapping and supported by a bearing wall.

Gable roofs can be run at right angles to each other and merge together. The angles formed where two gable roofs come together at right angles are called the valleys. Small gables can project at right angles outward from the main roof to contain windows.

ELEVATION VIEWS

Elevation views have an interesting characteristic. It is a view that you can never actually see. Take for example, the front elevation drawing of a house. It shows the windows and the doors and all of the features that are seen when looking directly at the front. However, if you actually stood in front of a house and looked straight ahead you would see only that which is directly in front of you the way the drawing shows. One end would be to your left and the other end to your right. These portions to the right and left would appear to you in perspective. The window to your right would actually appear as a parallelogram. If we were to draw a front elevation of a house in perspective, which is a lot more difficult, it would look more real, but we would be unable to take any dimensions from the plan in accordance with the scale.

Consequently, architectural elevation drawings are drawn as though you were standing directly in front of each horizontal point simultaneously so that there is no perspective. The advantage of this, is that the plan may be drawn to an accurate scale which is considerably more useful for the purposes of construction than a rendering in perspective.

It takes some practice to be able to translate the flat elevations of a plan into a three dimensional mental picture. The artists that draw architectural renderings in three dimensional form do exactly that. They look at the flat elevations of the scale drawings and translate them into a perspective view. Today there are computer programs which can do the same thing. They can

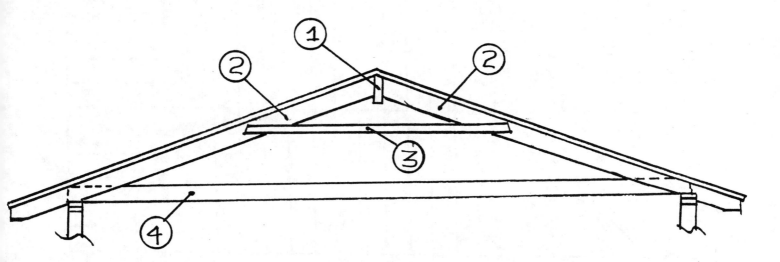

SECTION 4/12 PITCH
GABLE ROOF
FIGURE 26

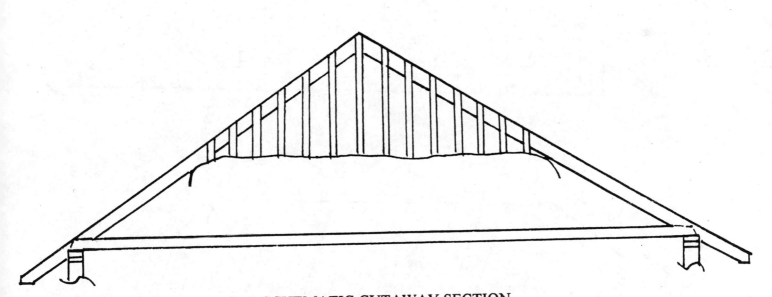

SCHEMATIC CUTAWAY SECTION
HIP ROOF END VIEW
FIGURE 30

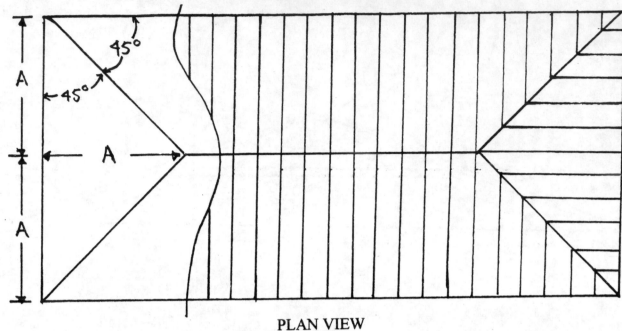

PLAN VIEW
FIGURE 27

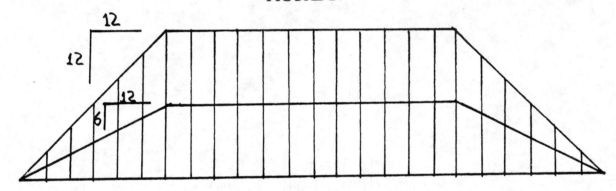

ELEVATIONS 6/12   12/12
FIGURE 28

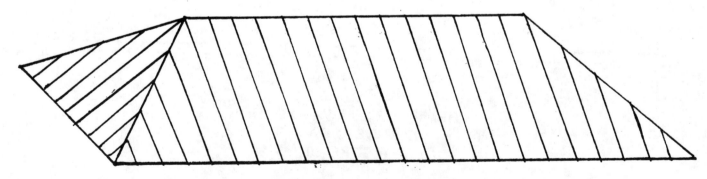

PERSPECTIVE HIP ROOF
FIGURE 29

SCHEMATIC FRAMING

146

produce a three dimensional representation from the flat plans. What is more, they can even vary the vantage point, the theoretical point from which the view is seen. These computer renditions are helpful but they still cannot match the realism and shading that a good artist can produce.

THE HIP ROOF

The hip roof is a modification of the standard gable roof, where instead of vertical gable ends, the ends are sloped at the same pitch as the front and rear slope. This requires the use of "Hip Rafters" which run from the corners up to the ridge. Figure 29, schematically represents the basic form of a hip roof. It is standard practice that the slope of the ends is always the same as the slope of the front and rear. This results in a uniform overhang.

Figure 27 shows a plan view of a hip roof. When the slopes are the same the hip rafters run at a 45 degree angle. The point where the hip rafters meet the ridge rafter is the same distance in from the end as it is from the front and rear. This holds true no matter what the pitch. Figure 28 represents an elevation view of a 6" pitched and a full pitched hip roof. Note that dimension A remains the same regardless of the pitch.

Figure 30 is a cut away schematic section showing how the actual wood members are arranged.

The hip roof is popular in Mediterranean and tropical designs and is frequently done with curved Spanish roofing tiles.

THE DUTCH COLONIAL

The Dutch Colonial roof is a style that originated in New England among the early Dutch settlers. It seems that houses were taxed on the number of stories they had not including the attic. The settlers realized that if they used the attic level for living space, they could have more living area without increasing their taxes. To improve the head room in the attic they cleverly put an outward bend in the roof and added small gables for the windows.

Figure 31 and 32 show a plan view and elevation view respectively. The nature of the roof is better understood by examining Figure 33 which is a structural section. You can see at once how the bend in the roof was accomplished. The framing of such a roof is complicated so that in modern times it has been simplified to a simulated design. In the simulation, the upper story is framed in the standard manner and then a false sloping roof is hung off to the sides. See Figure 34.

THE MANSARD ROOF

The Mansard style is a French style that was used extensively in America during the late 1800s and early 1900s. The upper story has very steep sloping sides treated with roofing. The roofing was usually done with slate or metal sheets. Slight dormers were required for the windows and they were often done with curved tops. The top of the roof was usually flat.

The Mansard style of roof is rarely used today for residential designs but enjoys considerable popularity on small commercial buildings. Rather than a flat roof these commercial designs use a very low sloping hip roof on top. The result is almost the same as illustrated for the Dutch Colonial simulation. Windows instead of being in small gables are installed in the flat wall

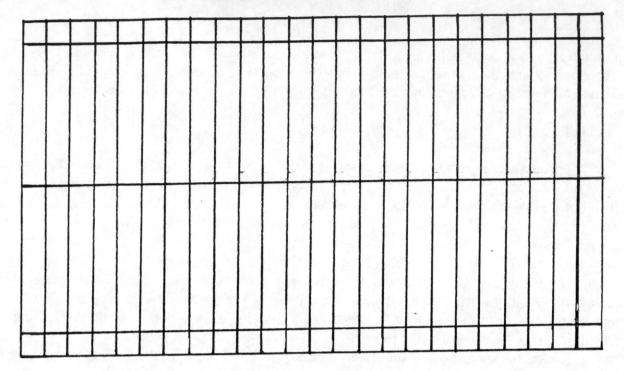

PLAN VIEW
FIGURE 31

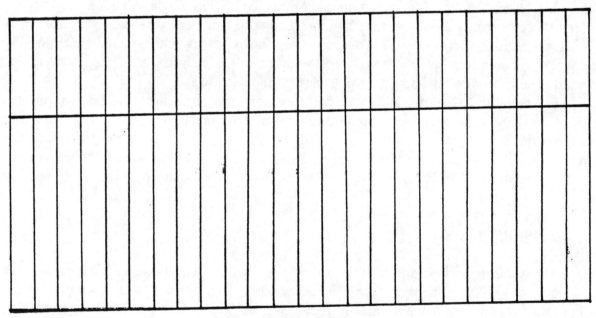

ELEVATION
FIGURE 32

SCHEMATIC FRAMING PLAN
DUTCH COLONIAL ROOF

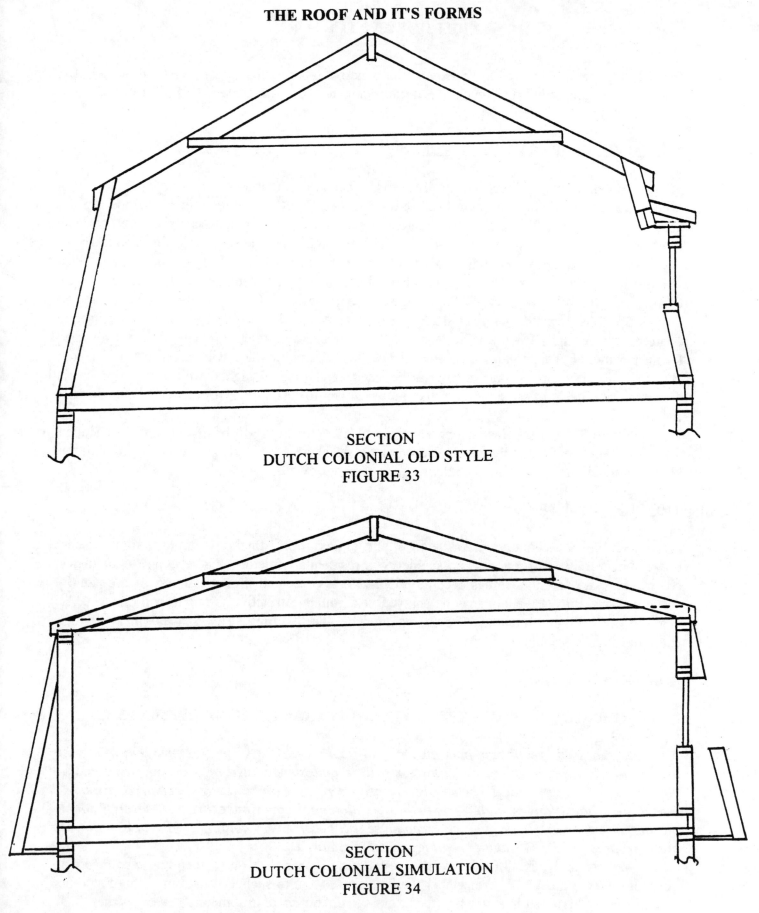

SECTION
DUTCH COLONIAL OLD STYLE
FIGURE 33

SECTION
DUTCH COLONIAL SIMULATION
FIGURE 34

and the sloping roof is cut out to expose the window. These cutouts are usually done with an arched top creating a hybrid French-Mediterranean style. The arrangement of the cut out window has been illustrated in Figure 34.

THE CONTEMPORARY CLERESTORY

Contemporary designs usually have roofs that are variations of the standard gable roof except that an interesting variation has been introduced. The front slope and rear slope are not necessarily the same. Where roofs of different slopes come together there is a short vertical wall to close the gap. Frequently, windows are installed in this wall and the inside finish follows the upward slope of the roof resulting in what is called a "Cathedral Ceiling". The windows are called "Clerestory" windows which have also been borrowed from Renaissance Cathedral design. Clerestory windows are very useful in passive solar design when they are south facing and provided with a means of summer shading. However, very often clerestory windows are used in contemporary designs for the effect and not for their energy gathering ability, and are installed facing northward. This creates a substantial heat loss situation which will be regretted in colder climates. If clerestory windows are to be used, and also skylights which are popular in contemporary design, consideration should be given to their solar orientation and summer shading.

Figure 35 is a schematic representation of a contemporary roof of two different slopes, forming a short vertical wall with clerestory windows. There are a variety of ways of framing this kind of situation depending on the internal arrangement of walls.

THE GREENHOUSE

Because a greenhouse is for the most part a glass roof, I think it is appropriate to discuss this architectural construction as an adjunct to a residential structure. There is no doubt that in recent years the greenhouse has become popular. It is presented in home shows as a delightful space where tropical splendor may be enjoyed year round. Attractive wrought iron dining tables promise the best in simulated alfresco dining. The ads featuring "Sun Spaces" make it look charming and irresistible.

RULE 46

A GREENHOUSE IS AN EXPENSIVE AND IMPRACTICAL DISAPPOINTMENT.

In reality a greenhouse presents many difficulties. In the spring summer and fall, when the sun falls on the greenhouse the interior will become superheated in the same way a closed automobile does in the sun. To be usable, extensive screening and shading is required, combined with large exhaust fans or high capacity air conditioning. In the winter, the glass, even if double glazing, is a poor insulator, and the greenhouse will become very cold. If plants and small trees are to be preserved a substantial heating system is required.

We are probably all familiar with a restaurant that has built on a green house to create an outdoor dining atmosphere. I remember the first time I went to such a restaurant with a few other people, we could not sit in a way that the bright sun did not glare in someone's eyes. As the

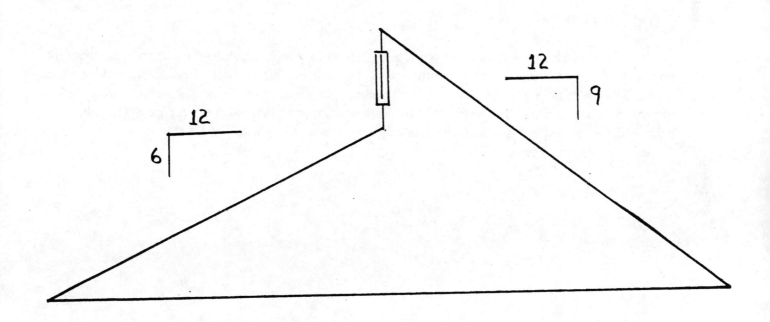

CONTEMPORARY CLERESTORY
SCHEMATIC REPRESENTATION
FIGURE 35

weather became warmer the temperature inside the greenhouse became so high that it had to be closed to use. The next time I went to that restaurant, dark shades had been installed over the entire ceiling and a large air conditioning unit put in.

If you ever visit a commercial greenhouse, the first thing you will notice are lots and lots of heating pipes and blower units. Up near the ceiling you will see large exhaust fans. In the summer, all of the glass is coated with a removable white paint. This has got to tell you how difficult it is to maintain an interior climate for the successful growing of plants. Without these arrangements any plants in your home greenhouse will burn up in the summer and freeze in the winter.

It has also been suggested that a greenhouse is an effective solar collector for use in heating a home. The means of collecting and transferring heat gained in a greenhouse are cumbersome, costly, and require an effective insulating shield between the living areas and the greenhouse at night so that heat energy gained during the day will not be lost at night by a reversal of the process.

A GARDEN ROOM

If you wish to create a room with a garden atmosphere, emulate the old style screened in porch. Keep the pitched roof and cathedral ceiling but insulate it well. Enclose the room with double glazed patio doors equipped with screens. The addition of blinds, a porch railing and a quarry tile floor will create a very attractive but much more practical garden room. This idea has been widely adapted in Florida where it is called a "Lanai, or "Florida Room".

CHAPTER 22

WINDOWS, DOORS AND SKYLIGHTS

Over the last twenty years there has been a concerted effort to develop windows of higher insulating value than the commonly used double glazed windows. Millions and millions of dollars of your money have been spent by the Government on this effort. The results have been very little. Never the less, some extravagant claims and misinformation about windows have been circulated to justify the enormous expenditure of public funds by the United States Department of Commerce and the United States Department of Energy.

Following is an excerpt of a paper I wrote on this subject:

WINDOWS AND ENERGY COSTS

It is an accepted proposition that windows are desirable. They give us light, heat from the sun, and the means to relate to our environment. Studies have shown that daylight improves the human mood, and increases productivity. Windows allow us to enjoy the view, keep tabs on the neighbors, and see who is at the front door. Since the development of glazing materials, windows have been used in a variety of ways both practical and artistic.

In the 1970s, with the advent of OPEC, energy costs rose sharply. The cost of heating and cooling our homes and workplaces increased accordingly, and we began to seek ways to lower our energy consumption.

The most readily available solution was to increase insulation. Up to then, homes were conventionally framed with 2x4 studs measuring actually 3 5/8" and later 3 1/2" in width. This permits the use of 3 1/2" fiber glass insulating batts, rated at R 11, between the studs. Two different approaches were taken to improve on this. It became common to frame with 2"x6" studs measuring actually 5 5/8" and later 5 1/2" in width, which permitted the use of 5 1/2" insulating batts having an insulating value of R 19.

The other solution was to use a layer of rigid insulating board on the exterior or interior of the 2x4" studs in addition to the 3 1/2" fiber glass thus achieving the same overall insulating value achieved by the 5 1/2" batts.

Under the stimulus of Federal and State tax credits, many further developments were made to reduce the energy requirement of heating homes. Super insulated walls, foam composite wall sections, active and passive solar heating systems, earth berming and geothermal systems were developed. Unfortunately when the tax credits ended public interest waned, as most of these techniques were not cost effective.

There are some very viable passive solar and insulating strategies which add very little cost and have reasonable payback periods. However, the public has shown little interest because of several drawbacks in passive solar design. Among these are the problems of glare, discomfort in direct sunlight, fading of carpet, furniture, and the loss of usable space because furniture must be kept back from the windows. Sun spaces and green house attachments also have problems. During the day they are too hot for comfortable use. At night, due to the poor insulating value of the glass they lose a great deal of heat becoming too cold for comfortable use. Usually these spaces must be sealed off at night to prevent excessive energy loss. If you have ever eaten in a restaurant greenhouse on a sunny day you noticed the extensive shading and air conditioning which was necessary to make the space comfortable.

The U.S. Department of Energy reports that 40% of all the energy consumed in this country is used in buildings. Lawrence Berkeley Laboratories put this figure at 20%. All agree that about 25% of the energy used in buildings is lost through the windows. This then represents from 5% to 10% of the national energy usage, equivalent to 1.7 to 3.4 million barrels of oil a day, or one to two times the entire annual output of the Alaska pipeline.

If the average American home loses 25% of it's heat through the windows it would appear that as we build more and more energy efficient homes the percentage of heat loss through windows will increase. For instance if we double the insulation efficiency of a building, then the percentage of heat lost through windows would become 50%, making windows a primary target for improvement in thermal efficiency.

HEAT TRANSFER THROUGH A WINDOW AT ORDINARY TEMPERATURES

Before we evaluate the current state of the art in window technology it will be helpful to discuss how heat is transferred through a window.

Heat transfers through a window by three means, conduction, convection and radiation. For our examination we will consider a standard double glazed window consisting of two opposing panes of glass, spaced apart, with air in the space. The inner pane of the glass absorbs heat from the room air. This heat is conducted through the glass and then absorbed by, and conducted through the intervening air. It is then absorbed by the outer pane, conducted through the glass, and absorbed by the exterior air when the temperature of said air is less than the temperature of the glass pane.

The second method of transfer is by convection. In a double glazed window the air which touches the inner pane is heated by that pane and tends to rise. The air in contact with the outer colder pane is cooled and tends to fall. This establishes a circular movement of the air between the panes. Thus we have a rotating or circulating energy delivery system where the air contacting the inner pane absorbs heat and circulates to the outer cooler pane where it gives up that heat.

The third method of heat transfer is by radiation. That is, heat in an infra red wave form which travels through the window. Infra red radiation is generally divided into two types, long wave and short wave. Short wave infra red radiation is given off by a source having a temperature of a thousand degrees centigrade or more. The wave length is less than 7500 angstroms. Long wave radiations are emitted by a source of less than a thousand degrees centigrade and have a wave length greater than 7500 angstroms. If a window is to be effective it must be able to control the transfer of both long wave and short wave radiation in either direction. In a heated space all of the surfaces, materials and objects emit long wave radiation which impinges on the window. Sun light and heat are short wave radiation which also impinges on the windows. To keep an interior space cool, it is important that the window be able to restrict the entry of short wave radiation from outside as well as controlling long wave radiation from inside.

Long and short wave radiations do not always behave in the same way. They both obey the laws of optics. When reflected the angle of reflection is the same as the angle of incidence however, they are not reflected in the same way. Sun light and heat, as an example of short wave radiation, is reflected to a greater or lesser degree by almost every surface it strikes. Light colors reflect short wave radiation to a greater degree than dark colors. Shiny surfaces, mirrors, water etc. reflect the short waves. However long wave radiation is not reflected by most surfaces but is absorbed. Long wave radiation can only be reflected by a non ferrous metallic surface such as gold, silver, copper and aluminum. The more the surface is optically polished the better it reflects long wave infra red radiation. Efficiency up to 90% can be achieved.

Short wave radiation passes readily through glass to an efficiency of about 90% for a single pane and a little over 80% for a double pane. However, long wave radiations are absorbed by glass. Short wave radiations pass through a column of air but long wave radiations are absorbed by a column of air.

STATE OF THE ART

Recent technology to improve the insulating qualities of windows addresses all three methods of heat transfer through the window. The air between the panes of the window can be replaced with another transparent gas such as Argon. This slightly improves the performance of the window because the gas is a better insulator than air and thus reduces conduction.

When the space between the opposing panes in a double glazed window is increased, the insulating value of the window is slightly increased. This may be attributed to the greater insulating value of the thicker air column and the greater absorption of long wave radiation emitted from the inner side of the inner pane as it passes through a thicker column of air. However, when the space between the panes reaches about one and a quarter inches there is no further improvement. This is attributed to the fact that at the wider spacing increased losses due to convection neutralize further reductions in conduction and radiation. It is known however, that when the space between the panes is reduced to about 3/8ths of an inch, there is no convection. This is due to a certain clinging effect the air has to the surface of the glass.

Most of the development work on windows has been done by M.I.T in Massachusetts and Lawrence Berkeley Laboratory in California, supported by Government grants from the Department of Energy and National Science Foundation.

MIT and LBL first approached the problem with regard to radiation. They developed low-E (low emissivity) coatings. These coatings are applied to a film or directly to the glass. In the case of the film it can be bonded to the glass or suspended between the double panes. These coatings are a finely disbursed film of metallic particles, usually silver, deposited on the base material in an extremely thin layer by a method known as sputter deposition. Other metals are now being used with improved optical properties. These coatings have the ability to reflect long wave infra red radiations. When the reflective coating is properly used in conjunction with a window, long wave radiations emitted from the surfaces and objects inside a heated room are reflected back toward the room reducing the heat energy transferred through the window. This increases the insulating performance of the window, from R2 to R3.

To understand a low-E coating we may think of it as similar to a screen over a window. Like the screen the film has millions of microscopic holes. These holes are small enough that the waves of long wave radiation cannot fit through and are reflected by the metallic surface. However, the holes are large enough so that short wave radiation in the form of light and heat can pass through. Just as the fabric of the screen blocks some of the light, the low-E coatings also block about 10% of the short wave radiations.

As previously mentioned, the use of a different gas in place of the air in the window, adds another 1 R of insulating value, raising the overall performance of a low-E window to R 4.

So called "Super Windows" developed by Lawrence Berkeley Laboratory utilize additional films suspended between the exterior panes. Depending on the number of films and coatings, these windows are claimed to have an R value of 6 to 8.

HOW GOOD ARE THESE WINDOWS?

The R rating is a simple numerical system to describe the insulating value of a material. A higher R value means better insulation, while a lower value means poorer insulation. To better understand the insulating value of the windows we have been discussing it will be helpful to compare them to a known standard. Let's take a batt of fiber glass insulation 12" thick as our standard. Although not a perfect insulator this is pretty good insulation and will serve as a fair basis of comparison. It has an R value of 40. An ordinary double glazed window has a R value of 2. Thus we see that such a window is only 5% as effective as 12" fiber glass. When the low-E coating is used the R value increases to 3 which is 7 1/2% as effective as our 12" fiber glass. When Argon is substituted for the air in the window the R value increases to 4 adding another 2 1/2%, for a total of 10% of the value of the 12" fiber glass. Finally, adding films inside the window raises the R value to 6 to 8 depending on the number of films. This yields a window 15 to 20% as good as our standard. "Super Windows" add 60 to 70% to the cost of the window. Low-E windows cost about 20% more, and gas filled low-E windows, about 30% more.

These "Super Windows" are not popular due to the high increase in cost and are offered by only two window manufacturers. Low-E windows comprise about 30% of new window sales.

LBL tells us that the low-E coatings have a 90% efficiency in reflecting long wave infra red radiation. As we have seen, when 90% of the radiation component of the heat transfer through the window is reflected, the insulating value of the window only increases by 1 R, or 2 1/2% against our standard. It seem reasonable to assume therefor, that very little of the total heat transfer through the window is by means of long wave infra red radiation. Even 100% elimination of the long wave radiation would add only another 1 R.

When two films are introduced between the panes of a double glazed window the R value increases by a value of 2. This improvement results from the elimination of the convection within the window when the spaces are reduced to at least 3/8ths of an inch. If eliminating 90% of the radiation loss and all of the convection loss only improves the performance of the window by a total of R 3, it must be concluded that the vast majority of the heat being transferred through a window of this kind is by conduction. Substituting Argon for the air in the window only improves the R value by 1. It appears that the avenue followed by LBL in their research was unrewarding in achieving any substantial improvement. They only addressed the minor aspects of the heat transfer process through a window, rather than the main matter of conduction.

THE REST OF THE STORY

LBL claims that the "Super Window" performs better than an equivalent area of wall from an energy standpoint. The rationale is that even though the insulating value of the window is less than the wall, the window admits solar energy which the wall cannot, and therefor on a total basis out performs the wall. This of course, is not an argument in favor of the technology of the window, but rather an argument in favor of passive solar design and the increase in window area used in such design.

It has long been known that a south facing double glazed window, over the course of a winter, gains more energy in the form of "Insolation", which is the term for solar energy gained through a window, than it looses through outward transfer.

IS THE SUPER WINDOW BETTER?

To fully evaluate the question we must have an understanding of "Shading". An ordinary pane of window glass blocks about 10% of the solar light and energy falling upon it. It is assigned a shading coefficient of 1. A standard double glazed window has a shading coefficient of .91. It blocks about 9% more of the "Insolation". A window with low-E glazing has a shading coefficient of .86 to .75. A window with low-E glazing and Argon fill, has a shading coefficient from .75 to .66, and a "Super Window" with three internal glazing sheets, two low-E coatings and Argon in place of the air, has a shading coefficient of .60 to .52.

As has been previously noted a standard double glazed window gains more energy than it looses at a shading coefficient ficient of .91. For the purpose of illustration let's assign some arbitrary values. Let's say that a standard double glazed window looses 100 units of energy through outward heat transfer when the outside temperature is lower than the inside temperature, and gains 110 units of energy from the sun for a net energy gain of 10 units over time. Now a "Super Window" with the maximum claimed R value of R8, cuts the heat loss by 20% when compared to our 12" fiber glass standard, or therefor to a loss of 80 units of energy in our example. The shading coefficient of such a window at .52 compared to the .91 of the ordinary double glazed window reduces the energy gain by .39 or 39% for a net gain of 71 units of energy. Thus we can see that a "Super Window" saves 20 units of energy by improving insulating value but looses 39 units by blocking "insolation" creating a net loss for the window of 19 units of energy.

It is demonstrated therefor, that low-E windows and super windows, because of their increased shading or blocking of incoming energy, keep out more energy than they save by their increased insulating value. These windows are energy negative. Rather than improving on an ordinary double glazed window, they are obviously not as good. LBL has reported that they have received about 20 million dollars from the Department of Energy to conduct their window research. Did the taxpayers get their moneys worth? The people who are purchasing these windows at increased cost in the expectation of saving money on their energy costs are in reality spending more for energy.(End of excerpt)

The remainder of the paper describes the construction and technology of a super insulating window invented and patented by this writer. This window can control the passage of both long wave and short wave energy in either direction and has a potential insulating value of R 20 with no increase in shading.

Due to the fact that the public and Government have lost interest in energy saving methods, the very substantial investment required to bring this invention to the market place cannot be justified at this time. Interested parties may refer to U.S. Patent Number 4,586,289.

THE DOUBLE HUNG WINDOW

The double hung window has been the most popular window design over the years. It has two movable panels, one over the other, which can be raised and lowered. For many years these windows required counter weights to keep them open and from falling down when raised. The counterweights, called sash weights, were concealed in compartments at the sides of the window and operated by the use of ropes and pulleys on either side. Eventually the ropes, which would break from age, were replaced by chains.

In the last thirty years or so, double hung windows were devised that slid up and down on spring loaded friction tracks which would keep the window panels from falling. This was a great advance and eliminated the sash weights, ropes and pulleys as well as the need to build compartments into the sides of the windows to hold the weights. A substantial decrease in price resulted.

Because the panels of double hung windows had to slide up and down in tracks which had to be loose enough to permit this, a major problem has always been air leakage. Especially when the wind is blowing. These infiltration losses led to the development of storm windows which can be put over the outside of the window and help to prevent the infiltration. Modern design and weather stripping have done much to eliminate this problem. If a double hung window cannot be reached from the ground, cleaning the glass is somewhat difficult. It is necessary to raise and lower the panels reaching under and over to get to all the area of the panes. Some double hung windows available today, permit the panels to be pulled into the room for ease of cleaning. This is certainly a big advantage but may sacrifice some of the air tightness.

THE FRENCH WINDOW

Another popular design of years past was the "French Window". This window opened like a pair of doors and had the advantage of being able to open the entire area of the window at the same time rather than the double hung window which restricts the opening to half of the total window area. After some time "French windows" would warp and loose their fit, making them very difficult to close tightly. They were even worse than double hung windows in preventing infiltration.

THE STEEL CASEMENT WINDOW

In the 1930s and early forties, the steel casement window was a popular replacement for "French Windows". They opened the same way and being made of steel they did not warp. As with the "French Window" the casement window was much easier to clean. One side could be opened while the other side remained closed, and it was easy to reach out to clean the outside of the closed panel.

Hundreds of thousands of apartments were built in the 30s and 40s using steel casement windows. Eventually however, rust became a major problem and windows started to rot out. It required a lot of maintenance expense to paint the outside of the steel frames to prevent rusting. Making of steel windows stopped and eventually most of them were replaced.

THE SLIDING WINDOW

Since the 1950s contemporary designed homes increased in popularity which gave rise to the increased use of the sliding window. They began to be made of aluminum as well as wood. Not requiring any counter weights or friction rails, the sliding window was simple to construct and therefor cheaper. It was widely used during the 50s and 60s in many developments. The sliding window usually has one panel fixed and the other movable.

CHUTE AND AWNING WINDOWS

During the same period, as the sliding window became more popular, contemporary designs used larger and larger glass areas. It was too costly to build these larger windows to fully open, so two modifications were adopted which previously had been used in commercial steel framed windows for factories and schools.

The chute window usually has an operable panel at the bottom of a fixed panel. The operable panel is hinged at the bottom and when opened, tilts inward forming a chute. The awning window is used in the same way as the chute window in combination with fixed panels. In this case the operable panels are hinged at the top and open outward as an awning, being held open by friction hinges at the sides.

These styles were widely used in commercial application where air conditioning and climate control reduced the necessity of having large areas of operable glazing.

THE PALLADIAN WINDOW

This window style although widely used in Early American colonial architecture, particularly public buildings, fell from vogue for a long time probably because it requires a high ceiling. During the great expansion of residential developments from the 50s to the 80s high ceilings were not considered economical, and were not used in residential construction except in high priced custom and contemporary designs.

The window, named for the architect, Andrea Palladio, who devised it, is characterized by a semi-circular top. The bodies of the windows were divided in small panes, and the upper arched portion was divided in panes like slices of pie.

In the "Post Modern" architecture of the 80s and 90s, the Palladian window has enjoyed a renaissance. This "Post Modern" style uses many basic geometrical shapes such as squares, triangles and semi-circles. It is also growing in popularity for residential construction, and in the last few years more and more window manufacturers have offered Palladian models. They really are very elegant, and if your budget permits you might be able to work them in. Bear in mind however, if your interior decor calls for window coverings, these windows require custom made drapes. Also be aware that they are high, and permit the entry of a lot of sun light when facing southward. Shades and blinds present special requirements.

WINDOW CONSTRUCTION

Since the 50s aluminum windows enjoyed increasing popularity because they are virtually maintenance free and do not rot or decay. They were a Godsend to housing construction in places like Florida, where the decay and rotting of wooden window frames, due to high humidity, was a serious problem. Wooden widows continued to require exterior painting and maintenance.

In the last ten or fifteen years, wood window manufacturers have developed wood windows that are clad in vinyl and protected from the elements. These are excellent windows but have a higher price tag than aluminum windows.

When the energy crunch came on, wood windows were advertised as better insulators than aluminum framed windows, which readily conduct heat through the aluminum frames. During this same ten to fifteen year period double glazed windows became pretty standard.

However the aluminum industry fought back and developed the "Thermal Break" frame which greatly reduced conduction. The windows are essentially made of an inner frame and an outer frame which are keyed together with an epoxy joint. In this design no metal is continuous from the outside to the inside, and energy loss is greatly reduced. Today a well made aluminum window is approximately equal to a wood framed window in overall insulating value, some of which has been achieved by increasing the space between the double glazing from 3/8ths inch to 1/2 inch.

WINDOW INSTALLATION

For many years there was only one basic way in which a window was installed. After the sheathing was applied to the wall frame the window opening was cut out. The window was inserted from the outside into the cutout and held in place with a few nails. Usually felt paper was put around the opening to form a sort of gasket for the window but this was pretty ineffective.

The problem with this type of installation is that it allows significant air infiltration around the frame. When a wind load is applied against the wall of a house there is movement and distortion in the shape of the house. Small cracks open up around the window molding permitting significant wind driven air to enter. This effect has not been widely understood by most framers and as a result infiltration reducing measures were not employed.

Today there is a good solution to the problem. Both vinyl clad wood windows and aluminum windows are made with a flange around the perimeter of the window. The window can be installed before the sheathing is applied by fastening the flange directly to the framing studs. When the sheathing is applied it fits over the flange right up to the sides of the frame resulting in a much more air tight installation.

RULE 47

DO NOT USE UNFLANGED WINDOWS.

If you remember the story of the two brothers. I used flanged windows. the other builder did not. That was one of the many energy saving provisions that added up to such superior performance.

INFILTRATION CONTROL OF OPERATING PANELS

The absolutely best window for infiltration control is the vinyl clad wood framed casement window. The operating panels open and close by use of a crank handle and when closed there are pressure locking handles which compress the window shut against the weather stripping. I have only seen one aluminum casement style window and that was poorly made.

The sliding aluminum, thermal break window, is for all practical purposes equally good. In the last 1/4 inch of travel when the window is closed, it wedges into tightly fitting weather stripping. I have tested both these types of windows in high wind by moving a candle around the frame without any detectable flicker.

STYLE AND APPEARANCE

Double hung windows are still widely used but are loosing popularity to casement and sliding windows which are more attractive in appearance. The panel over panel vertical appearance of the double hung window does not fit current architectural styles as the casement and sliding windows do. Both of the latter have side by side panel arrangement which geometrically blends more with the current mode.

In colonial styles the windows should resemble the early American windows which were divided into smaller individual panes. If you have ever washed a window of this type you know how much trouble it is cleaning all those corners. The window manufacturers have offered several solutions. Wooden window are available with removable frames imitating the authentic dividers which are called "Mutins". These frames are also available in a diamond pattern which is very attractive in Tudor and Mediterranean designs.

Aluminum windows are available with simulated mutins installed as a tape on the inside of the double glazing. They are now moving away from this to using a dimensional aluminum frame between the glazing which nicely simulates the authentic style. Due to the complexity of the construction they do not yet offer them in diamond pattern. The appearance and cost of these mutin panels and treatments varies greatly. Make sure you examine a sample of the window you will use before committing to an order. All good lumber yards have excellent window displays and samples.

FRONT DOORS

The front door is an important architectural element in the appearance of a house. It may make a statement about the architecture or the taste of the occupants, and is probably the most noticed by guests and visitors. In addition to appearance there are two other important considerations in choosing a front door. These are energy efficiency and security.

Nothing is more elegant than a multi-paned colonial entrance door with side lites and a sunburst window (Modified Palladian) over the top. These entrances are available in a great number of styles and are made with double gazing. In many cases the glazing in the door is only in the upper portion but in full height in the side lites. As the area of the entrance increases the area for heat loss also increases. However, this is one instance when I believe that energy conservation must come second to aesthetics. Our front entry is our best opportunity to express our personality.

This style has been adapted in contemporary design using rectangular side lites with a solid door.

There is an almost endless variety of styles for front doors. Wood doors are available with the most elegantly carved panels for every type of architecture. They range greatly in price depending upon the design.

THE DOUBLE DOOR ENTRY

Before making a final decision on the style of your front entrance, another option to consider is the double door entry. This is opulent looking, and works very well in designs with a center entry hall. For exterior appearance the double doors need to be centered on the facade. This does not always work out with every design, but I have been successful using a double door entry and covering one door on the inside by extending the wall. This results in an interior entry with a single door which can be off center and where the entry hall does not have enough width to allow both doors to open. One of the draw backs of wooden double doors is the problem of warpage. When one or both doors warp slightly they will not close evenly in the center. Great care must be taken in the installation and finishing of wooden doors to minimize warping. The door which remains closed must have top and bottom recessed bolts to hold it firmly in place so that the weather striping in the center can properly engage. You should make sure that when the doors are stained and varnished, the top and bottom edges are done as well to seal out moisture. Panels set into wooden doors are often made of more than a single piece of wood. When they dry and shrink a crack may open between the two pieces permitting daylight to show through. The panels may also shrink leaving a line of unfinished wood around the perimeter of the panel where the wood has drawn out of the retaining channels.

To preserve the beauty and finish of exterior wood doors they should be varnished a minimum of every two years. Perhaps by using some of today's very fine urethane formulations, that period may be lengthened. But bear in mind that once wood discolors from the weather it is impossible to restore the lost appearance.

STEEL DOORS

Steel doors do not warp and deform. They are also made with urethane insulation inside the panels, and are better insulators than wooden doors. Years ago when steel doors first appeared, they attempted to simulate some of the wood door styles by attaching moldings on the surface of the door. To my eye, this always looked artificial and cheap. However, in recent years, the technique of making steel doors has improved remarkably. The designs are now embossed into the door panels and copy the wood doors very well, except of course, they cannot imitate the appearance of the wood grain. The steel door can be easily painted in a variety of attractive colors which will create an individuality to the entrance.

DOOR COLORS

The use of color on architectural features has never been better done than on the "Painted Ladies" of San Francisco. These are Victorian homes that have been restored, with the intricate molding and detailing of the facades, imaginatively accented with both bold and pastel colors.

Several years ago I built a condominium project which was done with stucco and wood trim in an English Tudor style. The front doors were of steel with embossed paneling on the lower half, and with a leaded crystal glass panel of fitted beveled pieces in the upper half. It was a very elegant door and I decided that I would paint the door of each unit a different color. As there were four units to a building, I used four different colors. They were colonial shades of green, blue, red and gold with that smoky tone which is characteristic of colonial colors. I permitted each buyer to pick the color of his or her front door, so long as it was not the same as the one directly next to it.

I was surprised to find out how interested the buyers were in this choice. As I had hoped, it gave them the feeling that their unit would be individual. The choosing of the front door color became a serious and weighty decision. When visitors came to the model they would almost always comment favorably on the fact that the front doors were not all the same color. This taught me how important the individuality and appearance of a front entry is to most home owners. So I suggest to you, spend some time, thought, and perhaps some extra money, on making your front entry special.

Embossed steel doors are a very good option especially those that are equipped with magnetic weather stripping which works wonderfully well. Steel doors are excellent for the back door and also for the door from the basement to the garage if your design has an "in the basement" garage. Building codes require that this door have a certain fire rating which can readily be met by a steel door.

SLIDING GLASS DOORS

Sliding doors are also called patio doors, because they have been traditionally used as access to an outside deck or patio. For years tradition has placed the patio doors in the dining room. However, I have observed that when in a dining room, they are rarely used for going in and out. It doesn't seem to be convenient. Usually, we want to bring food and drinks out to the deck or patio. These refreshments originate in the kitchen. Therefor, that location for the sliding doors is preferable. If you are lucky enough to have your kitchen face the morning sun, the use of a slider will immeasurably enhance the cheerfulness of the room.

Another wonderful use for patio doors is in the master bath or master bedroom where the doors open to a private walled in garden. Very exotic!

Usually patio doors are sliding glass panels, with or without mutins, but they are also available as French style doors with either one or both doors operable. The French doors are more expensive but very elegant.

SKYLIGHTS

Skylights have become very popular because of their ability to make rooms light and bright. They can be used almost everywhere, and are limited only by your imagination. Remember however that the sun can beat down through a skylight, sometimes unmercifully, putting a heavy burden on the air conditioning. If you use skylights make sure that you have a means to shade them. Avoid skylights in bedrooms unless you don't mind waking up from the sun in your eyes.

Skylights come in a variety of designs and prices. A common type is a simple plastic dome which is doubled for insulating value. The dome has a flat flange around the perimeter several inches wide. It is installed directly to the roof using a mastic adhesive. The shingles are placed over the flange.

RULE 48

NEVER USE PLASTIC BUBBLE SKYLIGHTS.

These skylights are nothing but bad news. The plastic material they are made of has a very high coefficient of expansion and contraction. If you install them in the winter they will be fine until summer. Then they will expand so much that the seal to the roof is broken and they will leak, leak, leak. If you install them in the summer they will be fine until winter when they contract, and leak, leak, leak.

Sometimes the plastic dome is held in an aluminum frame and can open like a hatch way. They look good but beware. The plastic is held and sealed by rubber gaskets. After expansion and contraction the gaskets start to leak.

The manner in which a skylight is installed, and the type of flashing used, is critical if the skylight is not to leak.

Years ago in desperation I designed and built my own skylights and flashing system. I used tempered insulating glass panels. Glass has a very low coefficient of expansion and will not have the problems of plastic. However the frame and flashing design is tricky, and unless you know what you are doing I would not recommend that you try to make your own.

Good skylights are pricy, but if you are going to have them, you better get the best, and avoid the plague of leaky skylights that really can't be cured. I don't ordinarily recommend a particular manufacturer but in this case I would suggest that you buy skylights made by "Velux" or "Anderson". They are carried by almost all good lumber yards. They are attractive, well made, and when properly installed will not leak.

CHAPTER 23

EXTERIOR SHEATHING, SIDING AND MASONRY

During the discussion of framing and windows, I have made some references to sheathing and siding as it applied to the particular subject. However, It will be helpful to set forth a more comprehensive discussion of the treatment of the exterior of the house, and the options available.

SHEATHING

Sheathing is exactly what it sounds like. It is a sheath of material applied over the frame of the house to give the walls some solidity. In the days before plywood, sheathing consisted of tongue and groove boards which were nailed diagonally on the frame. Now we use plywood sheets which are dimensionally rigid, nailed to the frame. This of course is much faster, saving labor. The common type of plywood used is half inch thick CDX. This designation means that the plywood has been made with adhesives and resins which will not deteriorate from water. It must always be assumed that during the course of construction, the frame and interior of the house will be subject to rain and/or snow, before it is closed in and made weather tight. Non exterior grade plywood will warp, and the plys will tend to separate. CDX weather proof plywood should be used for sub flooring and roof sheathing as well as siding. If your floor joists and roof rafters are on 16" centers, 1/2" thick plywood will be adequate. If your spacing is wider, thicker plywood must be used.

More recently other types of sheathing panels have been developed which are manufactured from wood chips that have been formed into flat boards at very high pressure using water proof resins. This has enabled the use of types of wood which were unsuitable for cutting into lumber. These boards are sometimes referred to as oriented strand board, flake board, or chip board. Generally they are less expensive than plywood. There is another manufactured board called particle board which is not suitable for exterior use. It is generally employed as a flooring underlayment which we will discuss later. There are also some soft fiber boards used as siding which we will discuss later when we talk about aluminum and vinyl siding.

Sheathing is generally used when the exterior finish will be, stone, brick, stucco, or a nonstructural material such as aluminum or vinyl siding. Other options will be mentioned as we proceed.

BRICK

Brick is an ancient building material which was used by the Romans. When you see pictures of ancient Roman buildings, it is commonly assumed that they are made of stone. Of course the Romans built many structures from stone as they learned from the Greeks, but as their architecture developed they found that it was easier to build with brick, and cover the brick with stucco so that it looked like stone. They learned how to mold bricks in curved shapes for building columns. This construction can be seen at the ancient ruins of Pompeii.

Brick is strong, durable, wind tight and requires virtually no maintenance. It is available in a variety of colors and textures. For brick to enhance the appearance of a house it should be used with some artistry. There are many designs and patterns in which brick can be used, especially around doors, windows, and at corners. Covering a traditional ranch or colonial with plain red brick, can be dull, and even ugly. There is always the risk that the house will look more like a factory than a home.

If you are thinking about using brick, spend some time visiting local suppliers who have mock-ups of various types of brick. Save pictures from magazines of brick work you like, and take pictures of buildings that have work you admire.

Make very sure that you find a mason that is skilled and experienced in brick work. Check out some of his work. If you are satisfied that you have the right man, discuss your brick work and design in detail with him. Sketches of the various treatments are helpful, but if not available show him pictures of what you want.

Brick work is expensive compared to other siding options. Make sure you get a firm estimate early on in your planning, to make sure it doesn't break the budget. Your decision to use brick must be made before the foundation is built, because special provisions are necessary if brick is to be used.

Sometimes to save money, just the facade of the house can be done in brick, and the remainder in some complementary siding. Often brick can be used for half walls or accents at entrances. There are so many design possibilities that I cannot describe them here. Suffice it to alert you of the need to spend some time and effort in determining your use of brick. If the plans you are using delineate brick work that you like, then the problem is simplified.

THE BRICK LEDGE

In residential work, brick walls are usually built as a fascia one brick thick. This wall is backed up by the frame and sheathing. Metal strips are nailed to the frame at regular intervals and extended into the mortar between the bricks as they are being laid. This ties the brick wall to the structure.

A brick wall is very heavy and must be adequately supported by the foundation. This is normally done by creating a ledge in the foundation on which the bricks are erected. In our example foundation, we used 8 inch concrete block. To create a brick ledge, we would lay 12 inch block starting from the footing where we want to have the brick work above. The extra 4 inch width of the block is extended to the outside. The courses of 12 inch block are brought up to the elevation where the brick is to begin. This is usually just below the level of the planned final grade. The 8 inch block are laid on top of the 12 inch block flush to the inside, leaving the 4 inch ledge on the outside. If the final grade is to be sloping, the courses of bock may be stepped accordingly.

If you are planning to build a poured concrete foundation it is too costly to form a brick ledge into the concrete, because it would require special forms. The alternative is to lay 4 inch thick by 8 inch high block on the footing, and against the concrete, thus creating the ledge. Bring this block up to the elevation where the brick is to start as described above.

STONE

Stone is the oldest permanent building material known to man and was used because it was readily at hand. First fashioned into rude huts constructed from stone picked up from the ground, it evolved into structures as grand as the pyramids, as man learned how to cut and shape it to his needs. It's strength and permanence made it desirable for castles and fortresses. The historical aspect of stone, it's symbolic strength and durability, makes it appeal to all of us, when planning to build our personal castle.

Today, stone in a great variety of colors and textures is available for building purposes. It may be used in cut shapes or random shapes as found in the field. i.e. Field stone. It is used as sheathing on great skyscrapers. Granite and marble walls are common in large public and commercial buildings.

But for most of us, stone work is just too expensive to enable us to cover an entire house. Rather we use it as an accent, and in combination with brick, stucco or wood. There are also available, fiber glass panels made to look like stone, and prefabricated panels that are actually covered with very thin stone veneer These techniques make it easier and cheaper to get the stone look.

The support and backup for a stone fascia is the same as described for brick. Stone if not used well can make a house look cold, dreary and prison like. Heavy stone cheeks around an entry door which butt up to white aluminum siding, will never make the cover of "House and Garden".

I have seen so many houses that have a lot of expensive stone work that just don't look well. Sometimes it's a better idea to use the stone around the house rather than on it. A field stone wall in front of a colonial design or a wood contemporary, can look better than stone on the structure itself. Consider flag stone walks and stoops as stone accessories.

STUCCO

Stucco is a cement mixture similar to mortar. As mentioned, it was used by the ancient Romans, and has remained popular ever since. It generally is used as a surface coating applied over brick or stone to even out irregularities, and give a uniform appearance. Sometimes it is smoothed out and other times trowel marks are left to show. The trowel markings have come to be considered decorative. These rough finishes are associated with Mexican style, and are seen frequently in the southwest.

Stucco can also be applied over wood sheathing. Sheets of wire mesh called wire lath are first nailed to the sheathing and then the stucco is applied to the lath which holds it in place. To build up enough thickness the stucco is applied in three coats or layers. The first coat is called a brown coat because it is just made from a sand base. The white cement which is more expensive is used only on the final coat. The brown coat fills in most of the voids in the lath but much of the metal still shows through. A second coat is applied over the first coat which is also of brown material but this coat is called the scratch coat. After this second coat is applied it is scratched with a trowel or broom to create a rough surface which will help the final, white coat to adhere. The white coat is made from pure white cement, although if desired, colorings can be added. There are many different troweling techniques used depending upon the result desired. Each craftsman usually has his own particular style.

Stucco finishes have been very popular in warm southern climates but have not been used much in northern colder climates, because the stucco has a tendency to crack from the action of frost. Over a period of time stucco in cold climates becomes veined with hairline cracks If it has been applied over brick or block, it has the tendency to spall or break off. This condition is widely observable in many European cities. Even in warmer locations the stucco eventually tends to flake off.

Since the thirties, stucco has not been used much in the cooler portions of the United States, but recently over the last ten or fifteen years, the direction of modern architecture has been toward geometric white forms. Many modern homes, usually in the more expensive category, are typified by lots of windows and glass in a structure that appears to be solid white concrete. To the chagrin of some architects who were not aware of the problems of stucco, their creations began to crack and spall after a few years of cold frosty weather.

However, the demands of the market place prevail, and today there is available a marvelous new type of light weight stucco treatment that is applied over styrofoam insulating sheets and reinforced with layers of special fiber glass fabric. This is a beautiful material that does not crack or spall. It can be rough or smooth troweled, and can be grooved to simulate panels. I have been watching a building that received this finish about ten years ago when it was relatively new. So far the building, which incidentally is in a cold climate, looks the same as the day it was built. This wonderful new technique has liberated stucco treatment from the constraints of weather. There are several national companies that offer this stucco treatment as an integrated system and have trained and approved installers nationwide.

Stucco work is not inexpensive, and the cost of a stucco exterior is in the same range as brick.

"STUCATTO BOARD"

While on the subject of stucco I want to jump ahead a little and tell you about a hard board siding material called "Stucatto Board", which I have been using for more than twenty years with excellent results. Stucatto board is a proprietary product made by the Masonite Company. It is a hard board siding in 4'x8' and 4'x9' sheets consisting of dense waterproof Masonite panels over which has been applied an epoxy based coating, embossed to resemble, trowel marks. The boards are available primed or prefinished.

This siding material is approved as a single application siding. That means it can be nailed directly to the studs, and does not require sheathing underneath. The edges of the sheets are prepared with a ship lap joint. The manufacturer recommends the spacing for the nailing pattern which should be followed. I have used this material on many buildings for more than twenty years, and never had warpage or material failure.

This siding is most used to simulate English Tudor styling. The joints of the panels are usually covered with wide battens simulating beams. I have felt that the need to place a batten strip over every joint four feet apart was restrictive to developing more interesting trim and design patterns. I developed a technique of caulking the joints with a good quality caulking material not containing silicone which does not take paint well. After applying the caulking, we would smear the joints with a block of wood to make the appearance of the joint blend with the random trowel pattern of the material. I used the primed material and finished it with two coats of very good quality acrylic based sand paint. I used a product called "Thorocoat" made by the Thoroseal Company. The sand finish makes the siding remarkably similar in appearance to real stucco.

The use of this siding requires trim around windows and at corners. I would not recommend it for use on the very modern style of building previously mentioned. It is however, very adaptable to a variety of English and Mediterranean designs and is very economical.

HARD BOARD SIDING

There is a variety of hard board siding on the market, finished in many different wood patterns. Some resemble rough sawn boards. Many different wood simulations are available, even wormy cypress. These products are made by the major lumber companies. Hard Board sidings are approved for single layer application directly to the studs.

There seems to be two philosophies about making these sidings. There are those manufacturers who make their board as high density, and others who make their board in medium density. In my experience the medium density products have a tendency to absorb too much moisture which leads to warping and buckling. I would recommend that you stick with high density boards.

A major advantage of the hard board sidings is that they are factory finished resulting in substantial on the job savings. The manufacturers sell nails painted to match the color of the siding, and most guarantee the finish for ten years.

TEXTURE 1-11

This is a siding that has been popular for a very long time. It is a plywood sheet approximately 3/4 inch thick. It is made up usually of five plys with the surface ply being free from blemishes. Where blemishes occurred such as knots, they have been cut out and patched with a football shaped patch also referred to as a boat. After the siding is stained these boats are very difficult to spot. I have no idea why it is called Texture 1-11. In normal grade, a sheet is not supposed to have more than five boats. There is also a better grade that has no boats but due to the higher price it is rarely used. Normally the sheets of texture are grooved vertically in spacing of four, six or eight inches. There is a twelve inch pattern called reverse board and batten. In a normal board and batten pattern the joints where the individual boards meet is covered by a narrow strip of wood called a batten which stands out from the surface. In reverse board and batten it appears that there is a wide space between the boards with the batten strips behind the joints. Texture 1-11 is available in plain sheets which are rarely used.

Texture is approved as a single application siding and needs no sheathing underneath. It is necessary to finish the texture after installation. It readily accepts stain in a variety of standard colors both transparent and solid.

Texture 1-11 is very suitable for contemporary designs especially in the narrower patterns. In the wider patterns it can look contemporary or barn like. It is not appropriate for colonial designs. It can be used with good effect in combination with brick or stone. It is a durable material and should last many years without problems, but it requires staining every four or five years to keep the weather out of the wood.

Z FLASHING

When using Texture 1-11 or hard board siding panels on a two story house, there will occur a horizontal joint at the eight foot level. It is customary to use 8 foot sheets on the lower level and 9 foot sheets on the upper level. The extra foot covers the width of the floor framing between levels. It is very important to install a Z shaped flashing in this joint. this is prefabricated aluminum material made for this purpose. It is usually available in brown, white or unpainted finish. The upper part of the flashing fits up behind the upper sheet, the horizontal portion comes forward in the joint, and the final portion bends over the top edge of the lower sheet by abut a half an inch. This flashing is necessary to prevent water running down the side of the building from entering the joint. Even if the joint will be covered by trim it is essential to use the flashing. Expensive consequences can occur if you forget to install this flashing as I once did.

CEDAR SIDING

Cedar has been very popular as a siding for modern styles of architecture, particularly what I call California contemporary. This style is characterized by steep pitched roofs, contrasting angles, lots of glass, and frequently a clerestory. The cedar is usually used in the form of individual tongue and groove boards. A common width is six inch. The cedar can be installed diagonally, horizontally or vertically or a combination of same. No sheathing is required under the cedar.

Cedar is an excellent wood and will not rot or decompose, but it will discolor from the weather. Many people use cedar in hopes that it will eventually weather to that lovely satin like silvery patina often seen on old barns. Unfortunately the wood will not reach this condition for a very, very long time. Too often it just discolors from exposure to water and will turn a dirty brown or streaky dirty gray. It is most unattractive and shabby. There are products now available which will help cedar reach the silvery patina desired. These are bleaches and combination bleach stains.

There are several commercial buildings in my area that were finished with cedar. When they were new they had a beautiful pinkish golden tone. But soon the rain began the discoloring process. Within a few years these buildings became so shabby looking that they were all eventually painted.

If you want to keep cedar looking like it's original appearance, you must coat it with several coats of a good exterior polyurethane, and be prepared to redo it every few years.

REDWOOD SIDING

Redwood is very much like cedar. It is durable non rotting and has a beautiful natural color. It can be installed in the same way described for cedar. However, just like cedar, if the wood is not protected it will discolor and turn black. Once redwood or cedar discolors from the weather there is no way to reverse the process. Unlike cedar, redwood will not eventually turn a silvery color. It will turn black.

RULE NUMBER 49

BE VERY WARY OF CEDAR AND REDWOOD SIDINGS.

If you are thinking of using either of these two sidings take the trouble to inspect homes that have these sidings which are more than five years old. Make very sure that you will be satisfied with the result.

PINE AND FIR, BOARD AND BATTEN SIDING

Wide boards of pine or fir are used to create a barn look. As mentioned before, the joints are covered with batten strips. Because these boards will shrink, it is customary to nail only one side of the batten strips initially and wait a year before nailing the other side. If both sides are nailed at the beginning, splitting may occur due to the shrinkage. These woods are not as resistant to rotting and it is best to stain or paint them. If left alone they will eventually achieve the old barn look, but it takes a very long time.

ALUMINUM, STEEL AND VINYL SIDING

These are sidings which are installed horizontally. They have little or no structural strength and must be applied over a rigid sheathing. Sometimes in order to save money, fiber type sheathing panels such as "Homasote" are used in lieu of plywood or flake board. Because this material is not as structurally rigid, plywood or flakeboard panels are still used on the corners in order to keep the structure rigid and square. The aluminum or vinyl panels can sometimes simulate the width of an eight inch clapboard, or can simulate several four inch boards. Either material is factory colored. The aluminum is painted and baked and provides a very durable finish. Recently due to advances in finishing, steel siding has also been introduced.

Vinyl siding is made from colored raw plastic and consequently the color goes through the material and is not just a surface coating. Some people feel that the vinyl is less likely to fade although I have never seen aluminum siding that appeared to have faded either.

Aluminum and steel siding is subject to denting and must be handled more carefully. Stones thrown by lawn mowers can dent metal siding. However, these dents are difficult to see unless the light is hitting just right. Aluminum siding will expand from the heat of the sun and occasionally, if it has not been properly installed, it will buckle. There are special companion shapes for both aluminum, steel and vinyl siding for use around windows and on corners.

It appears to me that vinyl siding is becoming more popular than aluminum. It is too early to tell about steel. Both sidings now come with a thin styrofoam insulation backing.

The great appeal of both metal and vinyl siding is that they are virtually maintenance free. They are very adaptable to colonial styles and in the narrow board pattern look quite well on more contemporary styles. Both aluminum and vinyl sidings are available with a wood grain effect embossed into the material.

HORIZONTAL HARDBOARD SIDING

The manufacturers that offer hard board siding panels also make this material in horizontal panels similar to aluminum and vinyl siding. These horizontal panels simulate clapboard siding in various widths, and have embossed multi-colored finishes that are very durable. Unlike aluminum and vinyl, the hard board material does not require sheathing underneath, but diagonal corner bracing is necessary A large variety of natural wood simulations is available.

SHINGLE SIDING

Many years ago, shingles made of asbestos were popular as siding. They were very durable and maintenance free. There are still many old bungalows around clad with these shingles. Since the hysteria over products made from asbestos, shingles like these are no longer available.

Shingles made of cedar have also been popular as siding for a long time. They are available in two styles, hand splits and machine cut. The hand splits are rough and irregular in width. It requires a skilled carpenter to install hand splits as each shingle must be planed to fit. The machine cut shingles are rough textured but a lot smoother than hand splits. They vary in width but the side cuts are perpendicular and hand planing is not required.

Machine cut shingles are also available in horizontal panels with the shingles already mounted on lath strips. This greatly facilitates the installation and cuts down the labor.

Cedar shingles look well on New England style colonials, and are widely used on beach houses. They can also be used to good effect in combination with brick or stone for a rustic contemporary look.

Cedar shingles have the same problems of discoloration as previously mention for the tongue and groove siding boards. They will eventually weather to the silver patina which is very popular for beach houses. However it is a good idea to start them off with a coat of bleaching stain. They are also very attractive with brick and stone when stained with a dark opaque color.

ROOFING MATERIALS

The selection of the roofing material is possibly even more important than the choice of siding because so many popular architectural styles today feature steep sloping roofs with many gables and breaks. The roof displays more surface, and is more evident in these designs than even the siding.

SLATE SHINGLES

This is a roofing material that has been in use for a very long time. Long before the invention of modern asphalt shingles slate was one of the most durable roofing materials. In northern European areas slate roofing supplanted thatching. Slate is still in wide use today in England.

In this country there are plenty of old churches and Victorian buildings still sporting slate roofs. Some of them are done in different colored slate with complex designs. If you are willing to pay the price, there is probably no more impressive and long lasting roof than slate.

CLAY TILE ROOFING

In southern Europe, Mediterranean areas, and generally in warm climates, curved, orange colored clay roofing tiles are in wide use. This is what I call Spanish tile. We are all familiar with pictures of European villages where every building has an orange tile roof.

This roofing is also expensive to install but is very long lasting and durable. It has been used in this country principally on Spanish or Mediterranean styles, mostly in the southwest but also occasionally on northern beach homes dating back to the twenties and thirties. Many buildings in Florida, built in an earlier time, also display Spanish tile roofs.

There are manufacturers offering modern vinyl imitations of these clay tiles. These new tiles are lighter in weight and easier to install.

CEDAR SHINGLES

The same shingles we discussed as siding are also used for roofing. Because cedar is non rotting, a cedar shingled roof is durable and long lasting. The roof can be done with the rugged looking hand splits or the smoother machine cut shingles.

Cedar shingles are always allowed to weather when used for roofing, and in five to ten years will achieve the silver patina.

This is still a fairly expensive roof to do. In fact the aforementioned roofing materials should only be considered if there is a generous budget. If you need to control costs there are better options.

STANDING RIB ROOFING

Another old and durable roof material was copper. Copper does not rust and in a few years oxidizes to a light green patina which is highly prized. In earlier days copper roofing was used on some New England homes and barns. Sheets of copper were applied and the joints or seams stood up at a right angle, vertical to the roof, forming a series of troughs. Due to the higher and higher cost of copper this type of roofing was duplicated in tin and widely used on houses and barns. It eventually fell into disuse until it was duplicated in aluminum which of course is much cheaper. The aluminum panels are factory painted in a number of colors and provide an attractive and long lasting finish.

A standing rib roof is very eye catching and has become popular in recent years on commercial buildings, apartment and condominium projects. Some of our modern designs that feature steep roofs, almost in the French Chateau style, which incidentally did use standing rib roofing, would be very smart looking with this treatment.

ASPHALT FIBERGLASS SHINGLES

When asphalt shingles were developed they became instantly popular because of their much lower cost and ease of application.

Today most shingles are reinforced with fiberglass threads for greater life. Shingles come in 20, 25, 30 and 40 year qualities, and are warranted by the manufacturers. However if your roof fails don't expect to get much from the manufacturer. If you can't prove when the shingles were purchased you may get nothing. They usually prorate the life of the roof and offer you some new shingles equal to the value they took several months to decide. Not a good proposition if your roof is leaking and must be replaced immediately.

The simplest shingle is the plain color three tab shingle. The shingles are about 30 inches wide with the bottom portion which will remain exposed, notched into tabs.

Shingles are available in many colors which may vary according to the manufacturer. For a more interesting appearance, shingles are now offered in random varied shades.

There is another type of shingle available which is the dimensional or architectural shingle. In these shingles the tabs are of varied widths and every other tab is a double thickness. When these shingles are installed they give a textured look, simulating the thicker appearance of wood shingles. This is a very nice effect and makes a much more interesting roof. The additional cost is not much, and I highly recommend their use. There is one manufacturer that makes a very thick shingle which comes closer to the look of real wood, but the cost is a good bit higher.

Many roofers will apply the shingles directly to the roofing sheathing. However, is is said that if the shingles are applied over a layer of 15 Lb. felt paper, they will last longer. I have not noticed however, that the shingle manufacturers recommend this practice. Exposure to the sun, constant shade leading to mildew and moss, and ventilation under the roof lowering temperatures, are critical factors to the life of shingles.

CHAPTER 24

HEATING, VENTILATING AND AIR CONDITIONING

In the mechanical trades this is referred to as HVAC, and there are contractors who handle all of these installations. In residential construction, you most likely will deal with separate contractors unless you chose a combination heating and air conditioning system.

CHOOSING THE HEATING SYSTEM

Every heating system is composed of essentially two parts. The furnace which is the device that consumes the fuel and generates heat, and the delivery method which is the means of transferring the heat from the furnace throughout the house. In choosing a heating system therefor, two decisions must be made: What is the best fuel to use, and what is the best way to distribute the heat?

THE OIL BURNER

The oil burning furnace is probably the most popular heating device today. Over the years the size of oil burners has been substantially reduced, and the efficiency with which they burn fuel oil has been greatly improved. Back in the 1930s the oil burner came into use as an adjunct to the coal burning furnace. By installing the oil burning unit into the coal furnace the work of stoking the furnace with coal, shaking down and carrying out ashes as well as the need for an inside coal bin was eliminated. This was a huge step forward saving a lot of work, and getting rid of annoying and pervasive coal dust. For the first time, the furnace could be automatically controlled by a thermostat. The furnace however, was designed for burning coal, and was not very efficient for fuel oil.

The boilers produced steam which rose up through iron pipes and into cast iron radiators. This was a very efficient delivery system. The cast iron radiators were able to hold heat for a long period which evened out the highs and lows of temperature. However, the cast iron radiators were considered ugly. The valves on them which allowed the air to escape as the steam entered often hissed and sputtered, and when the condensed steam drained back down the riser pipe, loud banging and clanking frequently occurred.

After the Second World War and in the early 1950s, a great expansion began in the housing industry. Subdivisions and single family homes became more and more popular as people moved out of the cities. They wanted modern appliances and heating systems which were completely automatic.

The oil burner with a hot water boiler became the standard system. The heat is delivered by pumping hot water through a loop of baseboard radiators. This system works well, and maintains even heat levels. Today in the 1990s it is still a very popular and widely used system.

However, an oil fired system has several requirements. There must be a furnace or boiler room to contain the equipment which can be in an enclosed room or in an open basement. There are particular requirements for fire proofing ceilings and walls surrounding the furnace. Check with your local building department for these rules. A chimney must be provided to allow the products of combustion to escape, and an oil tank is needed to hold the fuel oil. Chimneys which were once made only of masonry, can now be installed using insulated metal pipe which is cheaper and easier. Fuel tanks, usually not over 200 gallon capacity, can be placed above ground in a basement or garage, but larger capacity tanks ordinarily must be buried. Most people today, prefer a larger tank because fuel oil is cheaper when purchased in greater quantity, reducing the number of deliveries necessary.

An oil burner has the possibility of a very unpleasant occurrence should the burner unit not ignite properly. This catastrophe is called a "Puff back". If a burner unit is old, or poorly maintained, sometimes the ignition rods in the unit do not ignite the oil quickly enough. When the thermostat calls for heat, the burner unit begins to spray atomized fuel oil into the fire box. Electrodes are in the spray, and are supposed to spark and ignite the oil. Sometimes the sparking of the electrodes is weak or intermittent, and the oil does not catch fire right away. Fuel oil continues to be sprayed into the fire box, and by the time ignition occurs a puddle of oil has accumulated on the bottom of the fire chamber. All of this oil suddenly ignites at once causing a small explosion which blows open relief doors in the sides of the fire box which have been provided in case of this problem. The small explosion does no damage, but it blows out the partially burned accumulated fuel oil in the form of dense, thick, black, oily smoke. That's the "Puff Back". If the furnace is in the basement, whether in a separate room or not, the thick oily smoke will permeate everywhere. If the basement is finished, it will coat the walls and ceilings and all the furnishings with a greasy black deposit.

I have noticed over the years, that oil burners have a certain perversity. When the control system fails, and the oil burner will not start up, chances are it will be on a cold Sunday morning when a service man is tough to get.

After I had a "Puff Back" in my home, which did thousands of dollars worth of damage, I vowed never to own another oil burner. Oil burners also have the tendency to rumble when in operation. I always knew when my oil burner turned on by the rattling of the dishes in the dining room china closet which was directly above the boiler room in the basement.

The United States produces an enormous amount of natural gas which is distributed throughout the country by an extensive pipe line system. Natural gas is available in most metropolitan areas and suburbs.

Gas burners can be installed as replacements for oil burners in the same furnaces. The gas burner eliminates the need for a fuel tank, and the possibility of oil spills during delivery. The primary popularity of gas as a heating fuel was based on the fact that it was cheaper to heat a house with gas than by any other means. However, over the last several years the price of fuel oil has gradually reduced, making fuel oil more competitive with gas.

ELECTRIC HEAT

After the Second World War in the late 40s and early 50s, the window air conditioning unit came upon the scene. This was a very popular appliance and people began to install them in their homes and apartments in great numbers. New commercial buildings and sky scrapers were equipped with central air conditioning, and older buildings in order to remain competitive, were retro-fitted with air conditioning. There was a veritable explosion in the use of air conditioning all of which ran on electricity.

The electric utility companies had to rapidly expand their generating capacity and distribution systems to keep up with the increasing demand. Every summer, in New York City, for example, under ground electrical lines would burn out due to the increased load. The utility company had no way of knowing how many air conditioners were being added to the system.

Actually the utilities did a very good job and expanded their facilities to meet the new and higher demand for electricity.

After a number of years of rapid expansion, the utilities realized that they had built an enormous system that was used only in the summer time, and that during the winter they had a tremendous amount of idle capacity.

To put the idle capacity to use, and earn some revenue thereby, the electrical utilities began a vigorous campaign to promote electric heat. The utilities promised their customers that they would sell them electricity for heating at a lowered cost which would make electric heat competitive with oil heat. The idea of the "All Electric Home" was promoted, and further price incentives were offered if a home used no other form of energy.

Electric heat has many very attractive characteristics. It requires no boiler room, no chimney, no storage tank, and provides the convenience of having a thermostat in every room. Heat in unused rooms can be turned down resulting in the ability to save energy without having to sit in a cold house to do it. Electric baseboard heaters are very trouble free. They require no repair or maintenance. The cost of installing electric heat in a new home is substantially less than a hot water system. If an electric heater is defective it will fail almost immediately. If it operates trouble free for a week the chances are it will continue to operate for years and years. In the 1950s electric baseboard heater manufacturers advertised that they guaranteed their heaters forever. The Government stepped in and said that this was unfair advertising because nothing could last forever. This of course, was typical of Government intervention when there was no need, and trying to fix what wasn't broke! The manufacturers just came back and changed their guarantee to the life of the building in which the heater was installed.

Some people criticized electric heat, claiming it was "Too Dry". I would remind them that a hot water system which contains the hot water in a sealed loop is just as dry, unless it was leaking.

By the 1980s millions of homes had installed electric heat, and the utilities had established a captive clientele. Although the various Public Service Commissions were supposed to regulate utility rates and keep them honest, gradually they allowed the utilities to raise the price of electricity used for heating until today the discount is for all intents and purposes, eliminated.

Without the lower price, people using electric heat found that every year their heating costs rose in comparison to other fuels. What could they do? The cost of installing an oil fired hot water system in a completed house was just prohibitive. Once again, with the complicity of Government, the public got screwed. If you think this is a rip off, just wait until electric cars are popular!

THE HEAT PUMP

The heat pump is a device that began to become popular in the mid 1980s. It's popularity has continued to grow, and more and more it is the heating system of choice. The heat pump has a unique ability; it can heat, and it can air condition. A Heat Pump consists of two basic sections. The compressor section which is located out doors, and the air handling section which is located inside. The compressor unit is connected by piping to the unit inside which contains the fan that circulates the treated air throughout the house.

To understand a heat pump it is best first to describe how an air conditioning system works. We are all familiar with an air conditioner, and we know that it is a machine that blows cold air into the house. We also know if we stand outside of an air conditioner, it blows hot air out of the house. By compressing and evaporating a refrigerant material it absorbs heat from inside, and expels that heat to the outside.

Along came someone with a good idea who said, if I can make an air conditioner work in reverse, I can absorb heat from the outside and expel it into the inside, thus having a system that can both heat or cool a space with the same mechanism. Indeed, it only required the addition of some extra controls to do the job.

The appeal of this idea is great, because for the price of a heating system you get a central air conditioning system as well.

How do you get heat from the outside air in the winter time? Even though the air feels cold to us, it contains a great deal of heat energy. The temperature must go down to a theoretical minus 460 degrees Fahrenheit, for the air to contain no heat. The heat pump is able to absorb some of this heat energy from the cold outside air and deliver it to the inside of the house.

Heat pumps run on electricity because they use electric motors to do their work. However, this use of electricity is much more efficient than the use of electricity for resistance heat, because the heat pump is actually deriving heat from the air. It is able to deliver about twice the amount of heat energy into the house as would result if the electricity used to run the motors, was used instead directly in a resistance heater. In simple terms, a heat pump although run by electricity, is twice as efficient as electric resistance heat and therefor costs half as much for the same result. This of course is an average.

As the outside air gets colder, it is harder for the heat pump to extract the heat, and therefor the efficiency begins to drop. At about 20 degrees F. the efficiency ratio is 1 to 1. When the outside temperature is warmer, say 50 degrees F., the efficiency may go to 3 to 1.

Besides extracting heat energy from the air it is also possible to extract heat energy from the ground. When you go down below the frost depth, you find that a temperature is encountered which is relatively constant all year. Because the ground at this depth is not frozen, the temperature must be above 32 degrees Fahrenheit. These constant ground temperatures will of course vary with the geographic location. In southern New York State for example, where I live, this constant temperature is 57 degrees F. It is more efficient to extract heat energy from a medium of 57 degrees F., than extracting it from air in the winter which can be much colder. However the mechanics of extracting the heat from the ground is not that simple. It is usually accomplished by burying air ducts in the ground and circulating air through them to absorb the energy. This can require an extensive system which does not lend itself to a heat pump system. However water extracted from the ground can easily be used in a heat pump.

For example, suppose we have a pond on our building lot. Even though the surface of the pond is frozen during the winter the water below the ice is not frozen and therefor must be at a temperature higher than 32 degrees F. Let's say it averages 40 degrees F. This means we can extract heat from a source that never goes below 40 degrees F., instead of extracting heat from air which can be much colder and therefor a less efficient source. Water is drawn from one end of the pond and run to the heat pump where the heat is absorbed by the uptake deck, and returned to the opposite end of the pond where it will gradually be rewarmed by the heat rising from the earth. If the pond is too small it may not be able to take up heat from the ground as fast as we remove it. The Heat Pump manufacturers have data which can tell how large a pond is required for a particular sized unit.

Where a pond is not available, water can be drawn from a well, circulated through the Heat Pump, and returned to the ground through another well called a "diffusion well".

Where there is a pond, the cost of piping the water to and from the compressor is not great. However, if wells are to be used, the cost of the installation must be calculated against the increased efficiency and the savings in operating cost. These calculations have been computerized by the equipment manufacturers who are more than happy to run a computer cost/energy analysis of your proposed system.

PRINCIPLES OF HEAT PUMP SYSTEM DESIGN

Unless you live in an area of extreme cold, it is likely that a heat pump is the best choice for you. I am going to explain the considerations involved, so that you will be able to make sure that you get a properly designed system.

AIR CIRCULATION

Air circulation is the only means used as the delivery system for heat pumps. The heat output coil of the heat pump does not get extremely hot, and therefor is particularly suitable for an air delivery system. In an air circulating system the most important factor is that the heated air is returned to the rooms only a few degrees warmer than the air being drawn out of the rooms and fed to the heating coil. This close temperature differential results in a very uniform temperature throughout the area being heated.

One of the major problems in using an air delivery system with a conventional furnace is the inability to keep this differential low. When a conventional furnace turns on, the heating chamber gets so hot that the air passing through it is heated too much. This results in that characteristic blast of hot air that you always feel when a hot air heating system goes on. Because the air is so hot, the thermostat is quickly satisfied and the blower shuts off. Then the space gets too cold before the next blast of hot air is delivered. This results in temperature cycling with repetitious highs and lows that are very uncomfortable. The heat pump avoids this problem by operating the heating deck at lower temperatures.

In cooling the air, this low temperature differential between intake air and output air is even more important. When we are air conditioning, the cooling deck, which is the same as the heating deck except that it is now being made cold instead of hot, performs two important functions. Firstly, it is cooling the air, and secondly, it is removing moisture from the air. This dehumidifying is as important to comfort as is the cooling. If the air is delivered to the rooms too cold, the thermostat will be quickly satisfied and the cooling will shut off. If the cooling deck is not cold, the humidity in the intake air will not condense and be removed. So in good cooling design it is very important that the system is not too large with over capacity. In such a case the delivered air is too cold and the system will shut off without dehumidifying. Many an air conditioning system does not work well because it is too large for the space being cooled.

RULE 50

NEVER OVERSIZE THE AIR CONDITIONING CAPACITY.

Some people oversize the unit in order to have more heating capacity. This will only result in unsatisfactory air conditioning.

The air conditioning requirement is calculated based on the area to be cooled, the amount of insulation in the structure, the exposure to the sun, the square foot area of windows, and the exterior temperatures expected. There are established formulas for calculating the requirement in terms of BTU (British Thermal Unit) requirements. The equipment manufacturers have computer programs that will make these calculations.

In most temperate climates, the capacity of the unit needed for the air conditioning will not always produce enough heat in the winter when the outside temperature becomes very cold. This problem is solved by having an electric heating coil in the system as an auxiliary source, if and when needed. Although this coil is the costly form of electric resistance heat, it generally comprises only a small portion of the overall energy used. The Heat Pump must be evaluated on it's overall performance for a whole season, which as has been stated, is twice the efficiency of ordinary resistance heat alone. The backup electric coil also has another important use. In the event of a compressor failure or condition which renders the compressor unit inoperative, an emergency heat selector on the thermostat may be used to turn on the back up electric heat coil, until the trouble can be corrected. This can be a very important function when the system fails on that inevitable cold Sunday morning.

HEATING, VENTILATING AND AIRCONDITIONING

In a good air conditioning system we want the air to be circulating over the cooling coil as continuously as possible so that maximum dehumidification will occur. This too, saves energy. You can be very comfortable at a temperature of 78 degrees F. if the humidity level is low. If the system does not run long enough to dehumidify, you will probably need to set the thermostat down to 68 degrees F. before you feel comfortable. Obviously this wastes energy.

The constancy of the air circulation is also important in eliminating heat differential between floors. In the winter time, heat rises, and the second floor may tend to become warmer than the first floor. However, at night, when the sun is not on the roof the situation may change. Conversely in the summer, the upper floor will be much warmer due to the sun on the roof, and will require more cooling than down stairs. This changes at night as well, when the sun is not on the roof. How are we going to accommodate all these differing changes and requirements throughout the day and for different seasons? It is really simple. It depends only on having the air ducts so arranged that return air from the second floor is continuously mixed with return air from the first floor, and the merged output air is delivered to both floors. The air of differing temperatures is constantly mixed to a uniform output temperature.

In a well designed and installed heat pump system, you should never be aware of interior changes of temperature, or a difference in temperature between floors. And you should never feel a breeze or be aware of the flow of the circulating air.

In hot climates, if the Heat Pump is sized according to the cooling requirement, there will be more than enough heating capacity available when needed.

DUCT DESIGN

It is poor duct design, more than anything else, that is responsible for Heat Pump systems that cannot achieve the operating characteristics outlined above.

Don't make the mistake that most people do, and frame up the entire house before calling in your HVAC contractor to work out a duct design. Many options may be denied because the construction is already done, and he will have to design the ducts to fit what you have built which may not result in the best arrangement.

BALANCING

When a duct system is put into operation there is always a task to perform which is called "Balancing". Each duct trunk as it leaves the blower plenum (the box where the air comes out), should be provided with an adjustable damper door which can regulate the amount of air which flows through that particular branch. By adjusting the various dampers, the amount of air delivered to each portion of the structure can be regulated in proportion to the requirement of that particular area. Additionally, at each air outlet in a room, there is provided an adjustable louver, which can further regulate the amount of air passing through. When balancing is done well, all the areas of the house will stay at the same temperature. Because hot air rises and cold air falls, it is usually necessary to rebalance the system for the opposite season.

Many people with heat pump systems complain about them not working properly because the installing contractor never showed them how to rebalance the system. This is not as complicated as it sounds. Once the proper settings are determined, the damper handles may be marked to show the desired setting for summer and winter.

DUCT LAYOUT

To operate properly, we want to deliver a large volume of air to a space at low velocity When the air velocity is too great, moving air currents will be uncomfortable, and noise will occur in the ducts and at the outlets.

In planning a duct layout, I like to separate the second floor from the first floor. Then I further divide each of these two areas into front and rear zones. These are the zones that are most likely to differ from each other depending on whether it is day or night, and whether the daytime sun is at the front or the rear. Besides delivering air to these locations we also want to gather the return air and bring it back to the air handler. To do this effectively we should have a return air intake centrally located on each floor. These are best located in halls where the return intake is more or less equally distant from each room. Air delivered into a room when the door is closed must have a way of getting out of the room and returning to the intake. Cutting an extra half inch off the bottoms of the doors will usually be sufficient for this purpose.

As you can see, under this arrangement there is a push pull situation. The air enters the room under positive pressure, and is drawn into the return grills by negative pressure. It does not make much difference whether the room inlet is in the floor or the ceiling. The air movement is adequate to keep the air inside a room, uniform in temperature.

In general we want the delivery ducts to go to their zones in the shortest way possible, and with the least amount of turns. The longer a duct is, and the more turns it makes, the greater the resistance will be to the air flow. This causes a loss of efficiency, and possibly duct noises.

RULE NUMBER 51

IN A PROPERLY DESIGNED AND INSTALLED SYSTEM, YOU SHOULD NEVER HEAR THE SOUND OF RUSHING AIR, OR FEEL IT'S MOTION.

Most HVAC contractors like to design the ducts with the delivery grills on the outside walls a foot above the floor level. When you install hot water heaters or electric heaters it is best to place these heaters on outside walls and under windows. These devices depend on rising air convection to circulate the heat. The rising flow from the floor level blocks the cold air from the windows. Contractors feel they must follow this rule in placing air vents. However, with forced air delivery, the air will be moving out from the delivery vents toward the center of the room rather than rising up in front of the windows. It is also likely that furniture will block the free movement of the air under these conditions. Further, running a three inch wide duct between studs that are only 5 1/2 inches wide leaves only two and a half inches to insulate the warm air ducts from the cold outside siding. This space is simply not adequate for a proper job, and if used will result in excessive heat loss and higher heating costs. Additionally, ducts installed in outside walls will create rising convection currents inside the walls, which will further increase heat loss. I cannot over emphasize this point.

RULE NUMBER 52

BADLY DESIGNED DUCT SYSTEMS CAN RESULT IN DOUBLE AND TRIPLE HEATING COSTS.

Delivery ducts and outlets for a first floor should be in the floor in front of the outside walls. In this way, the outlets can be placed in front of windows and will deliver their air upward which will not be blocked by furniture.

UNDER SLAB DUCTS

In the case of construction on a modified slab as described earlier in this book, the air handling unit will be located in a utility room or laundry room on the ground floor. If it is going to be placed in a garage area it must be enclosed by well insulated walls and a well insulated door. Generally one trunk can be run under the slab to the front and another to the rear. They can be "T'd" as necessary. Coordinate this layout with the plumbing lines so that there will be no conflict. Usually the air ducts can be run at a deeper level and pass under the plumbing lines. The return air duct, which is larger, can be more conveniently and directly run under the slab. When properly laid out at the location of the air handler the ducts can easily be made to fit to the unit. This should result in the shortest and most direct runs.

After the gravel is backfilled and compacted in the foundation, the trenches for the ducts can be quickly dug with a backhoe. The ducts should be made of galvanized steel coated with waterproofing compound or wrapped in sheet plastic. They should be surrounded with one inch thick high R insulating board. If the ducts are rectangular rather than round, the insulation is more easily done. Remember, the constant ground temperature under the heated structure will be reasonably close to room temperature so this level of insulation will be more than adequate. The branches from the trunk line leading up to the individual outlets should be installed to a height an inch above the final floor level. Wooden blocks should be carefully fitted into these outlets to keep concrete out during the floor pour, and to prevent the pressure of the concrete from crushing and deforming the rectangular shape of the duct openings If these outlets are deformed, the finished grill will not fit into the duct, and a lot of concrete chopping and patching will be required.

It is advisable to place the ducts deep enough to have at least eight inches of gravel over them when they are backfilled. This will be adequate to support the weight of the concrete and the workers if they should step on top of the ducts, which of course, will happen.

BASEMENT DUCTS

When the house has a basement, the ducts feeding the first floor may be run under the floor. If you intend to finish all or part of the basement you might want to make the basement ceiling a foot higher so the ductwork will be high enough for normal clearance. If the basement is unheated make sure that when you insulate the underside of the floor the insulation encloses the ductwork as well. If the air handler is located in the unheated basement it should be well insulated. We will say more about how this is done a little further on.

FEEDING THE SECOND FLOOR

This is much more difficult, and varies greatly according to the house design. If the floor joists are run the right way you may be able to feed the room that aligns with the utility room by running the duct between the joists and turning up for a floor outlet. Otherwise the best way would be to run a trunk line the length of the house under the second floor. Branches can be run at right angle to this trunk between the floor joists to feed every upstairs room through the floor. The down side of this arrangement is that the duct will be below the ceiling level of the first floor and will have to be enclosed by a soffit. Depending on the room arrangement this may not be acceptable but it is interesting to note that if you are aware of this need before the framing is done, usually a complete or partial solution can be devised.

If the up from the bottom method doesn't work out, then you have to go to a top down arrangement. This is usually done from the attic space above the second floor. To get the duct up to the attic level you can usually manage to rise through a closet. Remember there is a return duct to be accommodated too, which will have to go down through another closet. If you anticipate these requirements you can usually frame the closets accordingly, making them larger to accommodate the ducts. When such a space is closed in to form a vertical shaft it is called a "Chase".

If the space above the second floor ceiling is a crawl space, the ducts may be run more directly to the rooms to be served. I recommend using ceiling outlets. There are louvers for ceiling outlets that can distribute the air in a specified pattern. This should be determined by the location of the outlet in the room and the distance to the windows. Usually the outlet can be placed in the center of the room. In such a case a four way pattern would be used. However, if the outlet must be placed close to the wall opposite the windows, a three sided pattern can be used. These diffusing grills are also provided with damper vanes that can be opened and closed as needed.

With the return air leaving the room under the door, air will be drawn down from the ceiling toward the floor and good uniformity will be achieved. You might want to locate the outlet in the ceiling further from the door to create a more comprehensive circulating pattern. However, the delivery velocity of the air will be enough to reach all, parts of the room. If the room is very large, then you would use two outlets.

If the attic is going to be used for storage or even be finished, you will have to be more judicious about your duct locations. Frequently trunk lines can be run in the apex of the angle where the roof pitches down to the floor. In a finished attic this area would probably be closed off with a knee wall. Laterals can be run between the joists of the floor below.

Your contractor may suggest that instead of ceiling outlets the ducts should be run down the second floor walls, and outlets placed near the floor. This has the same problem as doing it on the first floor. Additionally, in order to turn a duct downward the top plate of the outside wall must be cut and the duct formed to a right angle down turn. This right angle will be in contact with the roof sheathing and be virtually impossible to insulate. Substantial heat loss will occur. Convection currents rising up beside the duct in the wall, escape through the cut plate. All these problems are readily observable when you study the way snow melts on a roof above this kind of arrangement. However, if that's the way you have to learn about the mistakes in your house it will be too late to remedy them.

INSULATED DUCTS

Rectangular ducts used in unheated spaces are often made from a dense fibre glass board. Round ducts are made of fiberglass matting wound around a wire spiral that maintains the shape. HVAC duct designers regularly specify these ducts to be installed in unheated spaces. They will tell you that the insulating material is effective and that the heat loss from the ducts is about 10%.

RULE NUMBER 53

HEAT LOSS FROM FIBER GLASS DUCTS INSTALLED IN UNHEATED SPACES CAN DOUBLE HEATING COSTS

Don't believe the 10% figure. The heat loss will vary depending on how cold the climate is and how much of the system ductwork is in the unheated space. Frequently they will place the air delivery unit in an unheated attic. These units are virtually uninsulated and will loose lots of heat.

If heating ducts loose heat in winter, imagine what happens when the ducts are delivering cooled air in the summer through attic spaces that can get as hot as 140 and 150 degrees F. More energy loss!

Ducts installed in an attic or crawl space must be insulated with a minimum of 12 inches of fiber glass and wrapped with poly plastic. Don't skimp on the insulation. The material is very inexpensive. The extra cost of 12 inches instead of 6 inches is negligible.

If the air handling unit is located in an unheated space it must be insulated. You can build an insulated closet but don't forget to glue 4 inches of styrofoam insulation on the inside of the door. You can make a removable enclosure out of rigid styrofoam around the unit, or you can wrap 12 inches of fiber glass around the unit. Usually where the ducts are attached to the plenum of the air handling unit, they are attached only with screws. Leakage can occur at these connections resulting in the loss of significant amounts of heated air. These joints should be sealed with an appropriate caulking compound. Builders silicone which we have previously learned about, is excellent for this purpose.

It takes very little extra effort to do the job right, yet this will rarely happen unless you are on top of the situation. If it's not done right you will pay for the mistakes for the rest of the time you live in the house.

REFRIGERANT LINES

Every heat pump system has a compressor unit which must be located outdoors for energy exchange with the air. A Geothermal unit exchanging energy with water, could be located indoors but due to the noise of operation it is always best to locate the compressor units outside. Be careful not to place the compressor under a bedroom window, where the noise might be disturbing.

The compressor is connected to the air handling unit by two copper lines which circulate the heated or cooled liquid refrigerant from the compressor to the evaporator deck in the air handler. Care should be taken to insulate these lines well. Usually the delivery line is insulated with a tube of foam rubber called "Armaflex". This surrounds the line with a sheath about 5/8ths of an inch thick. The longer the liquid lines run out of doors the more exposure to heat loss in winter and heat gain in summer. In winter the delivery line will be carrying liquid at a temperature of 100 degrees F or more. In temperatures below freezing the differential is great and therefore so is the resultant heat loss. The temperature in the return line will still be at approximately room temperature and this line should be insulated as well. Most contractors don't insulate the return line. Both of these lines should be insulated with much thicker "Armaflex" than is ordinarily used. The better the insulation the less wasted heat you will pay for over the years. Remember the cost of the additional material is very small.

AUXILIARY HEAT

One characteristic of circulating air heat is that all the rooms tend to operate at the same temperature. This may at times cause the temperature in the bathroom to be uncomfortably cool when bathing or dressing. With other systems you can put a larger heater in the bathroom to keep it warmer, but with air increasing the air flow will not increase the temperature very much. I have found that it is desirable to have an auxiliary ceiling heater in a bathroom so that you can always be comfortably warm. The best is a small electric heater with a fan. These are available in many combinations with exhaust fans and lights. They will warm up the bath quickly, and it is delightful to stand under when drying off after a shower. Infra red heat lamps are sometimes used but I have found them to be less effective.

SOLAR HEAT

In the 1970s and early eighties as a result of OPEC controlling and raising world oil prices, the subject of solar heat received a great deal of interest. The Government gave income tax credits to people who built houses using certain energy saving techniques.

Many systems were developed to collect energy from the sun and use it to heat our homes. These were generally divided into two groups: active solar, and passive solar. Active solar systems use mechanical devices and equipment to collect and distribute heat. Passive systems use no mechanical means, but depend on the orientation of the house, window placement, and natural absorption and convection. During that period there were many unbelievable claims made about the very low cost of heating that had been achieved by some experimenters. I remember one that claimed his entire seasons heating cost was ten dollars.

In general it proved out that active systems were not cost effective. The expense of installation of the equipment and the additional construction were such, that the savings in heating expense could not provide a reasonable payback, although many champions of these systems claimed otherwise.

Active systems using solar panels for heating domestic hot water did appear to be practical and have a reasonable payback time. However, in following up these systems through the years I find that none of them are still in use due to breakage, leaking and mechanical failure.

I remember reading an article about a small town in New York State that had built a new Town Hall using state of the art active solar collectors. The heat was gathered and stored in huge subterranean rock bins under the building, where it was retrieved by circulating air through the warmed stone. It was a one story building of about 5000 square feet in the usual drab contemporary style.

I arranged for a tour, and arrived there on a cold December morning with an outside temperature of 10 degrees F. When you entered the lobby you immediately noticed an impressive array of temperature recording devices with movable pens tracing lines on drums of paper. There was a graphic control panel for all the equipment in the system, complete with red, green and white lights, and a complicated mechanical diagram connecting them. The engineer who was conducting me explained that the entire system could be monitored from these panels.

We viewed the machine room which contained an impressive array of motors, fans, pipes and the like. The engineer proudly told me that the entire system only cost $250,000.00.

As we walked down the corridors of the building I noticed that the doors to the rooms and offices had no windows in them, so I asked if I could go into a few rooms to see how the air distribution system was working. When we entered the first office which was a large room in which about a dozen people were working, I was stunned to see that every person in the room was wearing their outdoor coat. When I asked why, the engineer explained to me that one of the limitations of the system was that it could not produce an ambient temperature above 63 degrees F.

So much for active solar systems and the waste of a quarter of a million dollars of taxpayers money. Lest you think this was an isolated case, I learned that it was a common limitation because the temperature of the underground rock could not be raised high enough to heat the air moving through it to more than a temperature in the sixties. A heating system that cost $50.00 a square foot and you still had to wear your coat!

PASSIVE SOLAR

Passive solar design depends on a few simple concepts.

1. Locate the house on the building lot so that it faces true south. This will create the maximum exposure to the sun as it traverses the sky during the day.

2. Increase the amount of windows on the south side so as to allow the warming rays of the sun to enter the house. A mistake that many designers made in increasing the south facing glazing was to increase the total square footage of glazing in the structure. Windows are poor insulators, and loose almost as much heat energy during the night as they gain during the day. The proper approach is to increase south side glazing by decreasing north side glazing. In this manner the night time heat loss through the windows remains the same, but the day time gain is increased.

3. Provide a means of absorbing the heat gained during the day and releasing it during the night. This was done by adding "Mass" to the inside of the home. This mass took many forms. It could be a stone or brick floor in front of the windows which would absorb heat from the direct rays of the sun. Sometimes a large and heavy masonry fireplace was constructed in the middle of the house. The mass of the masonry was to be sufficient to absorb the excess heat during the day and radiate it back during the night. Another method was to build a concrete absorption wall in front of the windows which would absorb the heat directly and later radiate it back. I remember seeing a picture of an absorption wall that an enterprising "do it your selfer" had built in front of his solar window array. The wall consisted of a rack holding 20,000 wine bottles filled with water. All of these approaches have drawbacks. The brick floor precluded furniture and wasted a lot of living space. The large fireplace and masonry work were too expensive, and who wants to live behind a concrete wall so that you can't see out the windows?

Most of the passive solar designers tried to apply the principles to conventional home designs. Ordinarily houses have an axial bearing wall running in the center from end to end which effectively divides the space into front and rear areas, making heat distribution by natural convection, impossible. The mass in the homes also had the effect of absorbing heat to the extent that it was difficult to raise ambient temperatures to a comfortable level.

What is needed for successful passive solar homes is a different approach to floor plan design and function. Once you start down this road many new and exciting living spaces can be created. Another problem was that the concept of "Mass", the way it was applied, was counter productive, space wasteful and expensive to construct.

There are many successful designs and approaches to passive solar which work quite well and do not increase construction costs, but to describe them all would take another book. Suffice it to say that passive solar was never developed to it's potential, but some of the simple principles listed above can be applied to any home with good effect.

WOOD STOVES

When energy prices skyrocketed, wood stoves became very popular. It seemed a store opened on every corner selling wood stoves. People ran around cutting trees and splitting wood as though their lives depended on it. Popular stories over a beer, were how well you could heat your house with how little wood. Bragging became worse than fish stories. As with most fads, after the novelty wore off it was just a lot of hard work. People became tired of cutting and splitting wood. Carrying in the logs on cold nights became uncomfortable work, as was the cleaning out of the ashes. After a few years only the die hard proponents were still at it. The wood stove stores gradually disappeared, and the stoves stood cold and silent.

However, if it is still your desire to have that early American ambiance, some very nice improvements have been made in stoves. There are models now which burn coal and pellet fuel. They are very efficient, burn for a long time, and produce little ash.

Bear in mind that most building codes require that a wood stove be installed a minimum distance from all walls, or the walls must be of fireproof construction. Complying with this requires more space for the stove than you would ordinarily allow, so plan accordingly.

FIREPLACES

The attraction of the fire place still endures. The homeyness of a warm fire on a winter evening or a place to hang the stockings for Santa, keeps the fire place high on the wish list of new home seekers. I remember when we had bought our first home we spent extra for a lovely corner style brick fireplace. One of my favorite times was to come inside after a brisk October afternoon raking leaves, and cozy up to the fire with a dry martini in hand. Just like the movies I thought. However, as the years went by, the trouble of lugging in the wood and cleaning out the ashes diminished the number of times the fire was lit. I got accustomed to my Sunday afternoon Martini next to an unlit fireplace.

As a heat producing device for a modern home, a fireplace is a negative. The conventional fireplace wastes more heat than it produces because the drafting up the chimney sucks the heated air out of a house faster than he fire warms new air. Since the energy crunch, many building codes require that new fireplaces be fitted with glass doors, and be provided with an intake of outside air to sustain the combustion.

These requirements gave rise to the metal bodied fireplace which was fitted with the necessary air intake, dampers, glass doors, and flue control. Additionally, they are made with a double jacketed space around the firebox, through which room air can circulate by convection. This increases the heating effectiveness of the fireplace considerably. With the addition of a small circulating fan inside the plenum, it can be increased even more. Today there are a number of manufacturers who make very good quality metal fireplaces that can be built in, and finished with brick or stone or any style you like. They can be made with tile surrounds, raised hearths or beautiful carved wood mantles. Heavy masonry construction is eliminated so that these fireplaces can easily be installed on an upper floor without the need for any special support. As a result they are finding their way into many master bedrooms. The chimneys are installed using insulated steel pipe and are light in weight. The fire boxes are constructed so that little or no clearance is required between the fireplace and the adjacent framing.

The manufacturers will gladly send you a brochure illustrating dozens of attractive fire place ideas and installations.

THE ULTIMATE LAZY MAN'S FIREPLACE

Lots of years have gone by since I sipped those Martinis by my first fireplace. Over this time I have become less and less inclined to even have to think about fire wood.

Recently I built myself a library-den as my personal work room, and decided I would like to have a fireplace, but one that would eliminate the usual work that goes with it. So I installed a prefabricated metal fireplace that operates on gas. The unit is beautifully trimmed in brass and black with a glass panel separating the fire box from the room. A set of very real looking logs sit on a grate, and if you didn't know they were made of a ceramic material you would swear that they were wood. The fire is created by a very cleverly designed burner which produces dancing yellow flames between the logs. Now here's the good part. If I am sitting at my desk and decide I would like a fire I don't have to get up. I just reach over and press the button on my remote control, and in a few seconds a bright and cheery fire is dancing in the fireplace.

This unit is a surprisingly good heating device. It has a plenum chamber to circulate the room air and I have added the small optional circulating fan. I used it every day during the cold 93-94 winter at a cost of approximately $50.00 for propane. Burners are also available that use natural gas. I could have bought a half cord of firewood for the $50.00, but it wouldn't have lasted the winter, and I might have gotten splinters and back ache.

CHAPTER 25

ELECTRICAL WIRING

INTRODUCTION

Over the years, in speaking to many prospective home owners, one particular statement seemed to emerge as almost universal: "I understand the framing and most of the construction that I can see, even the plumbing, but when it comes to the electrical, I don't know anything." Indeed, electricity to most people seems mysterious, because they cannot see it. You can always tell when the water is turned on, because it comes out of the faucet or the end of the hose. You can tell when the heat or the air conditioning is on by feeling the heaters or the air vents, but you can look at electric wires and panels all day long and not know whether they are "Alive" or not. The best rule to follow is to assume that electrical equipment is always energized, and that if you touch the wrong thing you can get a very unpleasant shock or worse.

Usually, the level of electrical voltage used in residences is not enough to kill you, or even harm you unless you have a bad heart. It is the reaction to an electrical shock that usually causes the trouble. We yank our hand back, or jump back, or lurch suddenly. Often this results in injury from banging against a piece of furniture or equipment. Sometimes by a sudden lurch, we may knock over a lamp or other appliance. I once jumped off of the top of a ten foot step ladder and landed in a barrel of scrap metal because I grabbed the wrong thing, got shocked, and automatically recoiled. Fortunately I was not hurt, but I learned a good lesson. I was lucky I didn't sustain a serious injury.

When installing the electrical wiring and equipment in a house, all of the wiring is usually completed before any electricity is fed into the system. Consequently the process of wiring is a mechanical one of routing wires through the structure and terminating them in the appropriate boxes and outlets.

A BASIC CONCEPT OF ELECTRICITY

You don't really need to know about electricity in order to build a house, however because so many people profess ignorance about the subject, I thought you might like to know a little about it. If not, skip down to the next heading.

Although it is not exactly the same in every respect, to understand electricity flowing through a wire or conductor, it is helpful to compare it to water flowing through a pipe. We all understand the idea of water pressure. We know that the pressure is the force that pushes the water through the pipe. If the pressure increases, the amount of water flowing through the pipe increases. In principal, if water pressure of ten pounds per square inch delivers three gallons of water per minute through a given pipe, then theoretically if we increase the pressure to twenty pounds per square inch we would expect to get six gallons per minute.

In electricity, the electromotive force (EMF), or pressure which drives the electricity through the wire is called the "Voltage". In the same way as increasing the water pressure increases the flow of water through a pipe, increasing the electrical voltage, increases the flow of electricity through the wire. The amount of the electrical flow is measured in "Amperes".

In both the flow of water, and the flow of electricity, what we are really interested in is the ability of a given flow to perform work. In the case of water, usually getting the amount of water we want, to the place we want it, is the work done. To make a better illustration, let's assume that the water coming out of the end of the pipe is hitting against a paddle wheel, causing it to turn and perform work. In measuring the amount of work that is accomplished, the concept of time must be taken into account. The length of time a given amount of energy is delivered determines the total amount of work done. In the case of the water, a given flow for a specific time equals the work done. Without getting into the definitions of work, we can measure the work being done by measuring the gallons per minute of water delivered.

There are two ways we can increase the amount of work the water does in that specific unit of time. As we have already seen, if we increase the pressure, we increase the amount of water delivered, or the gallons per minute. A second way is to keep the pressure the same but increase the size of the pipe. If we double the capacity of the pipe, then at the same pressure we can double the amount of gallons per minute delivered, or for the sake of our example, the amount of work done in the specific amount of time.

For electricity, let's hook our wire up to a motor which will be the equivalent of the paddle wheel. Similar to our water example, if we increase our electrical pressure (Voltage), then the flow of electricity (Amperes) will increase, the motor will turn faster, and do more work.

There is however, an interesting difference in the way electricity behaves flowing through a wire as compared to water flowing through a pipe. If we have a number of faucets attached to a water supply pipe, as we turn more faucets on, the pressure in the pipe cannot keep up with the demand for more flow, so the flow at each faucet will begin to diminish as the number of faucets turned on increases. Most people are familiar with the drop in water pressure in the summer when everybody is watering their lawn at the same time.

Electricity has a much greater ability to maintain the voltage (pressure) when the demand is increased. If we connect a group of lights to an electrical source, (just as the faucets were connected to the water supply pipe), as we turn on each light, the voltage is able to force more electricity (amperes), through the wires. As we turn on more lights increasing the demand, more amperes are forced through the wire to meet that demand. If we turn on too many lights, we can cause the ampere flow of electricity to exceed the amount that the wires can safely carry. When this happens the wires get hot. They can get so hot that they can start a fire or even melt.

The greater the diameter of a wire, the more electricity it can conduct without over heating. Consequently the greater the load or electrical requirement for the appliance we wish to connect, the heavier or thicker wire we must use to prevent overheating.

However we want to make sure that too much electricity can never go through a wire. If an appliance goes out of order and short circuits, it will demand more electricity than the wires it is connected to can safely carry. If we plug too many devices into outlets on the same circuit (wire), we may demand more amperes (electrical flow) than the wire can safely supply. Both of these situations can cause severe overheating and melting of the wire resulting in fire and disaster.

It is important therefor, to have a way of limiting the amount of electricity that flows through a wire or conductor to the amount that the conductor can safely carry. Such a device is the "circuit breaker". More on this later.

POWER

The amount of electricity we deliver to do work, which we call "Power", as we have seen depends on both the amount of the voltage (pressure), and the amount of the amperes (flow). A simple way to deal with this idea is to just multiply the volts times the amperes. The result is called "Watts". Thus the variations in the volts and amps which affect the total power are always taken into account. In the simplest form we say:

$$1 \text{ Volt} \times 1 \text{ Ampere} = 1 \text{ Watt}$$
$$\text{Thus: } 2 \text{ Volts} \times 1 \text{ Ampere} = 2 \text{ Watts}$$
$$\text{or: } 1 \text{ Volt} \times 2 \text{ Amperes} = 2 \text{ Watts}$$

You engineers will recognize that certain factors which influence this equation have been omitted for the sake of clarity in explaining the basic concept.

What we have shown so far, is the amount of power or watts at a given instant. To know the total amount of power delivered, or therefor work done, we need to know for how long the power was delivered and consumed. Just as with water we measured gallons per minute, in electricity we measure watts per hour or watt/hours. Because a watt is a pretty small amount, in order to keep the numbers from getting too large we usually measure the watts by the thousands or kilowatts. i.e. 1000 Watts equals 1 kilowatt. 1000 Watt/hours equals 1 kilowatt/hour. No doubt you have seen electric bills which charge by the kilowatt/hour. This is abbreviated as KW/Hrs. or KWH.

A KWH is that amount of electricity which would light ten 100 watt electric light bulbs for one hour, run a one horsepower electric motor for about one hour or operate a 1000 watt electric heater for one hour. The average cost of a KWH in 1995 is between nine and twelve cents. If you know what your utility company charges for a KWH, by taking the information from the name plate of any appliance which gives it's power requirements in watts or horsepower, you can calculate how much it will cost you to run the appliance for a desired length of time.

Houses receive their electrical power by being connected to the distribution lines of the local electrical utility company. In most suburban and rural areas these distribution lines are carried on the wooden poles with which we are all familiar. It is very much more expensive to place electrical distribution lines underground. In suburban and rural areas there are not enough customers per mile of distribution line to justify the cost of burying the lines. In cities however, there is a much greater density of users per mile, which makes burying the lines feasible.

In cities, the wires serving customers are carried in pipes or conduits which run from a buried splicing chamber to each individual building, usually entering underground into the basement. In suburban and rural areas the power is brought to the individual buildings either overhead or underground. The underground services are usually feeding stores and commercial establishments in the downtown shopping areas. When the power lines are carried on poles in these areas the wires are run down the poles inside conduits and enter the buildings underground.

ELECTRICAL WIRING

Residential services (the term used to describe the connection from the utility lines to the residence), usually are supplied by an overhead drop. That means the wires are draped from the pole to a point where they are attached to the structure and then down the side of the building to the meter.

The precise manner in which these connections are made is determined by the utility company. Sometimes the drop is made to a standpipe, which is a conduit extended upward into the air. This is used when the structure is not high enough to provide an attachment point at sufficient elevation for the draped wires from the utility pole to be high enough above the road and/or driveway. The manner of support of the stand pipe and attachment of the wires to the building are all determined by the utility company. Where the overhead wires are attached to the building, in most areas a special service drop cable is permitted to be run down the side of the building to the meter. The meter is plugged into a metal box called the "Meter Pan". In many cases the utility company will supply the meter pan without charge. Wherever possible, which is in almost all suburban and rural connections, the meter is required to be on the outside of the building, and at a height where it can easily and safely be read by a meter reader.

In cities, there is not room on the outside of the buildings to place the meter or meters. Consider an apartment building with sixty apartments. There must be sixty meters. In these cases the meter reader must enter the building to read the meters. In multiple occupancy buildings many utilities require that they be provided with keys to enable the meter reader to access the meter location. In single occupancies the meter man must be admitted by the occupant, a situation much more time consuming. When no one is present to admit the meter reader the utility company renders an estimated bill based on prior usage experience. Sometimes they will send the occupant a post card asking them to mark the position of the hands on the meter dials on a diagram on the postcard.

When the service connection is made overhead, the utility company usually does not want the wires to span a distance greater than a hundred and ten or twenty feet. If your house is further away it will involve erecting an additional pole. The utility company will erect the pole and in most cases charge you a percentage of the cost. If still more poles are required. the utility will erect them but you will have to pay the entire cost of the additional poles. Usually in these circumstances you have the option of erecting the poles yourself at your own expense. When the distances are great it is usually cheaper to hire a private contractor to erect the poles. An important consideration is the determination of who will maintain the overhead lines extended into your property in the event they are damaged. Usually the utility company will maintain the line if they installed it, and you give them a legal easement to enter on your property for that purpose. Otherwise, the maintenance may be entirely your responsibility.

When one or more additional poles are required to reach the house some people feel it is unsightly. The alternative is to bury the service conductors from the house to the point at the edge of your property where the utility pole is located. These wires may be buried directly in the ground if they are of the type approved for that purpose and are buried a minimum of 24 inches below the surface. If the wires must be buried at a shallower depth due to rock, for instance, they must be contained in a conduit approved for the purpose, to protect them from damage which might occur from landscaping or other digging. When you elect this option you will be required to pay for the entire underground installation but the utility company will give you a credit for the cost of the hundred feet or so of overhead line they would have had to supply under ordinary circumstances. The utility will usually take the maintenance responsibility for the underground when you give them the necessary easement.

When planning your electrical service you should also contact the telephone company and cable company to determine their requirements. Usually telephone and TV wiring can be installed on the same poles or buried in the same trench with the power lines. Make sure you determine the requirements of all these utilities before starting any actual work.

As mentioned before, the service entrances are solely within the jurisdiction of the utility company. They will set the specifications and make such inspections as they deem necessary.

The jurisdiction of the electrical inspecting authority, such as the National Board of Fire Underwriters, begins with the work after the electric meter. However when service conductors are buried underground, some inspectors claim the jurisdiction to inspect the installation. If you are installing an underground service make sure you check with the electrical inspector who has jurisdiction over your job, before backfilling the wiring trenches. Even though the inspector doesn't have jurisdiction, it is better to let him inspect than have him get mad at you later when he finds out the underground service is already completed. Remember the "Kowtow" rule!

TYPE OF POWER SUPPLIED

With rare exceptions, single family homes are supplied with what is called "single phase" power. This power provides dual voltage depending on the transformers used by the particular utility. The voltage supplied can be either 240/120 volt, 230/115 volt, 220/110 volt or 208/120 volt. Equipment which is designed to operate on 240 volts, such as a well pump, can also operate on 230 or 220 volt power without a problem but should not be used on a 208 volt system. If you have a 208 volt system all equipment designed to operate on the higher voltage should be specifically designed for use on a 208 volt system, such as: heat pumps, air conditioners, electric baseboard or duct heaters, laundry dryers, well pumps, shop machinery, large tread mills and motorized exercise equipment and others. Equipment designed for 208 volts cannot be used on the higher voltages without being destroyed.

Lighting equipment and small appliances can usually be operated on 110, 115, or 120 volts interchangeably although this may not apply to computers.

THE MAIN DISCONNECT

For every electrical service entering a building there is a requirement that there be a main switch or circuit breaker capable of disconnecting all of the electricity entering the building. This disconnect means is required to be as near as possible (within five feet) to the point of entry. This is a safety precaution. In the event of a fire the firemen know that they can find the disconnect means at the point of entry. They can use this switch to cut off the power to protect themselves from live wires, and to prevent possible short circuits which might reignite the fire.

Usually, the disconnect means is located where the power wires enter the structure from the outside meter. If there is a basement, that location will be used. If there is no basement the disconnect means is located on the wall inside the meter location. When these locations are undesirable either because of design considerations or future problems of accessibility, the disconnect may be located outside adjacent to the meter. In this case the equipment must be waterproof. There is special equipment available which combines the meter pan and the disconnect means in a single weatherproof housing. Today, in residential applications the disconnect means used is always a circuit breaker rather than the old fashioned knife switch and fuses.

THE DISTRIBUTION PANEL

After the power has entered the structure and passed through the main disconnect breaker it needs to be broken down into a multiple of smaller circuits which will be wired throughout the house to supply the various lights, outlets and appliances. For this purpose a circuit breaker panel is used. This is a metal box with a hinged door which when opened reveals two vertical rows of smaller circuit breakers. The incoming wiring connects to metal bus bars inside the panel and the individual breakers may be plugged into these bus bars as needed.

In most cases the main disconnect circuit breaker does not need to be installed outside, and for convenience is usually incorporated into the distribution panel box. When the door of the panel is opened the main breaker is at the top. When operated or moved to the off position it will disconnect all the power to the rest of the panel. Depending on the number of circuits that will be required in the house, circuit breaker panels are available in various multiples of branch circuits and circuit breaker positions. The most common are 24, 36 or 42 circuit panels. No single panel box is permitted to contain more than 42 circuits.

THE THREE WIRE SYSTEM

Previously we referred to dual voltage power supplied by the utility company. For the sake of illustration we will refer to the 240/120 volt variety which is the most common. The power is supplied to the house by three wires. Two of these wires are "hot" wires and the third wire is called the neutral. At the main disconnect switch the neutral conductor is connected to a ground conductor which may run to a water pipe or a metal plate or rod imbedded in the ground.

When an electrical device such as a light bulb is connected between one of the "hot" wires and the neutral, there will be a voltage across this load of 120 volts. However when an electrical device is connected between both of the "hot" wires then a total of 240 volts will be across the load. As we previously discussed, if the voltage is higher more current will flow through the load. Therefor, every device must be designed to operate at the voltage that will be applied to it and visa versa. Why do we use two different voltages? At the higher voltage we are able to deliver twice the amount of power than we would at the lower voltage, through wires of the same size. By using higher voltages smaller wires and equipment are possible. That is why utility companies transmit their power over the pole lines at very high voltages. The trade off is that the higher the voltage the greater the danger if a person was to come into contact with any live parts. It is for safety reasons therefor, that 120 volts is used for the distribution of power to things that the user might touch. All lights and wall receptacles are limited to 120 volts. 120 volts will give you an unpleasant jolt, but if you are healthy, should not harm you.

ELECTRICAL SHOCKS

What everybody fears is getting an electric shock but most people are not aware of the conditions from which a shock may arise. To receive a shock, electricity must flow through a part or all of your body. For electricity to flow there must be a completed circuit. Electricity entering a device must have a path to follow exiting the device so that it can return to it's source. Or put another way for electricity to flow through something, that thing must have the ability to conduct electricity and be part of a completed circuit. Electrical generators are connected to the ground and therefor the ground may be considered a return path. Remember we said before that the neutral conductor is connected to the ground at the electrical service, and that energy flows from the "hot" wire through the load and to the neutral (ground), thus completing a circuit. Even though the hot wire is connected to a device, if there is no connected path for the electricity to leave the device and return to the source, there is no circuit and no current will flow. Even though you may touch an energized electrical conductor, no current will flow through you unless you are also touching something that is grounded and enables the completion of the circuit. In other words, to be shocked you must be part of the path of an electrical flow of current. Another element in this matter is that electricity will always follow the path of least resistance. If a bird sits on a live wire nothing happens to it because there is much less resistance to the electrical flow through the wire than through the bird, and the power will not go up one leg, through the bird's body and out the other leg because it is much easier for it to stay in the wire which is the better conductor.

If I am wearing good rubber soled insulating shoes, I can touch the live parts of an electric panel and nothing will happen because there is no path for the electricity to go through me. If however, I stand with my bare feet in a puddle of water, thus establishing a conductive path from my body to the ground, and touch a live part of the panel, I will receive a very severe shock. The electricity will go through me because I have given it an exit path by which it can return to ground. If I put my hand into an electrical panel and touch a live part with my index finger, and the metal cabinet which is grounded, with my thumb, the electricity will flow through my index finger and thumb giving my hand a good shock. The electricity will not go through the rest of my body because it follows the path of least resistance which is usually the shortest path as well.

RULE NUMBER 54

NEVER TOUCH EXPOSED PARTS OF ANY ELECTRICAL EQUIPMENT.

Whenever checking or repairing any electrical appliance or device make certain that it is unplugged or the appropriate circuit breaker is in the off position. Not only is there the risk of shock but if you should cause a short circuit, wires can flash and spray molten metal into your eyes.

GROUND FAULTS

Today we use a lot of small electrical appliances in our kitchens and bathrooms that come in many forms. You also may use portable electrical tools. If an appliance is faulty you might receive an unexpected shock.

For example, let's consider an old style electric drill with a housing made of metal. As we have discussed, the drill receives it's power through two wires, one of which is "hot" and the other neutral. We know that if a hot wire and a neutral touch together there will be a short circuit, possibly a flash, and the circuit breaker will trip open the circuit. If however, inside the drill, the insulation on a hot wire becomes defective, and the wire touches the housing of the drill, the housing will become alive as an extension of the "hot leg" as it is called, but there will be no short because no neutral is also touching the housing. If you pick up this drill you will be holding a live housing, but you will not get a shock unless you are grounded. If you touch something that is grounded such as an electrical cabinet, a water pipe, or an appliance cabinet, you will complete the circuit, and get knocked on your a--.

You can imagine the hazard with all the appliances we use in the kitchen and the bath. If you pick up a device that has a "ground fault" which means that a live part is grounded to (touching) the housing, and then touch a grounded sink or faucet, wham!, back on your a--!

THE GFI

In order to protect against these hazards electrically there is a special type of circuit breaker called a "Ground Fault Interrupter" or "GFI". By electrical code, all circuits used in a kitchen or bath, for receptacles, lights or fans within five feet of the sink, must be protected by a ground fault circuit breaker. If a grounded appliance is plugged into an outlet protected by a GFI, the breaker is able to detect the small currents which are leaking into the casing. When it does so, it disconnects the circuit or "trips off". These breakers are very sensitive and trip off sometimes in response to dampness or moist air. To eliminate the inconvenience of having to go to the main circuit breaker panel to reset a GFI breaker, receptacles that have a built in GFI protector can be used in the kitchen and the bath. If they should trip there is an easy to see red "reset" button right on the receptacle. These built in GFIs can be wired to protect several receptacles in the vicinity.

In addition to the outlets in the kitchen and bath which must be GFI protected, electrical codes also require that all receptacles in a garage, and all outdoor receptacles be protected by ground fault circuit breakers.

With the development of new and tougher plastics, more and more appliances and tools are being made with non conductive plastic housings as additional protection.

MURDER IN THE BATH TUB

Well what about the whodunit where the killer drops the hair dryer into the water while the victim is in the bath tub? Is it likely the victim will die a horrible death? Of course not!

As soon as the hair dryer hits the water the ground fault circuit breaker will disconnect the circuit. If there is no GFI, the water will cause a short circuit within the dryer between the live parts and the grounded parts. The electricity will take the shortest path, and if enough electricity is conducted through the water the regular breaker will trip. But, maybe there aren't enough minerals in the water to make it conductive enough, or maybe the distance between the live parts and the grounded parts is too great, then nothing will happen. There is no reason therefor to believe that the electricity can conduct through the water, and through the victim's body which is not grounded. The porcelain coating of the tub is an insulator and does not conduct electricity. If the victim is touching the drain this might be a ground path if the drain is connected with metal piping. If the drain is connected with plastic piping the drain would not be a ground path. OK, let's say the victim grabs the spout which is connected to a grounded copper pipe. A circuit path becomes possible. However, if the current is not strong enough to short circuit within the dryer it likewise will not be strong enough to travel to the victim who therefor remains safe. Only if the victim simultaneously grabs the hair dryer, and touches a live part, will there be a completed circuit through the victim. As we have discussed, if the victim receives a shock he most likely will let go of the dryer and the spout reflexively, thus breaking the circuit.

All in all it's an improbable way to commit a murder. Script writers don't know as much about electricity as you now know, but don't try it out on your spouse for a joke.

APPLIANCE CIRCUITS

Many appliances that are used in the kitchen such as, toasters and toaster ovens, microwave ovens, waffle irons, electric cookers, food processors, mixers etc. require a significant amount of electricity for their operation. If too many appliances are used at the same time, and they are connected to the same circuit, an "overload" can occur which would cause the wires to overheat and the circuit breaker to trip. What if a circuit breaker malfunctioned and instead of tripping at 15 amperes it didn't trip until the circuit was using 20 amperes? In such a case the wires of the circuit could become severely overheated by carrying so much current, and a fire could result.

In order to prevent such a risk, the electrical codes require that kitchens be provided with special "appliance circuits". An appliance circuit must be wired for 20 amperes and be protected with a 20 ampere circuit breaker. Not more than two receptacles shall be served by an appliance circuit. A minimum of two appliance circuits must be furnished to the kitchen. This arrangement insures that the counter top area is provided with enough electrical power to safely use a number of appliances simultaneously.

LARGE APPLIANCE CIRCUITS

Refrigerators and washing machines operate on 120 volt power and can be plugged into ordinary receptacles but they should be on appliance circuits.

An electric range and an electric laundry dryer require significant power and are made to operate on the higher, 240 volt power. Larger air conditioners, heat pump compressors, air handlers and well pumps also require the higher voltage. Each of these devices must be wired with it's own individual circuit of wire size approved for the amount of current required by the appliance. These circuits are protected by two pole circuit breakers which plug into the distribution panel. A two pole breaker is like two single pole breakers attached together. Each pole controls one of the hot legs. If either leg overloads, the breaker will trip disconnecting both legs. The bus connections inside the distribution panel are staggered so that when a two pole breaker is plugged in each pole will be on a different leg or phase as it is also called.

CONVENIENCE RECEPTACLES

Convenience receptacles are those outlets which are installed around the circumference of a room. The codes require that there be an outlet for every 14 feet of perimeter. Any section of wall, such as might be between closet doors, that is 2 feet wide or more must have an outlet. The outlets must be a minimum of 12 inches above the floor. This insures that wherever a lamp or TV might be placed, there will be a convenient outlet. Extension cords are undesirable and constitute a safety hazard. Frayed cords can short circuit and start a fire. Normal receptacles are duplex type and permit two plugs to be inserted. In areas such as a desk or a music and entertainment center, double duplex outlets may be installed. Try to plan ahead as to where you are likely to concentrate electrical requirements so that you can make sure you have enough outlets.

Don't underestimate the things you are likely to need power for. At my desk for instance, I have a computer, an answering machine, a fax, an electric pencil sharpener, a CD and tape player, a desk lamp and a floor lamp all of which need to be plugged in.

LIGHTING OUTLETS

Years ago it was required to have a ceiling light in every bedroom. However ceiling lights have gone out of style in favor of the large variety of lamps which are now available.

If there is no ceiling light, the electrical code requires that at least one receptacle in a bedroom be controlled by a toggle switch at the door, so that a lamp plugged into that receptacle may be turned on without fumbling in the dark for the lamp switch. I would highly recommend that you have all of the outlets in the bedrooms half switched. This means that the upper half of every receptacle in the room is controlled by the wall switch and the lower half is alive all the time. Lamps can be plugged into the upper half and things that must stay on, such as clocks, fish tank pumps, answering machines etc. are plugged into the lower half. On entering the room you can easily turn on all of the lamps you choose. It's also a good idea to use this arrangement in the living room and family room.

The dining room will need a ceiling outlet as it is still popular to hang a chandelier over the dining room table. There also should be an outlet on an appliance circuit in the dining room to enable use of waffle irons, coffee urns, food warmers and the like.

RECESSED CEILING LIGHTS

Recessed ceiling lights, sometimes called "Hi-hats" used to be very popular but are loosing out today to more versatile and decorative track lighting. Recessed lights in a second floor ceiling can cause increased heat loss and air infiltration because they penetrate the usual insulation barrier. When insulation is packed around a recessed light, the light can become overheated. Today, specially approved recessed lights are required because of this. They are equipped with overheating thermal devices which turn off the light if it becomes too hot. Hi-hats have also been popular in hallways, but often the lighting result is unsatisfactory, and the hall seems gloomy.

Recessed lights are advantageous for closet lighting or over a tub or shower. A special vapor tight model is made for the latter purpose.

RULE NUMBER 55

RECESSED LIGHTS ARE USUALLY MORE TROUBLE THAN THEY ARE WORTH.

In a hall, wall mounted lights can be much more dramatic and effective They can illuminate up or down or both. There are also some very smart wall sconces that can very effectively accent dining room lighting. Wall lights went out of use when electricity replaced gas lighting but lately they are making a comeback.

KITCHEN LIGHTING

For years people have been building kitchens with poor lighting. Somehow it got carved in stone that a kitchen must be lit by a large fixture installed on the ceiling in the center of the room. From wagon wheels to elaborate plastic and wood fluorescent monsters, they all fail in their intended purpose. They simply don't provide the light where it is needed. When you are standing at the kitchen counter you are trying to see in your own shadow. To offset this problem, under cabinet lights have been used, especially over the sink, but they have limitations.

In my view, the only way to go is with track lighting. Tracks may be installed on the ceiling in line with the front edge of the counters. There is an enormous variety of track lighting available, from colonial style to modern. Hi-intensity lamps can be aimed downward at the counter tops. This will also provide interesting illumination patterns on the front of the cabinets which beautifully highlight wood grains. Track lighting units easily plug into the track, and may be moved to different positions. They can be individually aimed for the best effect. Good track lighting can make a kitchen come alive. Colored accents and accessories become dramatic and attractive.

BATHROOM LIGHTING

The best location for bathroom lighting is above or at the sides of the mirror. If you want to see your face to shave or make-up, the light must shine directly on you. Ceiling lights behind you just don't cut it. There are loads of attractive bath wall lights in many styles including theatrical lighting. Please avoid those funky glass tulips held by an old fashioned kerosene lamp chimney cup. Ugh!

NEW LIGHTING STYLES

There are some new styles of lighting which you may not be familiar with. New light bulbs are available which are miniature fluorescent tubes, but they are built on a traditional lamp base screw shell (Edison base). These lamps use much less electricity and have a very long length of life.

There are halogen long life lamps which give more light for less power. They are usually incorporated into floor lamps which bounce the light off the ceiling. Usually these lamps are equipped with a built in dimmer. However, if you are a talk radio fan, using the dimmer will make a terrible noise in your AM radio. As mentioned before there is a variety of high intensity, low wattage, track lighting available.

RULE NUMBER 56

VISIT A GOOD LIGHTING SHOWROOM EARLY IN YOUR PLANNING.

There are so many new and exciting development in lighting that you are sure to get some good ideas.

TELEPHONE WIRING

Most telephone companies will still come in during construction, and wire your telephone outlets. However their rates are more than it will cost you to have your own electrician do the work. You no longer are required to have the telephone company install the wiring. However, if they do, they will repair any wiring problems in the future, free of charge. they will also service the work you had installed by the electrician but of course, they will charge you for any repairs. Very little ever goes wrong with telephone wiring once it is installed. Problems are almost always with the equipment. If you supply your own equipment, which most people do today, make sure it is not defective before you call the phone company.

It is a good idea to put a phone outlet in the kitchen, the family room, the den, the office, and each bedroom. If you really want a conversation piece (pun intended), put a telephone in the bathroom next to the commode. I did that once in an upscale Condo project, and it was a tremendous hit.

Also plan a telephone outlet for your computer modem, your fax machine, your answering machine, and the base for your cordless phone.

CABLE TV

It is a good idea to wire in a cable outlet near every location you put a telephone outlet. Your electrician can do this which only requires that the special coaxial wire be looped from outlet to outlet. The cable companies prefer to make the final connections themselves, so don't worry about installing the cable outlets. If you don't expect to have cable, the outlets can be tied to a regular roof antenna, a satellite dish or one of the new small digital satellite dishes.

RULE NUMBER 57

PLAN AHEAD FOR THE INFORMATION HIGHWAY.

It is very easy and inexpensive to install telephone and TV wiring when you are building, and have open framing, so put in plenty.

EMERGENCY GENERATOR SYSTEMS

If you are going to live in a suburban or rural area where the utility wires are carried overhead on poles, you may be concerned about power outages, especially if there are a lot of trees near the power lines. High winds that accompany storms blow down limbs, and sometimes entire trees that can fall on the power lines and rupture them. Drivers, sleepy or drunk, seem to run off the road and hit utility poles, pulling down the wires, with annoying regularity. What is the feasibility of an emergency generator?

It can be done, and there is equipment available from totally automatic systems to small generators you can plug in. The major factor is cost, and that is mostly determined by the type of heating system you have, and how much power you will need to keep it, and the other essentials operating. If you live in a. warm climate, you will not have to worry about the heating system, but running the air conditioning is a big requirement. You can get along without air conditioning but if you live in a cold climate, being able to maintain some heat can be essential.

If you have an oil burner or gas furnace with a hot water circulator, you will have the heating system that requires the least amount of electric power, about 1500 watts. If you have a heat pump system or baseboard electric heat, you will need a minimum of 5000 watts and possibly more. With requirements in this range you can be getting into systems costing upward of $10,000.00 for a fully automatic installation.

An automatic generator system turns on when there is a power failure, disconnects your wiring from the utility lines, and connects it to the generator output. When the utility company restores power, it will shut off, and reconnect your system to the utility company's line. This automatic transfer switch is a pretty expensive item. There are ways to make a manual arrangement at much lower cost.

Lets consider a typical example. The house has a heat pump system of five ton capacity. It's just going to be too expensive to buy a generator big enough for that much load and the other things we want to run, so we are going to consider alternative heat. A fireplace might be OK if it is the type with air heating chambers, but if not it is energy negative, and not useful for our purposes. A stove that operates on wood, coal or pellets would be fine, but a pretty expensive proposition just for power failures. Well, maybe you are not into wood stoves and fireplaces. The best idea I know is to buy a couple of portable kerosene heaters, such as the ones made by "Kerosun". They produce about 18,000 BTUs, hold two gallons of kerosene, and will run about sixteen hours on a filling. A heater of this type would heat a good sized living room and dining room. These heaters are safe and odorless if you use them according to instructions. One of these heaters should cost under $200.00.

After heat, the next most important thing is to keep a water supply. If you are on a public water system you don't have to worry, but if you have a well and pump you will want to be able to keep your water system going. Additionally, let's add the refrigerator, the micro wave, the TV and the lights in the family room. We'll always have a couple of flash lights and fresh batteries on hand for getting around the rest of the house. So we have the following:

Well Pump	1000 watts
Refrigerator	500 watts
TV	300 watts
Microwave	900 Watts
Lights	300 Watts
Total	3000 Watts

If we have an oil burner let's add another 1500 watts for a total of 4500 watts. A 5000 watt generator should be obtainable for under $1000.00. This set up should be able to keep you operating and comfortable for an indefinite time.

Let's look at a minimal situation to cover the most common five or six hour outage. First we don't need to run the well pump. We keep on hand a couple of gallons of bottled water. We also remember that every toilet has one flush in it's tank so we should be able to manage that problem for a few hours. The food won't spoil in the refrigerator in five or six hours, so what do we really need, to be happy for a few hours? That's right! The TV to watch, a couple of lights to read by, and the microwave to heat a cup of coffee or something to eat. A 1500 watt generator will handle it. Cost? Probably under $400.00.

ELECTRICAL WIRING

THE EMERGENCY PANEL

When the main circuit breaker panel is installed have the electrician install a sub panel for the emergency circuits. The smallest panel is a 12 circuit. You will need about six circuits. The emergency panel should be connected to the main panel by means of a double throw switch. This is a switch that has two positions. In one position the emergency panel will be connected to the main panel. This will be the normal situation. When there is a power outage, you throw the switch. This will disconnect the emergency panel from the main panel, and connect it to a receptacle which will receive the feed line from the generator. It is important that the generator and the utility power never be connected to the same thing at the same time as this can be dangerous. The double throw switch prevents this from happening, and insures that the emergency panel is connected to one or the other. If the utility power comes back on, you merely need to throw the switch to the opposite position which will disconnect it from the generator input and reconnect it to the utility power. The extra panel and double throw switch should only cost a few hundred dollars more. Don't eliminate the double throw switch and think you can manipulate the circuit breakers instead. It may be possible, by why run the risk of blowing yourself up to save a $100.00 switch.

The circuits that feed the facilities on our emergency list should be run to circuit breakers in the emergency panel.

HOOKING UP THE GENERATOR

If you have a big generator you have to keep it outside in a shed. In this case it would probably be best to have the electrician install a permanent line to the double throw switch. Smaller generators such as 5 to 7 KW are usually mounted on wheels. I prefer to keep the generator in the garage out of the weather, and where it will be warmer in the winter, and easier to start. When you want to use the generator, wheel it outside. Do not run a generator inside the garage as there is significant danger from the exhaust fumes. Have the electrician make up an extension cord that will reach from the operating location of the generator to the receptacle at the double throw switch. If you are running a well pump you will need a generator that puts out 240 volt power. There are special receptacles and plugs for 240 volts. The connecting cord will need a plug on both ends. Always plug the extension into the generator last.

When there is a power failure do the following:

Place the generator outside.
Make sure the fuel tank is full.
Start the generator and let it warm up.
Throw the double throw switch.
Plug the power cord in at the switch.
Plug the cord in at the generator.

When the utility power is restored reverse the above procedure. Store extra gasoline for the generator outside in a safe place.

CHAPTER 26

PLUMBING

SEWER CONNECTION

In Chapter 3, I made reference to the laterals from a central water and sewer system which run into an individual lot. Now we are ready to make the necessary connections from these services to the house we are building.

The absolute most important thing in connecting a sewer line is the pitch of the line as it runs from the house to the connection. Ideally, it is desirable for the pitch of the sewer line to be about a quarter of an inch to the running foot. That means for example, that the end of a four foot length of pipe would be one inch lower than the beginning, with the downward direction being from the house toward the connection. There is a very important reason for having this pitch which we spoke about earlier.

When we are conducting waste material to a central sewer, we are putting paper, food and solid wastes into the drain line. Whether it be the flush of a toilet or the action of a garbage disposal unit, the solid material is always accompanied by water. The water tends to float the solid material thereby conducting it along the pipe, which could be as much as a hundred feet long. If the pitch of the pipe is too steep, the water has a tendency to run away from the solid material, leaving it behind in the pipe where it can harden and form a clog. It might take a number of years for a clog to develop but eventually the problem can arise.

If the pipe has too little pitch or no pitch, the solids will not move along and will accumulate in the line.

The pitch of the sewer line is dependent on the slope of the lot, and whether you are building with a slab or with a basement. Often, on relatively level lots the sewer line will enter a basement at some mid point in the basement elevation. If you plan to have plumbing facilities in the basement you must raise the elevation of the foundation accordingly. If raising the foundation is not desirable it will be necessary to use a sewage pump up system.

On a steep lot, the sewage line, of necessity, is going to also be steep. If it is steep enough, the force of the water running down hill in the pipe is enough to sweep any material left in the pipe, before it. If a clog starts to develop the weight of the water building up behind the clog is sufficient to clear the obstruction. The greater likelihood of a problem is with a pitch somewhere in between the optimum quarter inch pitch and the very steep. A pitch that is steep enough for the liquid to run ahead, but not steep enough for the following liquid to clear the obstruction.

CLEANOUTS

The proper answer to this problem, and what should be done no matter what the pitch of the line, is to provide an adequate number of easily accessible cleanouts. A cleanout is a pipe rising to or slightly above the surface of the ground, which slopes downward to the sewer line joining with it through a Wye connection. The cleanout will have a threaded cap. If an obstruction should occur, causing a backup into the lowest drain in the house which flows by gravity into the drain, the cleanout cap can easily be removed, and a plumbers snake inserted into the drain line to clear the obstruction. Good practice would be to provide a cleanout at the point the sewer line leaves the house, and every fifty feet thereafter.

THE TRAP

When connecting to a public sewer system most codes require the installation of a trap, sometimes called a grease trap, at the point where the sewage line leaves the building. A trap is a "U" shaped fitting with removable caps at the tops of the U. Grease will tend to accumulate in this trap, which keeps it from clogging the line further along or contributing to a clogging of the sewer main. If drainage flow becomes sluggish or there is a back up, the first thing to do is clean out the trap. If that does not relieve the problem it indicates that the clog is further down stream, and the cleanouts must be snaked.

If your plumbing layout is such that your sewer line will leave at some midpoint in the height of a basement, the trap and cleanout may be easily located there. If however, your trap and cleanout must be located below floor level it is necessary to provide a pit to contain them. The pit can be formed in concrete and be done concurrently with the pour of the floor slab. A steel plate can be made as the cover for the pit. Usually such a pit would be located in a garage or storage room, however if the room layout is such as to make that impractical, (you don't want to have a trap pit in the living room), most plumbing inspectors will allow the trap to be located in a pit just outside the foundation provided the pit is insulated against freezing and covered with an insulated lid. The warm temperature of the material running through a trap and sewer line, tends to keep these lines from freezing. Except for the trap, a sewer line when not in use is empty, and therefor freezing is not a major problem.

THE PIPING

Years ago it was always required that sewage lines be run in cast iron pipe. In many places it is still required, although neoprene joint fittings are allowed in lieu of the old method of oakum caulking and leaded joints.

There is now available, good plastic pipe which many jurisdictions will allow in place of the cast iron. This pipe is called ABS schedule 30, which designates it's composition and thickness. ABS pipe comes in ten foot or longer lengths rather than the five foot lengths cast iron pipe usually comes in. The cast iron is pretty heavy and longer lengths are difficult to handle. The ABS pipe is made with a factory molded neoprene seal at one end of every pipe length which is "Belled out" in shape so that the end of another length may be inserted. When the plain end is fully seated into the bell end, the pipes are very effectively sealed by the neoprene ring, and nothing further is necessary. This pipe may be cut and assembled with slip fittings by the use of an approved adhesive. ABS pipe is tough, durable, noncorrosive and less expensive than cast iron.

As has been pointed out, sewer lines being usually empty, cannot freeze, but depending on the climate in which you are building, it is desirable to bury them below the frost line. If rock prevents installation below two feet deep, the line should be covered with styrofoam. As a matter of principal, all lines should be buried at least two feet to protect them from damage from landscaping work.

SEPTIC CONNECTION

Because of the requirement for a septic system to be near the surface of the ground, the entrance to the septic tank is usually no more than two feet below the surface. The quarter inch pitch is still desirable for the same reasons as previously given. Unless the elevation of the house is substantially higher than the septic fields, basement plumbing facilities will not be feasible without an internal pump up system. If building on a modified slab, it is well to keep the elevation of the under slab drainage piping as shallow as possible so as to be able to achieve the necessary pitch to the septic tank.

Even when building on a steep or sloping lot the septic tank need only be a minimum of ten feet from the house. Establishing the grades to accomplish this should not be difficult.

ABS pipe can be run to the septic tank outside the building and will be allowed by most jurisdictions. The major consideration in keeping the tank ten feet away is that in the event that it should leak, no effluents will seep into the basement. If building without a basement, you can request permission to locate the septic tank even closer to the foundation because there is no seepage risk. The piping from the house to the tank is also done with an eye to prevent leaks and seepage.

Unlike a public sewer connection, a connection to a septic tank requires no grease trap. Whatever material would be accumulated in the trap is better allowed to enter the tank where it will decompose.

THE LEACHING FIELDS

The trenches and perforated pipe described in Chapter 3 are referred to as the leaching fields, which is descriptive of their function. Depending on the topography of the lot, the location of the well, and/or the proximity to water, the leaching fields may be located at some distance from the septic tank. These fields may be at a higher elevation or a lower elevation than the tank.

At a lower elevation the connection from the tank may consist of light weight 4 inch plastic pipe. The pitch of this line is not critical because it will carry only the effluent liquid. The solids are retained, and decompose in the tank. The connecting line terminates in the distribution box which feeds the lines of the leaching field.

When the leaching fields must be located at a higher elevation than the tank, a lift pump must be used to pump the effluent up hill to the distribution box.

EFFLUENT LIFT PUMP

This pump is different than a sewage lift pump which would be employed to pump the wastes from a basement toilet up and into the sewage line. The sewage pump must grind up the solid materials in the process of pumping. The effluent pump need only pump liquid.

A typical installation would be to install a pump pit next to the septic tank. This should consist of a precast concrete tank approximately three feet in diameter and about four feet deep. The outlet from the septic tank is connected to the pump pit with a 4 inch pipe. This allows the liquid from the tank to overflow into the pit. The bottom of the pump pit should be about two feet lower than the outlet of the tank. The pump used is usually a half horsepower submersible pump which sits on the bottom of the pump pit. It has a screened intake at the bottom and a discharge upward. The pump also has mounted on it a waterproof diaphragm switch. When the water level in the pit rises it exerts pressure on the diaphragm which closes an internal switch. This switch is wired to activate the pump, When the level in the pit goes down enough to relieve the pressure on the diaphragm, the switch opens and the pump stops. The output port of the pump must be connected to a line going to the distribution box. In this case a one inch PVC pipe is installed vertically from the pump, and then by means of an elbow and a removable flexible coupling, connects to a one inch PVC line running to the distribution box. A nylon rope is usually attached to the pump and secured at the top of the pit. If the pump has to be removed for servicing or repair, the flexible coupling is detached and the pump can be lifted out of the pit by use of the rope.

The top of the pump pit should have a flat steel cover flush with the ground so that it can be easily removed in order to service the pump. You can see why burying the pump pit lid would not be a good idea, especially in an area where the ground can freeze.

These submersible pumps are durable and should last a long time without giving trouble. In the event of trouble however, we want to be able to quickly install a replacement pump. The described arrangement would permit that.

The effluent pump offers another option to permit basement plumbing when the septic tank would ordinarily be too high for gravity outflow. The tank may be installed low enough for the flow of a basement drain. The pump pit is also made deeper accordingly with the bottom of the pit about two feet lower than the tank outflow. In this installation however, it is essential to provide easy access to the tank for pumping, as the removable lid may now be as much as five or six feet below the ground level. The best thing is to install a length of 12 inch diameter corrugated steel pipe or schedule 35 ABS pipe, vertically on top of the access opening. The pipe should be cut a few inches below the final ground level and the concrete lid from the tank access opening may be installed on top of this vertical pipe. The pump pit needs to be several feet deeper as well. If a suitable precast concrete box cannot be obtained you can use a length of corrugated steel pipe three feet in diameter, and cut to the necessary length. This pipe can be put into the ground as the pit. If the bottom soil is firm the pump can be installed on the bottom. if it is not firm an inch or two of concrete in the bottom will do the job. Concrete is sold at any lumber yard in pre-mixed bags. All it would take is a couple of bags mixed in a wheelbarrow with water, to make the necessary concrete for the bottom of the pit. Before ordering the corrugated pipe you should measure up from the bottom of the pit and determine the height of the tank outflow. Have the supplier of the corrugated pipe, when he is cutting the piece you ordered to length, also cut a four and half inch diameter hole in the side of the pipe the distance up from the bottom that you have measured to the outflow from the tank. This will facilitate the connection of the tank overflow to the pump pit with a piece of four inch plastic pipe.

As mentioned before the top of the pit should be covered with a steel plate. This plate should be given several coats of a good rust inhibitor before installation. If this plate, and the concrete lid on the tank access, are going to wind up in the lawn, they can be painted a dark green and will not be very noticeable. The absolute accessibility is worth any minor inconvenience.

PUMP ALARM

With any pump up system it is a good idea to have an alarm that will alert you if the pump fails to operate so you can take immediate steps before a backup occurs. For a normal alarm, an enclosed float switch is suspended in the pump pit just above the top of the pump. If the pump fails to operate, the liquid level will rise and operate the alarm switch. This in turn will activate the alarm bell which has been installed in the garage or some other convenient location. There is a silencing switch on the alarm control box which will stop the bell but a red light will remain lit until the liquid level in the pit is lowered and the switch deactivated. Frequently, the first time the alarm goes off you will find that the circuit breaker is tripped. Even if you reset the breaker and the pump runs, and the light goes out you should not assume that nothing is wrong. You should immediately investigate the pump and the wiring connecting it, to locate the cause of the tripout.

EFFLUENT PUMP WIRING

Ninety five percent of the time that there is trouble with an effluent pump it will be because of some failure in the wiring to the pump. Particularly, that portion of the wiring that is inside the pump pit. The effluent liquid in the pump pit gives off corrosive fumes. Over time, these fumes will corrode any exposed parts of the electrical connection. This will result in a degeneration of electrical contact causing overheating and eventual burnout. You cannot leave the wiring of your pump up to the electrician to do as he sees fit. Too often the electricians do not do what is needed to prevent corrosion.

The pumps are normally supplied with rubber covered cords already connected to the pump, and ending in a pin plug such as you would normally plug into a receptacle. A second rubber covered line comes from the diaphragm switch mounted on the pump and also terminates in a standard plug. The plug from the pump motor will have two receptacle slots built into it. The plug from the diaphragm switch is plugged into these slots, and the pump plug in turn, is plugged into a receptacle. The wiring within the pump plug is arranged so that the switch when plugged in, will turn the pump on and off.

An electrician seeing this arrangement would install an electrical receptacle at the top of the pump pit and would plug the pump plug into it.

There is a provision in the electrical code which requires that wherever there is an electric motor installed, there must be a disconnect means to turn off the power to that motor, within sight of the motor. In the case of small fractional horsepower motors, such as this pump, a plug that can be removed from a receptacle is considered a satisfactory disconnect means.

The reason for this requirement is to protect the safety of someone who might be repairing the motor or working on the machine operated by the motor. In the event someone would turn on the power without realizing that someone else was working on the equipment, the repair man could be seriously injured, and the equipment damaged. The idea of having the disconnect means within sight of the motor, allows the repairman to disconnect the power, and thereafter he able to observe if anyone goes to turn the power on.

The problem to all this, in the case of our pump, is that the receptacle and plugs are exposed to the corrosive gasses in the pit. Eventually the copper parts of the receptacle and plugs will corrode from these gases. When the copper parts corrode, it becomes more difficult for the electricity to pass through. As this resistance to the current increases, heat is generated at the contact points. The heat accelerates the corrosion, and eventually the heat will be enough to start melting and burning the insulation on the plugs until a short circuit occurs, and the circuit breaker trips off. However, if the hot parts are allowed to cool, as will happen with the breaker tripped off, the copper parts that were touching to cause the short may contract, and separate. When you reset the breaker, the pump will run and everything will appear to be all right. However, eventually the parts will heat up again and the breaker will trip again. After a few of these cycles the damage will be so great that the short circuit will remain and the breaker will instantly trip when you reset it. Because these pumps run for only short intervals, it may be some time between the first trip out and total failure. Probably a few days. That is why I said that it is essential to check for trouble on the first trip out.

"Ah'." you say, "all of this can be avoided if you just tell the electrician not to put the receptacle in the pit." But the electrician will tell you that he can't bury the receptacle, the code doesn't allow that, and we must have a disconnect means in sight of the motor so the only thing to do is to install a pedestal in the ground next to the pit, and mount the receptacle on the pedestal. The plugs can be passed out through an opening and plugged in. This of course is not very satisfactory. If someone pulls the plugs out the pump won't run. The alarm will go off in the middle of the night. Alarms always go off in the middle of the night, it's some kind of natural law. Besides, you don't want that ugly business sticking up in the middle of the lawn. "Why don't you just splice the wires together and eliminate the receptacle all together," you say to the electrician, "nobody is ever going to go down in that pit to work on that pump. If it needs to be repaired it will be removed."

At this point the odds are that you will hear a long story from the electrician as to how that would be a violation of the code, and his license means too much to him, and he is not going to jeopardize his means of making a living, and blah, blah, blah.

RULE 58

DON'T FALL FOR THE SUBCOTRACTOR'S SONG AND DANCE.

When you hear one of these it's a snow job!!!

I am going to pause in the story of the pump. As long as it has come up, I want to introduce you to what I call the subcontractor's song and dance, or the mechanic's snow job.

If you see something in the work that doesn't seem right to you, or doesn't look as if it's been done properly, and you ask the subcontractor about it, and he launches into a long story about how it's not his fault because the trade that worked before him didn't do right, and it's the best he can do, and by rights it's extra work, and how hard he tries to satisfy his customers, and how great a reputation he has, you will know that you touched a nerve, and put your finger on something that the subcontractor knows he didn't do right.

The amazing thing is, I have known subcontractors that were virtually illiterate, who would hand me the bill form and ask me to fill it out because they couldn't write, but boy could they give the smoothest and most creative snow job. Some of them were masterpieces. I wish I had recorded them. Some of these guys could give lessons to the fellow hawking the latest food chopper on a TV info-mercial. When they know that you are not a professional, but someone just building your own home, they will assume you are ignorant, and give the most outrageous excuses. When the fellow announces that he is going to "be honest with you" and not "BS" you, BEWARE!

These stories seem to proliferate toward the end of the job as you get into the finishing trades, and are dealing with the work that will show. The only way to counter the "Subcontractors Song and Dance" is to know the subject, and have the information.

That is what this book is all about. To give you the information you need, so you will know whether the job is being done properly or not. This is not a book to teach you how to do any specific work. You can buy tons of those in any lumber yard or book store. This book tells you step by step what is supposed to be done, and how to get it done.

THE LOCKOUT

Getting back to the pump problem, I have found that electricians always know about the code requirement for a disconnect means in sight of the motor, but they never know the second part which says, "or, (the disconnect) be provided with a means of being locked in the off position." This means that the disconnect switch doesn't have to be "in sight of the motor" if it can be locked in the off position so no one without the key can accidentally turn the power on.

There is an electrical switch called a "Safety Switch" in the trade. These switches have a handle that can be thrown upwards for the "on" position, and downwards for the "off" position. Next to the handle there are metal tabs with holes in them which allow a padlock to be placed through the hole and around the switch handle so that it cannot be operated.

The solution therefor, is to install a small, inexpensive, single pole, thirty ampere (the smallest size), "safety switch" next to your distribution panel, and wire the circuit for the pump through this switch. This will satisfy the code.

In the pump pit, a vapor proof junction box should be installed on the electrical conduit entering the pit. The plugs should be cut off the wires, and the wires should be spliced with approved connectors. The wires should be placed in the box, and the box should be filled with "duct seal" which is a putty like material available in any electrical supply house, and made for the purpose of sealing off electrical connections. A gasketed cover is placed on the box. This arrangement prevents any corrosive gasses from reaching the spliced connections but still allows for the easy disconnection of the wires in case the pump must be replaced.

It is important to make sure the electrician understands that the two wires that come from the diaphragm switch are to be wired in series with the pump feed. Otherwise he will probably do it wrong.

There are two cautions that must be observed. make sure that the electrician does not wire the pump alarm on the same circuit breaker as the pump, so that if the pump breaker trips off the alarm will still be able to operate.

The other caution relates to the diaphragm switch down on the pump. When the water in the pit rises and exerts pressure on the diaphragm, the air trapped inside the diaphragm must have a way to escape so that the diaphragm can be compressed. This is accomplished by the manufacturer, by running a small tube about an eighth of an inch in diameter inside the rubber covered cable carrying the wires up from the switch. At the plug on the end of this cord the tube opens to the air thus providing a vent line for the switch down in the pit. When the plug is cut off this line in order to splice the wires, care must be taken to strip back the rubber sheath far enough to keep the tube outside the splice box and open to the air in the pit. If this tiny tube is compressed or clogged, the diaphragm switch will not be able to operate and the pump will never turn on. There are also some new types of float switches that do not require a venting tube and where the connection between the switch and the motor is made at the motor.

PUBLIC WATER CONNECTION

Where there is a public water system, as we mentioned earlier, there will be, or should be, a lateral connection from the street main into the lot terminating in a curb box. In order to insure good pressure at the house it is customary to run the water service from the curb box to the house in one inch pipe. Generally there are two types of pipe used for this purpose. There is copper pipe and plastic pipe. When copper pipe is used it is made from a soft type of copper (type K), and comes in a roll which is easily straightened as it is laid into the trench. The copper pipe is long lasting and will not deteriorate in the ground over time. However, copper pipe is expensive. There is an alternative PVC flexible water pipe which also comes in a large roll, and can be rolled out in the trench similar to the copper.

The plastic pipe comes in 100 lb./sq. in. and 200 lb./sq. in. rating. The stronger pipe has thicker walls. I strongly suggest that you avoid the 100 lb. material and use the 200 lb. The lighter weight pipe is easily kinked if not handled carefully. Once the pipe has been bent, even if it is straightened out, a crease and a weak spot have been created in the wall of the pipe which will eventually fail.

If you live in a cold climate the water line should be buried well below the frost line. In the northeast we go down at least five feet. If rock or other problems prevent you going deep enough you should cover the line with several inches of styrofoam insulation board four feet wide. One inch of styrofoam is considered equivalent to one foot depth of earth. It is a common error to put insulation under the water pipe or to encase the line in "Armaflex" foam insulation. The line is kept from freezing by heat energy which is rising up from the earth. We want to put a cover or lid over the pipe which will retain that heat. We want the insulation to be wide enough so that the frost can not penetrate around it. Obviously insulation under the pipe keeps the heat out.

It is also important to insure that the bottom of the trench in which the line is to be placed is smooth and free from sharp rocks or stones. If there are stones in the soil, the bottom of the trench should be bedded with a layer of sand. Likewise, before backfilling stones on top of the line, if it is not to be covered with insulation, it should be covered with a layer of sand. Due to the settling of the earth, stones touching on the pipe may eventually bear down and puncture the pipe.

What is little understood about water lines, even by the plumbers and people in the trade, is that the line constantly moves in the ground in response to changes of pressure. If a line is touching a stone, the constant infinitesimal movement of the pipe can eventually wear a hole through.

To clearly understand this action you need only observe what happens to a water hose when the pressure is put into it. That's right! It wants to straighten out the bends. It takes several men to control the end of a fire hose when the pressure is on because of this phenomenon. When you turn on the water in the house, the pressure in the supply line reduces. When you turn the water off, the pressure in the line increases. Just like the garden hose and the fire hose, these changes in pressure cause the line to move. If it is in contact with an abrasive surface it will ultimately wear through.

The water pressure on a public main varies from place to place, but usually when there is no excessive demand, the pressure is higher than you want in your home. When your internal water pressure is too high, it causes a loud banging noise in the pipes when a faucet is closed. It must be remembered that water is not compressible, and does not cushion its behavior as air does. When the faucet is shut off it is like closing the door in front of a moving mass. It slams into the door. The remedy for this problem is to install a pressure reducing valve at the point where the water enters your home. If you are on a public system, doubtless you will be required to have a water meter at the point of entry.

You should plan the location of the water entry into your house to be in a convenient place where the meter and pressure regulator can be installed, and easily accessed. A basement or storage room is fine. Avoid the garage if in a cold climate because of the danger of freezing. Freezing can seriously damage a water meter, and they are not cheap to replace. If the garage is the only choice, then build a pit in the floor for the meter and regulator. Insulate the sides and the lid of the pit but not the bottom.

WELL WATER SERVICE

If you have a shallow well or a well point, all you will need is an above the ground pump installed in a suitable location inside the house. The same precautions should be taken against freezing as mentioned previously for locating a water meter. These pumps will be provided with a check valve that will prevent the water in the line from running back down in the well every time the pump shuts off so that the prime in the pump is not lost.

If you have a drilled well, the chances are that it will be at least fifty feet deep, and more likely a hundred feet or better. The weight of a vertical column of water in a pipe rising from a well can be very substantial and difficult for a surface pump to raise. Conventionally, in a drilled well, a submersible well pump is installed. This is a pump and motor constructed as a cylinder which will fit down into the well. These pumps are easily capable of pumping the water up through the well line and to the house. Being submerged they can never loose their prime. The deeper the well, and the heavier the load of water to be lifted, the greater the horsepower the pump will need to be.

THE PITLESS ADAPTOR

In times past a well head had to be in a pit so that the connections and lines leading away from the well could be in the ground and protected from the frost. Currently there is a device or a fitting called a pitless adaptor which is installed through the side of the well casing below the frost line. The service line is connected to this adaptor on the outside of the casing and run to the house. All the cautions and provisions cited concerning running of a water line from a public system apply equally to a line run from a well. Usually the well pump is attached to the end of a flexible plastic pipe, and lowered thereby into the well, together with the three electrical wires which feed the pump. Special waterproof electrical splicing devices are used for this connection. The end or top of this plastic line, after the pump has been lowered to the desired depth, is connected to a fitting which slips into the portion of the pitless adapter which is inside the casing. This effectively connects the well line to the service line. In the event the pump must be removed, the line is lifted up and the fitting disengages from the pitless adapter. After the installation is completed the excavation around the casing can be filled in, and all water connections will be neatly underground. The top of the casing which should be about a foot above the ground level, receives a cap with a special passage which allows the electrical wires to feed into the well from the top.

WELL PRESSURE SYSTEM

When a well pump is in use, unlike the public water main which maintains pressure into the house, a system must be used to maintain water pressure for interior use when the pump is not pumping. This is accomplished by the use of a pressure tank which is usually a small tank of about 30 gallons capacity in the center of which there is a rubber diaphragm. When water is pumped into this tank by the well pump, the pressure forces against the diaphragm, compressing the air which is trapped behind it. The diaphragm is used to keep the air and water out of contact. When a tank without a diaphragm is used, over time the trapped air dissolves into the water. As the amount of air decreases, the volume that can be compressed gets less, and therefor the amount of water that can be pumped into the tank becomes less.

The tank has a pressure switch on it which controls the well pump. When the pressure in the tank drops, the pressure switch turns on the pump, and water is pumped into the tank until the desired pressure is reached. When this pressure is attained, the pressure switch shuts off the pump. The pressure switch can be set for a high and low setting. Usually this would be a low of 30 Lbs./sq. in. to a high of 40 Lbs./sq. in. There is a check valve at the point that the pipe from the well enters the tank which prevents the water from rushing back out of the tank when the pump shuts off. A line leads out of this tank to supply the water for internal use. Pressure is kept on this line by the compressed air in the tank exerting force against the contained water.

One of these standard pressure tanks when fully filled to 40 Lbs. pressure holds about 16 gallons of water, which is a fair amount for domestic use so that you will probably not be aware of the changes in pressure as the pump cycles on and off. However if you do become aware of a rapid change and cycling of the water pressure from high to low in a short time, this indicates that the air or most of the air has leaked out of the pressure tank and it needs to be serviced.

If you have special water requirements a larger tank can be used, and the pressure settings can be varied.

Always remember that if you use a lot of water, especially for lawn sprinkling, you don't want to use water faster than your well can acquire it as was discussed in Chapter 3.

GAS SERVICE

The third piped in utility service entry that you might have, would be a gas service line. Most cities and suburban areas have gas utilities. Frequently it is the same company as the electric supplier. In more rural areas public gas service is rare. If your utility supplies gas, generally they will install the service main to the house. They will also install the gas meter.

L.N.G AND PROPANE

There are private companies which supply gas by placing a tank on your property and filling it as you consume the gas. While most utilities supply natural gas, a private company may supply LNG, which is liquid natural gas, or propane which is a manufactured liquid gas.

GAS USAGE

Natural gas supplied by the utility company is usually quite competitive with the cost of fuel oil, and is used for heating the home. It is also used for heating hot water, cooking and laundry drying. LNG and propane are usually too expensive to use for space heating, but are frequently used by people who prefer to cook on a gas stove. Don't forget the "lazy man's fireplace" previously described. Mobile homes are often equipped with heating systems that operate on propane.

INTERIOR GAS PIPING

In the old days interior gas piping was usually threaded iron pipe, caulked with string and "pipe dope". This will be the piping found in an older home. Today the gas piping is done with flexible copper tubing, and the fittings are flared compression fittings which are very leak resistant, and require no threading and caulking. Any competent plumber can install this work. Usually private companies supplying LNG or propane, are capable of installing the interior piping for you.

It is important that any gas piping system be properly pressure tested, before being enclosed in the finished walls. The gas utility or private supplier will service your system and gas appliances. Unless a plumber has had special training he usually will not know how to service and repair gas equipment.

HOT WATER BASEBOARD SYSTEMS

In Chapter 24 we covered the various types of furnaces and air circulation heating systems. It is appropriate here, to talk about hot water baseboard systems as they are a major part of the plumbing installation.

As we have described, the hot water baseboard system heats by pumping hot water around a closed loop of piping. The hot water is circulated from this loop through the baseboard radiators and back to the loop. The water is pumped from the boiler by a circulator pump run by an electric motor. When the thermostat calls for heat, the circulator pump turns on and the hot water is delivered through the radiators.

In most smaller homes up to about, 1500 square feet, the entire home is usually heated by a single loop. When the home becomes larger, the area to be heated becomes greater than a single loop can handle so an additional zone is created. Often additional zones are used to heat different areas of usage. For instance there may be one zone for the living areas, and a different zone for the second floor bedrooms. Usually when family rooms or recreation areas are separate, they are served by a separate zone. Each zone is controlled by it's own thermostat which enables the raising or lowering of the heat in accordance with the usage and time of day.

ZONE CIRCULATION

When there are multiple zones they may be supplied by a single circulator pump in combination with automatic solonoid valves which control the flow to the respective loops calling for heat. The alternate way, is to have each zone supplied by a separate circulator pump. This is more expensive and probably will not be included in the plumbers bid unless you have asked for it. Eventually, a circulator pump will wear out and fail. When there is only one pump, you will have no heat in the house at all, but if there is more than one, you will still be able to have heat in the unaffected zones. The multiple pumps may cost a few hundred dollars more but I believe it is worth it.

NOISE CONTROL

In all types of heating systems there is obviously a lot of expansion and contraction going on as heat is supplied or not supplied. When the radiators are not properly installed this can result in a lot of noise such as pinging and creaking. The pipe connection that feeds a baseboard radiator from the loop passes up through the floor. The plumber usually drills a hole through the floor and runs his pipe up. If this pipe is pressing against the edge of the hole, every time it heats up and expands it will rub on the wood making substantial noise. There are nylon sleeves made for putting in the hole to prevent this problem, but chances are you won't get them unless you specifically ask for them.

AIR BINDING AND BLEEDING

The water which is circulated through the heating system contains a certain amount of air which over time will come out of the water and accumulate at a high point, usually in a heater. When a heater becomes "Air bound", the hot water does not fill it, and the heater gives progressively less and less heat as the air accumulates. Every heater should have on it, a small valve called a bleeder valve. The bleeder can be used to purge the air out of the heater and restore it's operation. There are now automatic bleeder valves which let the air out as it accumulates. However, these valves may not always work properly. If you find a heater which does not seem to be giving enough heat, check the bleeder valve.

PIPING IN AN OVERHANG

There is a problem which often occurs in cold climates that must be guarded against. Many home designs, especially raised ranches or bi-levels are constructed with part of a floor projecting beyond, and overhanging the floor below. Straight ranches on basements and Garrison style colonials also have this characteristic. Where baseboard heaters are installed on the outside wall of the overhung room, the piping is run through the floor joists in the overhang. This piping is very subject to freezing in the event of a power failure.

I remember a time when there was a major power failure in the winter time which lasted for several days. When power was finally restored, and hot water circulators started to run again, water squirted out of pipes that had burst from freezing, causing flooding and damage in hundreds and hundreds of houses. The local plumbers made a lot of money that winter. This is a good argument in favor of having at least a small emergency generator that can run the oil burner and circulator.

DOMESTIC HOT WATER

There are three main ways that domestic hot water is produced. Hot water boilers, either oil or gas fired, have a coil of copper pipe contained inside the water chamber. As cold water is drawn through this coil it is heated by the surrounding hot water. The benefit of this system is that you never run out of hot water. A negative is, that the entire furnace must be kept in operation during the non heating season which is somewhat inefficient.

If gas is being used, an individual hot water heater is an option. One type of heater heats water stored in a tank. Another type heats a coil similar to the one described for the oil burner.

For homes using heat pumps, or homes in a warm climate where heating is only an occasional requirement, electric hot water heaters are used. Modern electric hot water heaters are very well insulated, and a tank of hot water will loose only a few degrees in twelve hours. If you should use a large amount of hot water and run out, the electric heaters have a fast recovery system that can heat ten gallons of water in less than fifteen minutes.

Many electric utility companies are now offering a "Time of Use" billing option. This means that power consumed during off peak hours is sold at a very substantial discount. Timers can be installed on a hot water heater so that it heats the water during off peak hours. Weekends and holidays are considered off peak time. This results in a very substantial savings.

INTERIOR DRAIN LINE NOISE

The interior waste lines from toilets, sinks, showers and tubs, are now normally run in plastic pipe. The only disadvantage of plastic pipe over cast iron is that the plastic pipe does not dampen the noise of the water flow as well as cast iron. Remember the roar when Archie Bunker flushed? This is not a great sound when entertaining guests. Good plumbing layout will keep waste lines from running down through living room and dining room walls. These lines can also be wrapped with sound deadening material or contained in a chase that is insulated with sound board.

TOILET CONNECTIONS

Toilets usually are positioned between other bathroom fixtures and generally must be placed exactly where shown on the plans. Often the toilet location will fall on top of a floor joist which the plumber will promptly saw through. This leaves the ends of the floor joist without support. Proper headers must be installed to support the ends of the joist where it has been cut. If possible get the framers to do it while they are framing. The toilet location can be measured off the plans and ascertained. This is another one of the details that will not get done unless you bring it to the carpenters attention. If the plumbers do it, insist they do it correctly using joist hangers, not just toe nailing in a couple of cross pieces. If the Building Inspector sees an improperly cut floor joist he'll give you a violation so you will wind up having to do it any way. The important thing is to get it done when the appropriate workers are present on the job, rather than have to try to get someone to come back.

WATER PIPING

The water piping is pretty cut and dried. Most jurisdictions require it to be done with copper pipe, but more and more areas are permitting the use of plastic pipe instead.

There is currently a concern about lead being in drinking water. Solder used to solder the copper pipes must be a lead free type.

Care should be taken to insure that water feeders to bathrooms containing showers should be at least 3/4 inch pipe so that water flow in the shower will not be affected by water use elsewhere in the house. If you are planning a whirlpool tub that requires a lot of water, you may want to consider increasing the size of the water supply line so that it may be filled faster. Also make sure that your water heater has enough capacity to fill the tub.

Running the water pipes is pretty straight forward. Lots of holes need to be drilled through joists and studs to accommodate the lines. It is important that the pipe be far enough back from the surface, that sheet rock screws and finish carpentry nails cannot puncture it.

RULE NUMBER 59

IT IS ESSENTIAL THAT ALL WATER LINES BE SEALED AND PRESSURE TESTED BEFORE THE WALLS ARE CLOSED.

The pipes must be closed off and air pumped in under pressure, and measured by a gauge. No pressure should be lost in the system within twenty four hours. If the pressure falls off it means there is at least one leak. Every time a leak is found and corrected the test must be repeated to make sure there is not another leak.

It is a lot easier to test the lines when installed than have to cut through and patch finished and painted walls and ceilings when the water is turned on and a leak is discovered. Lots of plumbers don't do this test. You must insist on it.

THE AIR CUSHION

We previously mentioned that when water pressure is too high a banging can occur in the pipes. There is another measure taken to dampen any of this water hammer effect if it occurs. At the high point in the plumbing, for instance at a second floor bathroom, the hot and cold water lines are fitted with Ts where they connect to the faucet supply, and are extended upward past the Ts for about two feet. The tops of these pipes are capped. When water pressure is allowed into the line air is trapped in these top portions of the lines above the Ts. The air, being compressible, dampens any hammering tendency.

UNDER SINK CONNECTIONS

The final connections that are made under sinks which connect the supply lines to the faucets, are usually made with smaller diameter plastic tubing. The fittings on this tubing are also plastic, and if they are tightened too much they may break. As a result these connections are frequently not tightened sufficiently, and may leak after the water pressure is turned on. The first week after pressure is on, these connections should be checked often for leakage. An oversight here could result in a water damaged ceiling below. Repair of this damage will require a sheet rocker and taper and a painter who are no longer on the job. The dry wall man will have to come at least twice to do two coats of spackle. It's a big hassle that can be avoided.

WATER CONSERVATION

Some states have laws requiring that special water saving toilets and shower heads be used. This of course assumes that you are getting your water from a public system. However the old type toilets may not be available. These new toilets hold much less water in the bowl and tend not to always be cleaned completely by a single flush.

Water saver shower heads are also in my opinion not very satisfactory. Usually the water reduction is accomplished by a rubber ball inside the shower head. This ball is easily removable.

If you are going to have your water supplied by your own well you'll probably get the new type fixtures anyway unless you specifically ask for the old style. Even then you may have to obtain them from another state.

WHIRLPOOL TUBS

Luxury bathroom fixtures are becoming more and more popular. No doubt you will want to have a whirlpool tub in you bathroom. These tubs operate by use of a pump which in almost all cases, is mounted to the tub. Most of these tubs are designed to be dropped into a platform. After the tub platform has been covered with tile or marble as they usually are, the pump cannot be accessed for repair without removing the tile etc. There are some tubs available where the pump is not attached to the tub frame. Whenever I designed a bathroom to hold one of these tubs, I always tried to get one end of the tub to back up against a bedroom wall where I was able to locate a closet. I always constructed a removable panel in the back wall of the closet which gave access to the area under the tub platform where the pump had been positioned. `This solution may not work in every case but if you are aware of the problem, chances are you can work out some answer.

CHAPTER 27

INSULATION

Of all the steps in building a house, insulating it correctly is one of the most important operations, yet routinely, insulation is poorly done and improperly installed. It is the one aspect of the construction that bears a yearly price in terms of the cost of heating the house. Poorly executed insulation, over the years, can cost thousands of dollars in unnecessary fuel expense simply because the right things were not done when the house was built.

There are three basic ways in which heat energy is lost from a house. The first is the loss of energy through the walls, ceilings and windows. The second is the loss of energy by moisture migration, and the third is by means of air infiltration. We will discuss these aspects in turn, and how they should be properly dealt with.

HOW INSULATION WORKS

Of course, the purpose of insulation is to prevent the transfer of heat energy through the walls, ceilings and windows of a structure. Different substances have different rates of heat conductivity. Generally metals are very good conductors, gold, copper and aluminum being the best. Non metallic substances are less good. One of the poorest conductors of heat energy is air, and it is air which forms the insulating basis of almost all insulating materials. As we previously noted in discussing windows, Argon gas is a slightly better insulator than air but does not have the convenience of use as air, and would have to be hermetically sealed in a medium to prevent it's loss.

By far the most widely used insulation material in use today is spun fiberglass. Glass is a pretty good conductor of heat, why then is spun fiber glass a good insulation? The glass is not the insulating medium. It is the millions of tiny cells of air that are trapped within the fiberglass material that provide the insulating ability. All the fiberglass does is hold the tiny cells of air in place, and eliminate any movement of the air cells, or convection, as we previously learned.

The heat energy must be exchanged from air molecule to air molecule as it passes through the medium. The heat will always move from the area of higher temperature to the area of lower temperature. The greater the difference in these temperatures, the faster the rate of exchange. The smaller and more immobile the cells of air, the better the insulation. That is why plastic foam insulation's are more effective than spun fiberglass. In the foams, the cells are actually tiny enclosed bubbles rather than just spaces between the woven strands. In foam insulation the gas inside the tiny cells will not be air, but the gaseous material resulting from the chemical reaction used to form the foam.

The R value of fiberglass insulation is about 3R to the inch. Most of the rigid foam board insulation's are about 5R to the inch and some with reflective backing are a little higher.

RULE NUMBER 60

INSULATION DOES NOT GENERATE HEAT.

There is a common misbelief that if you surround something with enough insulation it will not freeze. Insulation can only contain the heat that is already there. If there is no input of heat the existing energy will gradually dissipate, and the item will freeze.

A lady for whom I had designed and built a home, called me one day and said that we must have left out the insulation in the bathroom wall because she found the wash cloth in the tub, frozen. It turned out that it was the guest bath which was on the north side of the house. The glass enclosure for the tub was kept closed and because the bath was not used the thermostat was kept down at fifty degrees. The glass enclosure kept the room air out of the tub area which gradually got colder and colder as the heat transferred through the outside wall. Eventually, when the temperature one night fell below zero, the temperature inside the tub got below 32 degrees and the wash cloth froze.

I explained to my client that insulation only reduces the rate at which heat passes through the wall, and that if heat energy is lost at a faster rate than it is supplied, the space will become colder until an equilibrium is reached.

The solution was to leave the glass door enclosing the tub, open.

FIBERGLASS BATTS

Fiberglass insulating batts are quite inexpensive compared to rigid material, and much quicker and easier to install. The fiber glass of course, is installed in the spaces between the studs of a wall, or joists of a floor or ceiling, while the rigid boards must be applied to the surface of the frame. Cutting and fitting the rigid material between the studs takes much more time and does not fit as well. There are certainly appropriate uses for the rigid materials, but for walls, floors, ceilings and roofs, the fiber glass material is much more desirable.

PAPER FACED BATTS

Fiberglass insulation is quite porous, and air under pressure can move through it quite easily, so for years the most commonly seen insulating batts were fiberglass faced with paper. The paper is to restrict air movement through the batt.

Unfortunately, among those whose job it was to install this insulation, there was never an understanding of the proper way to do it. Getting the material between the studs, any way possible, was all that mattered. The insulation batts are made in the proper width to fit snugly between the studs which are usually on 16 inch centers. Down each side of the batt is a continuous paper tab about 3/4 inch wide. Customarily the batts were pressed in between the studs with the paper facing forward, and the tabs were stapled to the insides of the studs to hold the batts in place. If there was an electrical wire running through holes in the center of the studs, the batt would be stuffed behind the wire and against the outside sheathing.

This is the worst possible way to install this insulation yet it is done over and over again. I have attended seminars given by a utility company on the proper way to insulate houses, and been shown movies of paper faced batts being incorrectly installed as described above.

This method of installation commits four basic errors and reduces the insulating effectiveness of the material to about fifty percent of it's rating.

CRUSHING

A 12 inch thickness of fiberglass insulation, insulates twice as well as a 6 inch thickness, because the width of the entrapped air cells through which the heat must be conducted is twice as much. If we begin to squeeze the batt, we reduce the number of air cells and the thickness of the batt. 12 inches of fiberglass insulation squeezed down to a 6 inch thickness is a worse insulator that an ordinary 6 inch batt because twice as much glass has been compressed into the space, causing more of the strands to touch together. This provides more conductive paths through the glass fibers which are themselves fairly good conductors of heat.

Crushing the paper faced batts between the studs so as to be able to staple the tabs to the insides of the studs, reduces the thickness of the batts and the number of insulating air cells. This reduces insulating value.

CONVECTION

When the sheet rock is installed over the crushed insulation, large spaces or voids are created between the crumpled insulation and the inside surface of the sheet rock. Convection currents occur in these spaces which accelerate the loss of heat.

AIR INFILTRATION

The purpose of the paper wrapping is to prevent air currents from moving through the insulation. When the tabs are stapled to the insides of the studs, gapping occurs between the staples, and the air can freely move through.

DEFORMITY BEHIND WIRES

The fourth error is in the deforming of the insulation and stuffing it behind electrical wires. If a batt is stuffed behind a wire running through the center of the studs in a 2x4 wall, the insulation thickness is reduced to about 1 1/2 inches. This virtually eliminates the insulating properties and creates a large void.

THE RIGHT WAY

The proper way is to first fluff up the batt to it's full size and fit it between the studs with the paper face forward so that it fills the entire space, especially the rear corners. The tabs should be extended over the face of the studs and stapled in place. This prevents crushing of the batt and creates a flush surface. When the sheetrock is applied, the tabs are sealed against the studs and the insulation touches the inner surface.

If there is a cable passing through horizontally, the batt should be cut and fitted tightly above and below the cable so that it is completely surrounded without the insulation being crushed. The cut should be sealed with an adhesive tape.

This method of installation takes a little longer and requires a bit more care. Most insulation installers are paid on the amount of insulation they install, so their primary concern is the fastest way, not the best way.

MOISTURE MIGRATION

Moisture will migrate from the interior of a house to the exterior by evaporating into a gaseous state and passing through the walls of the building. Just as heat will move from a location of higher temperature to a location of lower temperature, water vapor will move from an area of higher humidity level to an area of lower humidity level. In the winter time the humidity level outside a house is invariably lower than the level inside.

The reason this migration is important is that the water vapor carries a great deal of heat energy out of the structure by virtue of something called "The latent heat of vaporization".

We know that it takes one BTU of energy to raise the temperature of a pound of water by one degree Fahrenheit. We also know that it takes more than a hundred BTUs of energy to transform one pound of water into water vapor without raising the temperature. The energy is required just to change the physical state of the water from liquid to gas.

Inside a house in winter, moisture is continuously evaporating, taking up large amounts of energy in the transformation. The resultant vapor migrates out of the structure, taking the absorbed energy with it.

THE VAPOR BARRIER

Because of the loss of energy due to moisture migration it has become good insulating technique to install a vapor barrier to prevent this loss. Faced insulating batts are made with a moisture resistant paper to accomplish this but a better practice is to install a continuous sheet of polyethylene plastic over the inside of the walls after the batts have been installed between the studs.

When the poly vapor barrier is used it is customary to use unfaced fiberglass batts. Without the paper the batts can be more easily installed and made to "Bloom". Blooming means that the batts fluff up and expand, thereby increasing the amount of air that is entrapped. The unfaced batts are also less expensive. It is very important that a batt be installed so as to fill the entire space between the studs without voids and gaps. They should be slightly folded forward in the center when placed, rather than just pushed in. This technique insures that the batts fill into the rear corners rather than being held back by friction against the sides of the studs.

It is important that the vapor barrier be installed on the warm side of the wall. If a vapor barrier is installed on the outside of the wall, the moisture vapor would be able to enter the wall but not be able to pass through. It would condense from the colder temperature inside the wall, and water log the fiberglass insulation. Wet and soggy fiberglass becomes virtually worthless as insulation. Because of this danger I am against the installation of rigid foam board insulation on the outside of the house which is often done.

INSULATING CEILINGS

It still is a wide spread practice to use paper faced insulating batts when doing the ceilings, but you will almost never see it face stapled as it should be. It is used to provide the mechanical means of keeping the insulation from falling out of the ceiling until the sheet rock is installed. Secondly, there is a widely held belief that ceilings should not be totally impermeable to moisture migration, or condensation will occur in the sheet rock, making it soft. I do not agree with this idea, and find it to be baseless. I routinely insulate ceilings with unfaced batts covered with a continuous sheet of poly plastic. I have never observed any interior condensation as a result.

Condensation may occur at the high point of a cathedral ceiling in the summer time if there is insufficient ventilation, but it has nothing to do with the insulation. More heat is lost through the ceiling than anywhere else and it is important to insulate the ceiling in the most efficient manner.

INTERIOR WALLS

There is one instance where I would recommend the use of paper faced batts and that is in an interior wall between a heated and an unheated area, such as between a kitchen and a garage. With the studs completely open on both sides, unfaced batts will not stay in place, and tend to fall or be knocked out before the sheet rock is applied. The paper face and tabs provide the necessary means to hold the insulation in place. The paper should face the cold side and the poly barrier should be applied to the warm side.

FLOORS

When a house is on a basement, and the basement is not to be heated, it is necessary to insulate the floor above the basement. Many insulators will wrongfully use paper faced material stapling it to the floor joists. This leaves a space between the insulation and the flooring above in which condensation might occur. The proper technique would be to install unfaced batts between the floor joists, up against the bottom of the flooring. To keep these batts in place and prevent their falling out, there are stiff wires used which can be wedged between the joists up against the bottom of the insulation. These wires are referred to in the trade as "Tiger teeth".

ATTIC SPACES

When the house has a low pitched roof, the attic space created is not considered usable. In these cases there is another insulating option. Instead of installing batts from the ceiling side, insulation may be blown in to cover the attic floor to the desired depth. This insulation might be loose fiberglass or a fire retardant cellulose material which is also used.

The problem with this installation is that it cannot be done until the ceiling sheet rock is installed. The vapor barrier poly would have to be installed when the rest of the insulating work is done, and then at a later date, the insulating contractor would have to return with the blowing equipment to insulate the attic space.

I find no advantage in creating the extra step and potential disruption that blown insulation requires. I prefer to get all my insulation done in one shot by the same people.

Further, if the roof has a higher pitch, and the attic area is intended to be usable, some kind of flooring needs to be installed, and is best done during the framing. If the flooring is omitted to allow insulation to be blown in, the flooring material will have to be carried up sheet by sheet through the house. It might be difficult to get it up into the attic area if a hatchway or pull down stair is used.

MISCELLANEOUS INSULATION

When we described platform framing we indicated how floor joists were supported by the outside walls. The joists rest on top of the wall plate and their open ends are closed by the band. In a two story house, when the walls of the first floor and second floor are insulated, the band area which is the thickness of the floor is not included and must be insulated separately. Special sized pieces of insulation are made for this purpose and are referred to as "Beam ends". They must be introduced between the joists and placed against the outside band. Unfortunately there is no easy way to create a vapor barrier between these joists and it is one of the lacks of standard practice.

When door jambs and window frames are installed in the framing there are always small spaces between the jambs and the studs. These spaces should be carefully packed with fiberglass.

Where an interior wall meets perpendicularly to an outside wall, a pocket is created which we discussed earlier under framing. Attention should be paid to see that these pockets are stuffed. This is an item that insulators rarely do unless specifically directed.

AIR INFILTRATION

This is the third way heat is lost from a structure. We discussed earlier, some of the concerns about infiltration but there is another important factor.

All building codes require attic ventilation. This is usually done by having louvers in the soffit of the roof overhang to allow air to enter, and other louvers at the gable ends of the roof in the attic space. The soffit vents can also be done with a continuous louvered strip, and the top vents can be done by the use of a ridge vent. When a ridge vent is used the roof sheathing is kept back from the ridge rafter to create a slot through which air can exit. The ridge vent is a device which is placed over this slot. It allows the air to exit but prevents rain from coming in. Ridge vent comes in various lengths. It can be capped at the ends or connected together to form a continuous run.

In the summer time, when the sun beats upon an attic roof, the very humid air in the attic rises to a quite high temperature, often as much as 140 degrees Fahrenheit. In the nighttime when the outside air cools, and the roof becomes cool, the moisture in the hot and heavily laden air inside the attic, may condense on the underside of the roof sheathing which can lead to deterioration of the material. The idea of venting is that when the air in the attic heats up it rises out of the vents at the top, and is replaced by cooler air drawn in through the louvers in the soffit overhang at the bottom. This creates circulation which will keep the temperature of the attic lower, and which ventilates the attic preventing condensation.

This is fine in the summer, and by keeping the attic cooler, air conditioning load is reduced. However, in the cold of winter this venting is very undesirable, yet the substantial negative factor, thus far has been ignored by building codes and architects.

When cold winter winds blow they strike against the side of the house and drive upward through the venting louvers. This causes a positive air pressure in the attic and helps force the air out the top vents. However, during the positive pressure which lasts as long as the wind blows, air is forced into the interior of the house through every possible crack, opening and crevice.

Recessed ceiling lights which pierce the vapor barrier allow cold air to blow into the heated area. Poorly sealed and uninsulated attic hatches, allow air to blow in. The air under pressure easily finds it's way into the wall cavities, and wherever there is an electrical outlet box, blows into the house. Air can leak out at the baseboard level where the sheet rock doesn't quite meet the flooring. This is concealed behind the base molding and is not easily seen.

Houses built on hill tops, and exposed to high winds can leak like sieves.

REMEDIES

Follow the hints already given about using flanged windows, the proper installation of the exterior house wrap, and the sheathing tips given. On the inside make the poly plastic vapor barrier as continuous and well sealed as possible. This barrier blocks air currents. Do not penetrate this barrier with recessed lights.

Make sure that the poly vapor barrier on the walls comes down to the floor and folds forward a little. Install additional flooring on top of this plastic at the perimeter. Underlayment, hardwood flooring and carpet padding can be installed over the plastic. The poly must be cut back to glue down vinyl or tile. In this case the junction between the base molding and the flooring material should be caulked with a thin bead

Insulate all electrical outlet boxes in outside walls. Spray cans of insulating foam are available. The space between the sheetrock where it has been cut around the electrical box should be sealed with foam. The inside of the outlet box should be filled with foam to seal it's many openings. This is best done after the wiring device, such as a receptacle or switch, has been installed in the box, and of course, before the finish plate is put on.

Attic hatches and pull down stairs should be weather stripped where they close. Glue a piece of styrofoam insulation on the back of the attic hatch or attic door. Nobody ever bothers to do these things but they are enormously important, and will save a lot of money in heating costs. Remember the story of the two brothers.

Once someone came to me who had a severe winter air infiltration problem. His house was located on an open hill top where the wind blew all the time. We did some of the obvious things without tearing the walls apart, and improvement was made, but it was not enough. I advised him to buy a roll of adhesive backed plastic package sealing tape, and tape over the louvered vent strips in his soffit overhang. This prevented the wind from blowing in, pressurizing the attic space, and virtually cured the problem.

CATHEDRAL CEILINGS

The code venting requirements apply to cathedral ceilings just as they apply to attic spaces. A cathedral ceiling must be vented so that air may circulate between the insulation and the roof sheathing. This exposes the cathedral ceiling to the same infiltration problems, and vapor barrier penetrations should be avoided.

In order to insulate a cathedral ceiling with 9 inch fiber glass batts which I consider the minimum, ceiling rafters need to be 2x12s to allow a sufficient space for the air circulation.

When the batts are installed at the lower end of the ceiling into the soffit, they may block off the vents. To prevent this there is a shallow trough made out of quarter inch thick rigid foam which should be installed in each bay at the lower end to insure the circulation. The troughing comes in four foot long pieces for this purpose.

If you want to insulate the ceiling with a higher R value you can install 12 inch batts between the 2x12s. This of course uses up the air space but the installation is approved if the plastic troughs are extended continuously in each bay from the soffit up to the ridge vent opening. Although the trough width is not the entire width between the rafters, the amount of ventilation they permit is considered adequate to prevent condensation.

BASEMENT AND GARAGE ACCESS DOORS

Usually the doors leading from the heated area of a home to the unheated basement or garage area are ordinary doors. In the case of the garage a steel door might be used to meet fire requirements. However these doors are never weather stripped or insulated, and they should be. Exterior garage doors do not fit very tightly and when the wind blows it can easily enter the garage causing positive pressure. The air travels around and under the access door causing substantial infiltration losses.

HIRING THE SUBCONTRACTOR

When you hire your insulating subcontractor, make sure he understands exactly how you want the insulation installed. Tell him that if it not done properly you will make him do it over until you are satisfied. No matter what he may say, he knows that the things you ask for should be done. Chances are when he sees that you know what you are talking about he won't give you an argument.

Insulation prices are based on the square footage of the different thickness and types required, plus troughs and beam ends. You can figure out these square footage's and check out the price for yourself. Some contractors will give you a good square foot price but they will over state the amount required and try to rip you off.

RULE NUMBER 61

FOLLOWING THE INSULATING INFORMATION GIVEN IN THIS BOOK WILL INCREASE THE THERMAL EFFICIENCY OF YOUR HOUSE BY 50 PERCENT.

CHAPTER 28

DRYWALL AND TAPING

The days of plaster walls are gone, and today all interior walls are finished by applying drywall board, gypsum board, or sheetrock, which are all names for the same thing.

Sheetrock as I like to call it, comes in 3/8ths inch, 1/2 inch, and 5/8ths inch thickness. 3/8ths inch is a little iffy and may not give as firm a wall as desired. If used on ceilings, over time it might develop bellies between the joists. The most commonly used is 1/2 inch thick material which does a good job for all ordinary applications. Some people like the 5/8ths inch board just because it is extra solid and firm. The boards are four feet wide and come in eight foot, ten foot, twelve foot, fourteen foot and sixteen foot lengths.

WALLBOARD TYPES

Regular sheet rock is made from gypsum which is like plaster, covered with a heavy paper. It is reasonably strong but you can knock a hole in it with a good whack from a hammer. The paper bonds well to the taping compound or "Spackle" which is used to conceal the joints. It takes paint well and does not require sizing or any special preparation for wall papering.

There is a special fire retardant type of sheet rock which is referred to as "Fire Code" type, or type X. This is generally required on garage walls. In order to meet the fire code requirements, fire code sheet rock is usually used in 5/8ths inch thickness. Usually if fire code sheetrock is applied to both sides of the wall in question, the 1/2 inch thickness will suffice. Check with the building inspector for your local requirement before ordering any wall board.

There is a waterproof type of sheet rock which comes in a light green color so that you will be able to distinguish it from the ordinary rock. This type is generally used in bathrooms which are subject to high moisture and especially around tubs. If you are planning to tile around a tub which will contain a shower head, or if you plan to have a tiled stall shower, there are special tile backer boards which should be used. These are very resistant to moisture deterioration in the event water penetrates through the grout cement between the tiles.

FASTENING THE WALL BOARD

For many years sheetrock was nailed to the joists and studs. This produced an effect which would usually begin to appear six months to a year after installation. It is called a "Nail pop". A certain percentage of the nails would begin to withdraw and cause a small eruption on the wall where the nail had been plastered over. By the action of the drying of the lumber in a heated house, some of the nails become squeezed out of the wall just like tooth paste out of the tube. These pops tend to occur in ceilings adjacent to outside walls where the changes in temperature and absorbed moisture may have a greater effect. However, nail pops can appear anywhere.

Many attempts were made to eliminate nail pops. Nails were made in a spiral shape, and others coated with rosin to help them stay in better. Nevertheless, there were still pops. One idea was to nail the board with nails in groups of two. This held the board better but did not lessen the nail pops.

SCREWING IT UP

Finally with the advent of light weight drills that could drive screws, some contractors began to screw the sheet rock rather than nail it. It cured the problem. The screws held well and did not pop. The down side was that the screwing took a lot longer to do, and the screws were a lot more expensive than the nails.

As time went on magnetic screw driver tips were developed that held the screw so it could be driven with one hand. You still needed the other hand to put the screw into the bit, but the process got faster as the installers acquired practice.

Today there are power screw guns that feed the screws automatically. Using this equipment, screwing the sheetrock is faster than nailing, and one hand is free to help hold the sheet in place.

CEILINGS

Sheetrock is heavy, and holding it up against the ceiling is difficult and requires at least two men. Often when holding a board up against the ceiling, in order to secure it in place the installers will nail the edges and then afterwards screw the rest. They do this because it takes two hand to use the screw gun if you don't have an automatic feed. The result is that even though you are supposed to be getting a screw job, a lot of nails are used at the perimeter of the sheets which could eventually pop.

There are props to hold the sheet rock up. There are even mechanical lifts that can raise a sheet up against the ceiling, but most installers don't like to use these devices because it takes too long.

Ceilings are always done first. The room dimension is rarely an exact multiple of four feet and the sheet rock must be cut at one side of the room.

WALLS

The board is always installed on the walls horizontally starting at the top. This places a straight factory edge against the ceiling board which will result in a nice straight joint line. The bottom board is put up last and will leave a space from the bottom edge of the board to the sub flooring of one inch. If you will remember, rough framing ceiling height is eight feet one inch. Now we see the reason for the extra inch. This eliminates the necessity for cutting the bottoms of all the wall boards if there are any variations in the ceiling height which can occur from lumber shrinkage.

There are jacks that look like little see-saws which are slipped under the bottom edge of the board. When the installer steps on the outer end the board is lifted up bringing the joint in the middle tightly together.

If there are electrical outlet boxes in the wall their location will be measured, and the sheet rock carefully cut to fit over the box. There are some places where the electrician may have installed a wire but did not install a box. These are usually a wire to feed a light over a medicine cabinet, or a wire to feed the light in an exhaust hood over the stove, or a feed for a water heater or an air handler. Because these wires are to run directly to the appliance, no box is used. The sheetrocker when he sees these wires should make a hole in the sheetrock and bring the wire through. Most of the time he forgets to do it or brings it through in the wrong place. This means that when the electrician comes to finish he may have to cut walls to find his wires or cut new holes when they are in the wrong location. This will result in the need to patch and paint already finished walls which is a complication that can be avoided. I always ask the electrician to staple the wire against a stud so as to protrude forward at the point he wants it to exit the wall. The sheetrocker will not be able to close this in, and must cut a hole for it to come through.

It is also customary when hanging sheetrock to cover right over the doors and windows and then cut out the opening with a small hand saw.

END JOINTS

Because of the weight, it is difficult to handle sheets more than fourteen feet long. If the room is longer there will be end joints. Good practice requires the staggering of these joints which will minimize the visibility of the joints in the finished wall.

CURVES AND CORNERS

It is possible to sheetrock around curves if the radius of the curve is not too small. This is done by soaking the sheetrock with water which will soften the gypsum and make it flexible. Sometimes the use of the thinner 3/8 inch thickness facilitates this process.

Corners are protected by installing a metal corner bead. This is a right angle shaped length of metal with a strong vertical rib at the angle. It is nailed over the corner and should be applied everywhere there is an outside corner formed by the sheetrock.

Many types of windows in use today do not have jambs which are as wide as the wall. This requires that sheetrock be installed at right angles to the window frame to form the "Return". The edge of the sheetrock which meets the window frame might be a cut edge which does not always provide the neatest result. A metal or plastic strip called a "J" bead, because it's cross section looks like the letter J, can be slipped over the rough edge of the sheetrock. J bead should

SOFFITS

An item that is frequently forgotten during the framing are the soffits. A soffit is a dropped portion of the ceiling. Frequently soffits are built over the top kitchen cabinets so there is no opening above the cabinets. This style is becoming less popular however, and more and more the open space is left above the top cabinets. Drop soffits are frequently used in bathrooms over the tub or shower or even the vanity. They do tend to improve the design in these areas. Before starting the sheetrocking make sure all the soffits you want are framed out.

TAPING

Taping is the method used to cover over the joints, which are apparent after all the sheetrock has been hung. It is so called because a strip of heavy paper or "Tape" is embedded in the "Joint compound" which is used like plaster to smooth over the joints.

Compound is first troweled over a joint filling in the crack and then the tape is applied over the wet compound and smoothed over with the trowel. This embeds the tape in the wet compound. The edges of the sheet rock at the joint, have been beveled down at the factory to provide a slight recess so that the application of the tape and compound will not result is a raised bump.

The tape has a slight groove pressed into it which runs lengthwise down the center. This facilitates the folding of the tape at right angles so that it may be applied to inside corners and at the joints of walls and ceilings.

A slight amount of compound is troweled over each exposed screw head. At the corner beads a heavier coat is applied because the corner rib is slightly raised forming a sort of recess for the compound. The compound is "Feathered out" away from the corner usually for eight to twelve inches. The surface of the metal angle is roughened and has holes which enable the compound to adhere.

After the first coat of compound is dry a second coat is applied, and the edges are feathered out further than the first coat. If the taping is being done in cold weather, it takes a very long time for the compound to dry. It is necessary to use some form of temporary heat to hasten the drying process. The usual device used is a propane fueled heater called a "Salamander". Both the products of combustion and the drying of the compound put an enormous amount of moisture in the interior air and it is essential that windows be left partly open to permit ventilation.

SKIMMING

When a light is held close to a wall and allowed to shine across the surface, every tiny trowel mark, dent, scratch and bump will be very visible. Sometimes windows are positioned so that at a particular time of the day, sunlight will fall across a wall in this manner. Often light from windows shining upward across a cathedral ceiling will create this problem. Curves made in sheetrock might be a little bumpy from the shaping. All these conditions can be improved by the taper applying a very thin coat of compound and troweling it out smoothly. This is called skimming and requires a great deal of skill. Usually this will not be done on ceilings because there are better ways to deal with that which we will go into later.

SANDING

No matter how skilled the taper, there will always be rough spots and trowel marks. These can easily be smoothed out by sanding. A sanding pad on a pole with a flexible joint at the head is used for this purpose. The flexible joint allows the head to fit flat against the wall or ceiling regardless of the angle of the pole. Compound sands well, and a lot of work is not involved. However, many contractors are lazy about the sanding and try to get away without doing it, but it should be done, and will result in a much better paint job.

HIRING THE DRYWALL CONTRACTOR

Drywall work does not require any big investment by the contractor and requires only a few simple tools. For this reason, in my experience, this trade attracts a lot of fly by night operators. They are here today and gone tomorrow. Unfortunately, my experience has been that four out of five drywall contractors will try to rip you off. I am going to tell you how they do it and how you can prevent it.

TAKING THE COUNT

Sometimes there are contractors who only hang the sheetrock and others who only tape. I try to avoid dealing with two different contractors, and make one contractor be responsible for the whole job. If he is only a taper, let him hire the rockers. If you hire the rockers separately, chances are the taper will complain about how the lousy hanging job is increasing his work. He'll claim that the joints are too open, there are too many joints, the screws aren't all the way in etc., etc. You don't need this hassle.

The price for hanging and taping sheetrock is based on the total square footage of the sheets of material that are consumed. Note I said consumed not hung. The contractor will quote you the price as so many cents per square foot. There can be a lot of difference here and it is important for you to get several quotes.

By all means, you want to buy the sheetrock. Probably the contractor wants you to buy it too because he doesn't have the credit at the supply house. If he did there is a chance that he may never pay for it, and you'll get stuck with a lien. But you should make it clear that he is to furnish the compound, the tape, the corner bead and J bead if needed. If he runs out of compound he can't complain that you are holding him up and costing him money. When taking the bid ask the contractor to measure up the job and give you a count of the number and sizes of the sheets that will be required. Also tell him to keep the count separate by floor because it is delivered to each floor by the supplier. You will have to tell him where water proof type is to be used, and where fire code type X is to be used so he can count those separately.

When the contractor is measuring he has one idea in mind. That is to have the fewest possible joints thereby lessening the taping work as much as possible. If a room is 12 feet 6 inches long he will ask for 14 foot long sheets so that the walls and ceilings will have no butt joints. If the shorter wall is say, 9 feet long he will ask for ten foot long sheets and he will figure it to run right over the windows and doors. All the pieces that get cut off and cut out of the door and the shorter wall is say, 9 feet long he will ask for ten foot long sheets and he will figure it to run right over the windows and doors. All the pieces that get cut off and cut out of the door and window openings will be thrown away as waste but they are included in the total square foot count which is used to determine the price.

The contractors final count will list the quantity of each size sheet he needs in each location. The square footage is calculated and totaled. The answer is multiplied by the square foot price, which gives the job price. However, if there are special conditions required by the job such as scaffolding to do a cathedral ceiling, skim coating on curves, or his quote does not include furnishing corner bead, he will ask for an additional amount.

Customers, including builders, almost never check out the contractors count. I am telling you that it is essential that you do so. It is a very common practice for the count to be over estimated. For instance if a 12 foot long sheet is required a 14 foot piece may be listed. This increases the count by about 15% and adds that percentage to the final price for which no work will be done. It is also a common practice to include extra whole sheets beyond what is needed. During the installation the extra sheets will be cut up into smaller pieces and thrown on the waste pile, and you will never know the difference. I have been given a count on a job for 10,000 square feet which was ultimately done with 6,300 square feet. Not only is the contractor overcharging you, but you are also paying for all the extra material that he throws away.

RULE NUMBER 62

YOU MUST CHECK THE SHEETROCK COUNT.

Sit down with the plans and figure out the total square footage of the ceilings. Measure all the wall perimeters and multiply by eight and you will have the square footage of the walls. Don't forget the closets. Add them together and you have the total square footage. Add another 10% to cover waste. If there are a lot of angles. sloping ceilings and dormers, add another 5%. If the count you have been given is more than the answer you have arrived at somebody is trying to rip you off. Tell the contractor you think he made a mistake, and ask him to go count up again.

ROUGH DOOR OPENINGS

When your framers frame the inside door openings they use a standard height which assumes that an additional layer of flooring will be installed. If you are building on a slab or are using a single layer flooring you should coordinate the opening height with the framers. Usually I have them lower the opening 3/4ths of an inch. If this is not done, when the door is set in place the top trim may not cover the opening completely and patching is required. Or If the door frame is set higher there will be a visible space at the bottom of the jamb trim.

MAKING THE AGREEMENT

You must make certain requirements clear:
1. All sheetrock is to be screwed and no nails are to be used.
2. Large pieces more than three feet long are to be used.
3. Any full sheets left at the end are to be deducted from the count.

4. All joints, corners and screws are to receive three coats. If you don't specify, Sometimes the screws get only two coats. Sometimes the insides of the closets get only two coats. Sometimes the garage gets only one coat.

5. All compound joints and screw heads are to be sanded.

6. All scrap and waste is to be picked up and deposited where you say. (Probably a garbage hole or a container.)

7. All floors are to be swept up and left broom clean.

8. Globs of compound are to be scraped off wood and concrete floors.

SHEETROCK DELIVERY

When you order the sheetrock, tell the supplier how many sheets of each size and type you want for each floor, basement and garage. The supplier will load the truck accordingly so that it can be delivered to those areas in sequence.

The supplier will use a truck with a boom and cradle that is capable of lifting the sheet rock up in the air and next to a window. The sheetrock is standing on edge on the boom cradle and is manually drawn into the building.

When you are framing the house it is important to give consideration to how the sheet rock will be put inside after the sheathing and siding are applied. It will require a window with at least a four foot high unobstructed opening to get the sheetrock in. Sometimes the window sash, (The frames holding the glass) must be removed.

If there is not going to be an opening adequate for the sheetrock delivery then a piece of sheathing and/or siding must be omitted until the sheetrock is inside.

Experienced delivery men will put protection on the rough window sill to avoid damaging window channels. They will distribute the sheetrock among the rooms and stand it against outside walls. The sheet rock when standing together weighs a great deal. Dividing the material between the rooms spreads out this weight. Stacking at outside walls insures that the weight is carried on the floor joists close to the bearing walls.

When sheetrock is carried on a truck, often bundles of sheetrock strips are used as spacers. The deliverers will usually throw these off the truck and leave them where they fall. The amount is not insignificant. If you don't make sure they put this material back on their truck, you will get stuck with the clean up job.

CHAPTER 29

INSIDE FINISHING

During the sheetrocking, white dust gets everywhere. White footprints are tracked in and out of the house. Now is the time that the job be cleaned. If you have a vacuum or a shop-vac, it is helpful to clean up all the remaining dust on the floors and the window frames.

TRIMMERS

Many carpenters who do the framing for custom homes, also do the interior trim and finishing. However, if your framers only frame, you will have to hire what are referred to as "Trimmers". These carpenters specialize in the inside finish work such as installing underlayment, stairs and railings, doors, cabinetry, molding, closet poles and shelving.

UNDERLAYMENT

The first consideration is the flooring. If you are planning areas of wall to wall carpeting, because of the cost, most people do not install hardwood flooring in those locations.

Assuming the forgoing is the case, the first thing to be installed is the second layer of the flooring called the underlayment. First the entire floor surface should be covered with a layer of red rosin paper. This will prevent any squeaking between the layers. Particle board is the least expensive and most commonly used underlayment beneath carpeting. It is used in 5/8ths inch thickness. This board is pressed from what appears to be sawdust, and has a very smooth finish. The sheets should be installed in a staggered pattern so the joints are not continuous. It may be nailed or screwed down. If proper twist flooring nails are used there should be no future squeaking. However, there are now extension screw guns which permit the screwing down of underlayment from a standing position. If your carpenters have this equipment it makes the superior job.

What is nice about applying a second layer of flooring is that the result is a clean smooth floor which is easy to sweep. Where hardwood flooring is to be used, no underlayment is required but the red rosin paper should be installed.

BATHROOMS

For bathrooms that will have tiled floors, particle board should not be used because the adhesives used to glue down the tile can degrade the surface of the particle board, and cause the tiles to loosen. In this case you should use a 5/8ths inch thick plywood which is available as smooth on one side only. This cost less than smooth both sides.

THE KITCHEN

If the kitchen floor is to be tile or vinyl, the smooth one side plywood should be used. If vinyl is to be used the installers will use a special quick drying flash patch material to smooth over all the joints so they will not show through the vinyl.

If the floor is concrete the tile or vinyl can be glued down directly.

INTERIOR STAIRS

Stairs are usually not made on the job unless they are very unusual. There are companies that specialize in building stairs. They sell direct or through a lumber supplier. When the framing is completed it is the time to call in the stair builder who will take exact measurements for the height and width of the stairs.

There is a variety of styles and materials for stairs depending on how they will be positioned and finished. If the stairway is to be closed on both sides or if you want a more contemporary look, you can use stairs with closed sides. This means that the steps are formed between the side pieces which are called the "stringers". This is the kind of stair you often see coming down from a deck. In a contemporary design where the stairs are not enclosed underneath, an open tread design can be used. That is, there are no vertical pieces (risers) closing in the rear of the steps and you can see right through.

If the stairs are to be partly or fully open on one side you might use exposed treads where the open stringer supports the steps from underneath. This is a so called colonial style where each tread has a "Nose", to the side as well as the front. The stairway may be partly closed and partly open, requiring a combination of both styles.

The material the stairs are made from greatly affects the price. If you are going to have open tread stairs uncarpeted or with a carpet runner you will probably want the stairs to be made of oak with the wood nicely finished. If you use stairs with exposed side stringers and a "Waterfall" carpeting which fully covers the treads and risers, a hard pine is very nice and finishes well.

If your stairs are going to turn at a landing half way up, which is the case in a raised ranch or bi-level design, you must have the framers build the mid platform so the top of the platform is exactly half way between the floor levels. The stair builder will need this platform to be completed, in order to take his measurements.

You need to discuss with your stair builder how the stairs are to coordinate with the sheetrock finish. If there is a stringer against the wall a space may be allowed for the sheetrock to fit behind, or it may butt to the top of the stringer.

There are stairs with landings near the bottom that turn. This design allows a stair to be fitted into a smaller length. A normal stair requires about nine feet of forward space with at least another three feet to allow for dismounting at the bottom. If the space is smaller; a platform can be built two or three steps from the bottom with the final steps entering the room at a right angle to the stairway. I call these "Archie Bunker" stairs which were often seen in the memorable TV show.

There is also a variety of railing styles, including newel posts, railings, balusters etc. Follow you plans on this, and check with your stair builder. Railing materials are available at any good lumber yard and your trimmer should know how to install them.

Contemporary railings can be made in so many different styles and materials that you should rely on your plans or your designer for help here.

If you are planning to use a spiral stairway, you need to plan the clockwise or counter clockwise turn so the stairs start and end at the right place. Spiral staircases are available in wood or metal and in various diameters. The manufacturers will provide diagrams and advice for their installation.

THE SECOND FLOOR NOSE

For design purposes the second floor level is considered the top step. The stairs will be constructed with a nose piece that fits against the edge of the floor. The height of this nose must be made to come flush with the final floor.

For instance if the floor is to be hardwood, the nose should be raised by the thickness of the hardwood flooring to come flush. If the floor is to be tile, the nose height should be adjusted to the thickness of the tile. If the floor is to be carpeted, the nose should be flush with the underlayment. The carpet will be wrapped around the nose. Carpeting over a nose that is too high or too low creates a very dangerous footing to anyone starting down the stairs, and a serious accident could occur.

INTERIOR DOORS

Interior doors come in three general styles. There are flush doors which have a completely smooth surface and paneled doors which have recessed panels in various configurations. These are usually referred to as colonial. There are also louvered doors which allow air to pass through.

Flush doors are usually "Hollow core" which means that the door is hollow inside but contains a honeycomb core strengthener. Flush doors are available as solid wood but they are considerably more expensive and are generally not used unless sound proofing or break in resistance is desired.

DOOR MATERIALS

Doors come in natural wood, molded wood, plastic and steel. Each material has its advantages and disadvantages.

Before deciding on doors you must make a basic decision about your final decor. Do you want to have doors stained and finished to display the natural wood grains, or do you plan to paint the doors to coordinate with a decorating scheme?

The most commonly used and the cheapest doors are flush wood doors made of Luan mahogany. This wood has a rather porous grain and does not finish very well with varnish or urethane. The course grain makes it unsuitable for painting. Personally, I hate them.

If you want a good looking flush door that is smooth grained and takes stain and varnish very well, purchase flush doors made of birch. They have beautiful grain patterns and only cost a few dollars more than the Luan. They also take paint well and result in a smooth finish. Flush doors with other woods are available usually by special order. Order early and allow plenty of time for delivery.

Wood louvered doors are made with full louvers from top to bottom or as a half louvered door with inset panels on the lower half. I always liked to use louvered doors on linen closets or hall closets for their extra decorative quality.

The techniques of molding doors have improved enormously. You can buy a molded door embossed to look exactly like the more expensive wood paneled door. If you are planning to paint the doors these are a good choice.

Steel doors have generally been used on the exterior or for the door to the garage in order to meet fire code requirements. There are some steel louvered doors which are used at times on utility closets and laundry rooms but these to me, are cheap looking.

PRE-HUNG DOORS

Almost all doors can be purchased fully assembled and hung in the door jamb. No longer does the carpenter on the job have to build the jambs and hang the doors. The doors are pre-drilled for the latch sets and often supplied with the bolts already installed. The bolt is the part of the door latch that has the tongue which engages the striker plate on the jamb.

The carpenter sets the entire door and jamb in the rough opening, making the door level and square by using shims and spacers between the jamb and the jack studs. When the door is square the jamb is nailed into the studs.

DOOR OPERATION

The most common operation is the hinged door. Currently hinged doors are supplied with three hinges. These doors are supplied as "right handed" or "left handed". Sometimes they are referred to as "hinged left" or "hinged right". These are not the same thing. When you are ordering doors you must make sure that you and the person taking your order are using the same nomenclature. Usually doors are described from the inside. That is when you are standing inside a room, and you pull the door towards you to open it. If the knob is on your left it is called a left hand door. Sometimes it would be described as hinged right. If the knob is on your right it would be a right hand door or hinged left. Make sure that the person you are talking to is describing the door from the inside as you are. This is the customary way but sometimes it gets mixed up.

RULE 63

WHEN ORDERING DOORS DOUBLE CHECK THE NOMENCLATURE.

What could be worse that to have all your doors delivered only to find that they all operate opposite to what you wanted.

TYPES OF DOOR ASSEMBLIES

In addition to the standard hinged arrangement of a door other arrangements are available which are primarily used on closet doors.

Sliding doors are hung in pairs, and hang by rollers from a track at the top of the jamb. Either door can slide to the opposite side. The limitation of sliding doors is that only half of the closet can be opened at a time.

Double doors are also used on closets and are supplied prehung. In this arrangement both doors can be opened at the same time giving easier access. One of the draw backs of double doors is that if there is any slight warpage, the doors will not meet evenly at the bottom. Magnetic catches would normally be used to hold the doors closed at the top.

Another limitation is that double doors are usually not available for an opening greater than six feet. Closets that are going to be much wider than that should be divided into two closets with two sets of doors. Closet doors that are three feet wide may be inconvenient when opened into the room. To overcome this problem there are bi-fold doors. This would be a pair of doors where each door is split and hinged in the middle. The closing edges of the doors are guided by a track above. To open these doors a knob is mounted at the split in each door. When the knobs are pulled each door folds in half as it opens outward toward you and simultaneously slides to the side.

INTERIOR HARDWARE

There are five basic types of door hardware for interior use.
1. The passage set. This is an assembly with a knob on each side of the door which when turned unlatches the door.
2. The privacy set. These are used primarily on bedrooms. The inside knob has a push or turn latch which can lock the door from opening from the outside.
3. The bathroom set. This is the same as the privacy set except the outside knob is brass but the inside knob is chrome to match the bathroom fixture trim.
4. The lock set. This unit has a locking mechanism which must be opened with a key from the outside but can be locked with a turn handle on the inside.
5. The dummy knob. These are made to resemble a standard knob but do not turn. They are used on double closet doors or bi-fold doors as pulls.

Here is something that nobody ever tells you but can be very important if a child locks him or herself in the bathroom or a bed room, and then can't open the door. In the center of the outside knob on all privacy sets there is a small hole in the middle. Packed in every box containing the set there is a small tool which is a straight wire about three inches long with a handle bent at a right angle. This tool can be inserted into the hole in the center of the knob, and by pushing will unlock the door. Nobody ever seems to know this, and the carpenters always throw these "keys" away. Ask for them to be saved for you so that you can keep one available in a handy place.

DOOR SWING CONFLICTS

This problem often crops up in bedrooms where a closet door, if left open, obstructs the inward swing of the room door resulting in a clash. If you anticipate this problem, see if the shorter bi-fold door will eliminate the problem. If not, sliding doors on the closet will solve it. Mirrored sliding doors are readily available for closet doors which are both attractive and functional. If you are going to have a double entry bath be alert for swing conflict problems.

DOOR AND BASE MOLDINGS

The moldings that go around a door are referred to as casing. With a prehung door the casing is already applied to one side of the jamb. The casing for the opposite side is furnished in a package with mitered angles already cut.

There are generally in common use, two styles of door casing. One is called "clam shell" which is distinguished by a curve at the top blending back to the wall surface. This molding is regarded as "modern" but it has been around so long that it really looks dated. The other is called "Colonial" and has an "Ogee" molding cut at the top. (S shaped) This design is pretty universal and can go with Tudor and Mediterranean styles as well as Early American. For a more contemporary look I have been using square cut trim.

Base moldings come in the same styles as the casings but are a little bit wider. For specialty uses you can use rough sawn cedar or the more expensive 1x3 oak.

CORNICE MOLDINGS

Cornice moldings are those moldings which are run around the top of a wall against the ceiling. They were out of style for a long time but are now coming back. They come in a multitude of designs from very elaborate to quite simple. This type of specialty molding can be very expensive and that is doubtless why it fell into disuse. However, if you want to achieve an elegance there is nothing approaching the commanding look of really good cornice work.

Cornice molding is coming back into style largely because it can now be manufactured from molded plastic, greatly reducing the cost. There are also many styles of molding for chair rails and wainscoting crown. Wainscoting is wood paneling which is installed on the lower third of a wall. It can be barn boards or very ornate oak or mahogany paneled millwork. It is especially effective in a dining room, library, or den.

Other molded plaster forms which were so widely used in turn of the century homes are again available in molded styrofoam. Ceiling rosettes and even shell shaped wall niches are again being made.

These trim modules can add a distinctive look to a variety of designs besides Early American. They were borrowed from French and Italian motifs and can simulate those elegant styles.

WINDOW SILLS

A lot of windows in use today make the use of a wooden window sill optional. There are windows that mount flush to the inside wall and are finished with a casing frame like a picture. I personally do not like this style. When I am inside it makes me feel as though I were outside.

During my years as a builder I can only recall a single customer who ever said she had no interest in house plants. The vast majority of people seem to like plants, and particularly prize window sills on which they may be kept.

Aluminum widows that mount to the outside of the sheathing do not have a jamb the thickness of the wall as most wood windows do. As previously mentioned these windows can be finished by returning the sheet rock to the frame. This creates a good geometrical contemporary look, and the sheet rock sill may still be used for plants although some protection is probably advisable.

Lumber yards sell a pre-routed window sill stock which can be cut to the desired length. This lumber however is rather thin and narrow and makes for a cheap looking window sill.

For a very nice looking sill leave out the sheetrock return at the bottom of the window. Have your finish carpenter use a piece of 8 inch, by five quarter, clear pine. The sill should be notched into the opening to meet the frame of the window but go past on either side for a few inches. The edge may be chamfered, or routed with an "ogee" bit. The corners may be made square or are easily rounded. This sill may be stained and urethaned to a beautiful glossy or satin finish, and will make a very eye catching accent to your interior trim. For Tudor or Mediterranean styles, cut out a couple of "S" curved brackets and mount them under the sill to simulate supports. Treat the edges of the brackets the same as the edge of the sills. With the cost of the wood, the labor and the finishing, this will probably cost you around $100.00 a sill, but is well worth it in terms of the elegant effect.

FALSE CEILING BEAMS

False beams can do a lot to soften the severity of a cathedral ceiling or add warmth to the family room or den. Beams painted in an accent color can add interest to a kitchen or even bathroom ceiling. They are easy and inexpensive to do, and with a little imagination you can simulate many of the effects of more expensive post and beam construction.

If you want to have your beams in a natural wood finish there is nothing nicer than using real clear oak. However, this material can get pretty expensive. As an alternate I like to use "Inland cedar" either clear or number three with some knots. This cedar usually comes rough sawn on one side and smooth on the other so that you can choose the texture you like best. For contemporary styles I usually use the smooth side out but for Tudor and Mediterranean I like the rough side out.

Usually the false beams on a ceiling will run in the same direction as the ceiling joists or rafters so it is a good idea if you are going to have false beams, to have the framing carpenters install some "cats" (cross pieces) between the joists or rafters where the beams will be located to provide for fastening. Divide the ceiling into an equal number of spaces, usually between four and six feet wide to lay out the beams. For a really professional look plan for a half beam against each end wall.

I have seen the home improvement experts on television demonstrating the installation of ceiling beams by trying to first pre-fabricate the entire length of beam and then fasten it to the ceiling. This is definitely the hard way. The easy way is to have the carpenters snap the chalk lines on the ceiling where all the beams will be located. This gives you a chance to check the layout and see if it looks all right to you. You might decide to increase or decrease the number of spaces. Next nail a 2x4 on the center of each line for the length of the run. Joints may be made on top of the prepared cats. If you did not install any cats ahead of time, the 2x4s may be fastened to the ceiling using toggle bolts. After the 2x4s are all secure, nail your finish material cut into strips the same width as the 2x4 (3 5/8") along their length. Next nail on the side strips which have been cut to come down a half inch lower than the flat piece just installed. Square pieces may be installed as the final trim on either side of the beam where it meets the ceiling. In these simple steps you have created a very substantial and smart looking beam. All the parts for a single beam can be cut from a single 3/4 x 12 inch board which is really 11 1/2 inches wide.

For a more contemporary look install the side pieces first, even with the bottom of the 2x4. Then install the cap piece overlapping the side pieces but keeping back on each side a 1/4 to 3/8 inch reveal.

If you are putting up beams in a small room like a bathroom and you want a small beam, just use a 2x3 base piece.

CLOSET SHELVES AND POLES

There are a lot of prefabricated closet shelves, racks and organizers on the market which can increase the storage capacity and usability of your closets. If you are thinking of using this type of thing, look into it early in the game so that you can make sure your closets will be framed the right size.

Some people find these closet systems too expensive and prefer the traditional system which is quite simple.

A linen closet for instance, will usually have five shelves. The shelves are supported on 1x3 strips of wood nailed to the sides and rear of the closet. If you have saved the larger pieces of your roofing and sheathing left overs, you will have enough material for your shelving. Most builders only put 12 inch deep shelves in linen closets which usually wastes half of the available space. There is no law against a two piece shelf.

In a regular clothing closet there is usually a shelf at a height of six foot six inches with a pole suspended below for hangers. The shelf is supported in the same way as in the linen closet. 1 1/4 inch round pole material is carried by any lumber yard and can be cut to the correct length for the closet. A simple pair of "Rosette" sockets is mounted in the closet on the shelf support strips to hold the pole at either end. For shelves wider than three feet there is a metal shelf bracket with a pole support hook which should be mounted in the center to prevent sagging of the shelf and the pole. These brackets are quite inexpensive and should be used generously. Although much particle board is sold as shelving, in time it will sag terribly. Plywood is better. The wooden poles enable easy sliding of hangers. They can also be stained and look attractive.

CHAPTER 30

CABINETRY AND APPLIANCES

KITCHEN CABINETS

Kitchen cabinets are available in a very great variety of woods and styles, and range equally as much in price. This is another time when budget discipline should be exercised if it is a consideration. It is easy to get carried away in a kitchen showroom where cabinets are displayed under brilliant lighting with color coordinated backgrounds designed to appeal to the eye. All kitchen cabinets do pretty much the same job and do it well. True, there are some appealing features like built in cutting boards, lazy Suzans and pull out storage racks etc., but by and large the difference in cost is based on the difference in appearance and quality of materials. Good lighting and imaginative color and accessories can do more to enhance the beauty of a kitchen's appearance than expensively worked oak or cherry cabinets.

RULE 64
DESIGN YOUR KITCHEN AS A WHOLE.
DON'T GET CARRIED AWAY BY CABINETS ALONE.

For example, a laminate counter top can look just as good as expensive granite, tile or "Corian", and I assure you will be a whole lot easier to keep looking well. Beveled, contrasting colored edging can create a very custom look.

Laminate counter tops are available in an almost endless variety of colors and designs. Tile counters look great when they are new, but the edge tiles have a habit of falling off and breaking, and the tiles will crack if a heavy pot is accidentally dropped on them. It also takes a lot of work to keep the grout between the tiles clean and good looking.

Granite and marble are absolutely stunning, but despite what the sales person tells you they will get spots and rings and require a lot of care to keep them looking the way they look when they are new. They constantly need to be siliconed and polished and waxed and buffed.

Avoid very dark colors or imitation slate with rough surfaces as they are the devil to keep clean looking. Every pass of the cloth or sponge shows up as streaks when dry.

"Corian" is a durable, but pricy material. In my experience it water spots easily and always looks sloppy unless you make a career out of wiping it down with a dry cloth or paper towels after every wetting.

If you are looking for very modern design cabinets, the best I've seen are made in Sweden and Germany but, be prepared for high prices.

To stay at the low cost end there are a number of manufacturers that offer plain white contemporary styled cabinets. These cabinets are finished inside and out with a vinyl skin. An interesting counter top with perhaps some custom edging feature together with these cabinets can make a knockout kitchen at very reasonable cost.

COUNTER STYLES

Most kitchen suppliers offer a selection of the most popular laminate counter tops in what is called "Post Formed" style. In this type of counter the laminate is a continuous piece that rolls over the front edge with a little raised portion to keep liquids from running off, and then goes flat back until it curves up into the rear rail, curving again over the top. This design which eliminates joints is very easy to clean. However, these tops must be made in the factory and therefor are made only in the most popular laminate designs. If you find a post formed top style you like it will probably cost less than half of the usual square edge, made to order, counter top.

BUYING YOUR KITCHEN

There is no point to my describing every variety of kitchen cabinet because what you should do is go to several lumber yards or big chain home suppliers that have extensive kitchen display show rooms and get proposals. These showrooms can generate a kitchen layout by computer graphics so make sure you bring the plan or dimensions of your kitchen along. If you stick to national brand cabinets you cannot go far wrong, but please go to more than one place.

There are custom kitchen suppliers and contractors who will design and install your entire kitchen but this route can be very, very, expensive.

BATHROOM VANITIES

Kitchen cabinet companies also make vanity cabinets, so shop for these at the same time you look for your kitchen. A very popular idea for the master bath has been the double vanity with two sinks. This is a good looking set up. However, over the years I've asked clients if they ever used both sinks at the same time and I never found any one who said they did.

There are one piece vanity tops with the sink basin molded in. This is referred to as "cultured marble". My experience is that over time this material checks and cracks. I would recommend using drop in sinks in a vanity with a laminate top.

INSTALLATION

It is not particularly difficult to install kitchen cabinets, and your trim carpenters should be able to do it without any problem. Because floors and walls are not perfectly square the cabinets should be installed before any flooring or back splash.

The base cabinets must be leveled using small wedges. The slight space that results can usually be covered by the flooring especially if tile or some thicker material is used. If sheet vinyl which is quite thin is used on the floor, a bead of appropriately colored caulking can seal the crack. This is not something that is routinely done by flooring installers so you will have to specify it.

Often the back rail of the counter top does not fit perfectly flush to the wall because of undulations in the sheetrock, especially at corners. If you install a tile back splash, which is very practical and smart looking, the tile will cover any space. If no tile is to be used, and the fit is poor, the installers should cut the back rail into the sheetrock using a razor knife. A fine bead of caulking will finish the job neatly. If the variations are small, a bead of caulking alone will probably suffice.

It has been the tradition to install upper cabinets with their top at a height of seven feet above the floor. This tradition grew out of the practice of building a soffit above the cabinets one foot down from the ceiling. As previously mentioned, soffits are out of favor, but unless you specify otherwise, the top of the cabinets will be installed at seven feet high. Many women are not tall enough to reach the top shelves comfortably at this height. There is no law against installing the top cabinets six or eight inches lower. You must decide this however, when you are ordering your cabinets because the cabinets that fit over the refrigerator, stove and sink, will need to be less high by the amount you lower the installation.

APPLIANCES

Before you can finalize your kitchen design you must also decide what appliances you are going to have so that the appropriate spaces can be planned in the kitchen layout.

THE REFRIGERATOR

Most refrigerators will fit in a 33 inch wide space. However the very large double door units, especially those with the ice dispenser in the door, require a 36 inch space. Even if you don't plan on it initially, it's probably a good idea to provide a 36 inch refrigerator space anyway so that you will be able to fit one in the future.

Usually in kitchen layouts, the refrigerator, because it is deeper, is placed next to a wall. This can result in a problem. Modern refrigerators have wide shelves in the doors. If the refrigerator door can only open at right angles because of the wall, there will not be clearance enough to pull out the storage bins without them conflicting with the door shelves. The door needs to be opened more than a right angle. The new big units have double doors, so the problem can occur on either side. This can usually be solved by planning the refrigerator on the end of the run next to the door entering the kitchen. Often a two foot deep end wall is built at the end of the run. The refrigerator is deeper than the two feet, which is the same as the counter depth, and the doors will be able to swing back without obstruction.

This problem is relatively new, and is not being addressed in many kitchen layouts.

RULE 65

DO NOT PLAN YOUR REFRIGERATOR TO GO AGAINST A WALL.

A few years ago I bought a new double door refrigerator with the "in the door" ice dispenser for my home. I congratulated myself for having had the foresight to plan the kitchen originally with a 36 inch refrigerator space. However, when the unit was put in place, and we opened the freezer door it hit against the wall, and could not open enough to be able to pull out the shelves. Half of the opening is obstructed by the deep compartments in the door, and you have to be a contortionist to put things in an out of the freezer.

THE RANGE AND OVEN

There are basically two options regarding these appliances. You can use a separate range top and wall oven, or a conventional one piece range and oven.

A wall oven requires a large cabinet to hold it. This cabinet can add substantially to the total cabinet cost. It also takes up a lot of space. Some people want to have a double oven, and in that event the wall cabinet is essential, although unless cooking is you avocation, the need to use two ovens at the same time is rare. The separate range top is easily installed into the counter top. Wall ovens and range tops are usually only available as electric units.

The alternate is to use a conventional one piece range and oven unit. These come in both electric and gas units. The one piece electric units also offer the continuous cleaning and self cleaning features.

The continuous clean feature eliminates some oven cleaning but does not eliminate it entirely. The self cleaning oven virtually eliminates all oven cleaning, and is a very desirable feature in today's busy world.

THE MICROWAVE

Increasingly we are finding new uses for microwave ovens. It is invaluable for heating up leftovers and consumes much less energy than heating up the oven. More and more foods are being offered for microwave cooking and it has become an indispensable appliance. Any kitchen being planned today should certainly include a microwave oven. There are compact units designed to be installed under the cabinet above the range. These are fairly small units and are better for retro-fit than a new installation. Any microwave unit can be kept on the counter top and there are also top cabinets designed to hold them.

THE ONE PIECE MULTI UNIT

In recent years appliance manufacturers have been offering a one piece, free standing kitchen unit consisting of a normal range top and oven below, and a microwave oven and exhaust unit on top. These are very well designed and economical in cost, especially the ones offered by General Electric. The whole unit is arranged to plug into a special range outlet and is easily removed if necessary. I have used this type of unit extensively and recommend it highly.

THE EXHAUST HOOD

It is necessary to say a word about this very misunderstood appliance. When the idea of ventilating a kitchen first came along it was done by using through the wall exhaust fans installed as near to the stove as possible. These worked pretty well. Then the idea developed to put a hood over the stove to increase the efficiency. However the problem was, that rarely in a kitchen layout is the range on an outside wall. Although these exhaust hoods were ducted, few people realized that the ducts were simply blowing the greasy air up into the attic space. Additionally, the early models did not have filters, and over time the fan housings would become literally filled up with oil. Sooner or later the inevitable happened. Fires started in the grease laden ducts and a lot of homes burned down. I remember watching my neighbors house burn from this very cause. I went home and removed my exhaust fan only to find it full of dangerous grease and oil. I cleaned it out, and then disconnected it.

Unless a kitchen exhaust hood can be properly ducted to the outside with no more than six feet of duct it should not be used. If the duct is too long it will accumulate grease and oil.

Ductless exhaust hoods are now common and are provided with filters that remove the grease from the air and return the air to the room. This type of hood eliminates the waste of heat from blowing it outside, and also provides a system that can be easily cleaned and maintained. Although they may not be as good as exhausting to the outside, they can be mounted anywhere and are a lot safer.

THE DISHWASHER

Dishwashers are offered with a multitude of options, push buttons and cycles. My research has shown that although these extra features seem initially attractive, people that have them say they never use them. Most people prefer the basic wash, rinse and hold cycles. The extra cycles can add significantly to the price, and increase the possibility of electrical control malfunction.

Often the dish washer is positioned in a kitchen layout where it will fit the easiest, not where it will be the most convenient. If you are right handed the dishwasher should be to the right of the sink. If you are left handed there is no law against the dishwasher being on the left of the sink where it will be more convenient to you.

THE GARBAGE DISPOSALL

This is essentially a grinder installed in the sink drain. It is used to grind up and dispose of food wastes and requires the water to be running to operate. There are several draw backs. Only a very small amount of the waste we need to dispose of is food waste, so the advantage of the unit is small. If you are on a septic system the food waste may overload your system, hardly worth the small convenience.

In general I believe it is bad practice to ever put food waste and cooking waste down the sink. It only contributes to grease build up, and eventual maintenance problems. Grease and oil from cooking should be saved in a separate container for disposal, and never allowed down the drain.

THE GARBAGE COMPACTOR

Most of our household waste is paper and packaging materials. If we are already separating out plastic and glass for recycling, probably more than 90% of our garbage waste is paper. Paper waste takes up a lot of space and necessitates emptying the kitchen garbage container frequently. A Compactor can crush down this waste into a very small volume, making taking out the garbage, a much less frequent and easier chore.

ORDERING CABINETS AND APPLIANCES

The biggest problem in this area is timeliness. Often things are ordered only to find out that they are out of stock, and the next shipment from the manufacturer will not be in for eight weeks. This happens more often than you would believe. This equipment should be ordered well in advance of the time it is needed. Allow at least eight weeks.

Another problem is to receive equipment at the last minute and find that cabinets are damaged.

On more than one occasion I ordered appliances from a major national retailer which were defective. I had occasions when people moved into their new condo, turned on the oven, and it exploded. Another time a brand new refrigerator was plugged in and wouldn't run. What a hassle to get replacements from that company. I learned to get my appliances in time to test them out, and replace them if defective. However, I never had those kind of problems with GE equipment. While others took eight weeks for delivery, GE never took more than a week.

RULE 66

ORDER CABINETS AND APPLIANCES AT LEAST EIGHT WEEKS IN ADVANCE.

APPLIANCE SERVICING

In the course of most building, the manuals, directions and guarantee cards that come with all appliances get thrown away by the workmen. Make sure that when appliances are unpacked these materials are given directly to you. Most appliance delivery services, for a few extra dollars, will uncrate the appliances, and deliver them to their permanent location. They will also remove all the empty cartons and crates. This service is well worth the few extra dollars it costs, and can save serious damage to newly installed vinyl flooring.

Make sure you send in the warrantee card, and save the shipping ticket to prove the time the appliances were delivered. Keep this where you can find it when you need it. Most major companies are very good about servicing appliances under guarantee if you can establish when the appliances went into service. If you sent in the warrantee card they will have the information in their computer when you call.

OUTLET WAREHOUSES

If you live in an area where there are any outlet warehouses of major retailers, you may be able to save a bundle by buying slightly damaged appliances. You might get a refrigerator at half price because there is a dent in the side which occurred during shipping. If that side will not be exposed in your kitchen, you can make the saving.

CHAPTER 31

FLOORING

HARDWOOD FLOORING

If hardwood flooring is to be used in some or all areas, it should be installed over the red rosin paper the same as for the underlayment. This prevents squeaking caused by the two layers rubbing together.

Hardwood flooring is usually installed by a special subcontractor who will lay the flooring, then sand it and finish it. Hardwood flooring should be laid right away as the interior trim is being done, but should not be sanded and finished until after all interior painting and decorating is completed.

Generally hardwood flooring is made of oak and used in random lengths ranging from 1 to 6 feet. Good practice is never to have adjacent boards with butt joints next to each other. The boards are made with tongues and grooves, and are nailed through the tongues so that no nails are visible when the work is finished. Oak flooring is available in several grades or qualities, and the price varies accordingly.

In some colonial designs random width pine flooring may be used. Maple flooring is also used both in wide board form and tongue and groove. When wide board flooring is used, generally it is nailed from the surface using hand wrought nails to imitate the original method.

Hardwood flooring is available as prefinished boards in a variety of woods and stain colors. It is also widely used in parquet squares in a great variety of patterns and stain colors.

If your sub flooring is a concrete slab, conventional hard wood board flooring cannot be installed. There are methods of imbedding nailers or building up a platform, but they are difficult and costly.

Prefinished hardwood parquet flooring squares can be laid directly on concrete and set with appropriate mastic. This is a much more satisfactory and economical way of installing hardwood over concrete.

TILE FLOORING

If you have never been to one, a trip to a modern tile showroom will astound you.

Magnificent and beautiful tile is made in almost every country in the world. The principal ones are Italy, Spain and Brazil, but you'd be surprised at what you can get from Ireland or the Netherlands for example.

Tile flooring comes as small pieces glued to a square mat, or individual pieces in squares and oblongs up to 12 inches. They can be plain colors with a shiny glaze or a matte glaze. Tiles are painted in an almost endless variety of floral and geometric patterns. Many have companion border and edging tiles.

For use in bathrooms many of the larger tiles do not have companion base and corner pieces. Some are available with crown and cap pieces and others are not. However if you improvise and combine, the possibilities are almost endless.

If you are building on a slab, a tile floor is a very good solution for the kitchen. It can hide the rough spots, cracks and imperfections in the concrete which can be a problem when laying vinyl. As a kitchen floor, tile is very easy to care for. Spills are easily wiped up, and all that is needed is an occasional damp mopping. A tile floor can be kept looking spiffy by running a vacuum cleaner over it. The rotating brush polishes and shines the tile.

Don't overlook the possibility of a tile floor in your entry hall. Not only is very practical for wet and snowy feet, but can be stunningly beautiful.

Unglazed Mexican clay tile, quarry tile and slate tile, are a horse of a different color. These are porous materials that must be sealed. They are the very devil to clean when the construction is finished, and it is time to apply the sealer. It's a tough hands and knees job with a lot of paper towels. These materials will hold moisture. They must be protected until they are thoroughly dry before the sealer can be applied. The sealer will wear off and the floor must be periodically refinished. If you have a dog who wets a floor with sealer, the sealer will turn white and create an ugly stain which cannot be removed without stripping the floor. If you are determined to have this kind of floor then keep every body off it, no easy task in construction, and apply three of four coats of sealer. When the sealer is hard, apply several coats of good quality paste wax.

MARBLE AND GRANITE

These materials are available in 12 inch squares and can be used and laid in the same way as tile. Your tile showroom should have samples of these as well.

A gorgeous bathroom can be created by using marble on the walls and floors. With a little imagination you can have a "Roman Bath" fit for Caesar.

VINYL FLOORING

In residential applications the use of vinyl flooring in individual squares has given way to the use of sheet material, largely because it is less costly, but also because many new patterns and designs have been developed. The key factor in laying vinyl flooring is to have a perfectly smooth surface underneath. If there are cracks, joints and knots they will show through the vinyl in a short time.

When laying vinyl on concrete as well as wood, careful preparation must be made of the base surface. Flash patching and smoothing is a must. The second very important factor is cleanliness. The slightest lump, speck of plaster or wire clipping under the vinyl will be very apparent in the finished job. Vacuuming of the base surface is highly recommended.

If the floor surface requires a lot of preparation the vinyl installers may ask for extra payment. This is pretty traditional, and they are entitled to extra if they have to spend a lot more time preparing the floor.

One disadvantage I find to vinyl flooring is that it seems to be easily marked and scuffed by rubber heels. These marks are not easy to remove and are quite unsightly on a light colored floor.

WALL TO WALL CARPET

Wall to wall carpet is a very popular floor covering, and for good reason. It makes a colorful, warm and elegant finish to any room and is by far the lowest cost flooring you can put down. As previously mentioned, if you are going to put down wall to wall carpeting there is no need to invest in an expensive hardwood floor underneath. Foam urethane padding retains it's springiness and will not rot or mildew like the old fiber padding.

The quality of carpeting is based upon the number of fibers to the square inch in the weave. The thicker the carpet the nicer it appears. The cost is relative to this fiber density.

The new space age fibers wear very well and resist staining and mildew. Carpet is much less work to clean than other floorings. It requires only a once over with a vacuum cleaner, while hardwood for instance, requires regular dusting and polishing.

BUYING CARPET

Carpet is sold at a price per square yard with an adder per square yard to cover the cost of padding and installation. Dealers will usually figure 3/8 inch padding but for a few pennies more you should use 1/2 inch padding which makes a much nicer job.

When you have made your selection the carpet salesman will want to measure up the job to determine how many square yards will be required. He will come to the house and carefully measure the dimensions of each room and then tell you he will lay the job out on paper to see exactly how much carpet is needed. He will come back to you with the final yardage figure multiplied by the cost per yard for the carpet, padding and installation, and ask you to sign an order, and give him a deposit so that he can order the material from the mill.

RULE 67

YOU MUST DOUBLE CHECK THE YARDAGE FIGURE.

Sorry to say, but in my experience most carpet salesmen over estimate the amount of yardage required for the job. Customers accept the yardage figure and never know that they are being overcharged, sometimes as much as 10 to 15%.

Carpet men are a lot like the sheetrock men. They will try to avoid making seams wherever possible to save the labor. For instance, in measuring a bedroom they will measure all the way into the closet even though it means that a big piece becomes waste. They could measure half way into the closet and piece out the rest with the waste. Who cares if there is a seam in the bottom of a closet. Anyway, a properly made seam is virtually invisible.

Another usual trick is to not install the padding under the carpet in the closets. This saves them only pennies yet unless you specify that you want padding in the closets you won't get it. If you complain afterwards they will tell you that the installation price does not include padding the closets.

Most carpet comes in 12 foot widths. If you lay out the carpet the long way in a ten foot wide room, the two feet cut off will be waste. The run could be made two feet shorter and the cut off piece seamed onto the end. Most installers will tell you that turns the carpet ninety degrees, and that the grain will not match. If the seamed area is in a high traffic location the seam may become a little visible. However, in most cases the two feet at the end of the room will be under the bed or other furniture and it will not matter.

If you are using the same color in more than one room then pieces from one area can be used in another. If the hallways and stairs are to be carpeted in the same color, lots of small pieces can be used up on the stairs by using the cut and tack method rather than using one continuous piece down the stairs in what is called a waterfall. When either of these methods is used it's hard to tell the difference in the final result.

Figure out the square footage of each area to be carpeted by color. For the area of stairs multiply by three. Divide by nine to determine the total number of square yards required for each color and add 5% for waste. If the estimate yardage you have been given is much more that, it is probable you are being ripped off. Any good carpet layout man should be able to keep his waste within 5%. If you disagree with the figures given you, ask him to measure again, and show you his layout plan. There must be a layout plan because the installers need to have it to follow, so that they will cut and lay the carpet the way it was planned.

It is also advisable to be present when the installers come and make sure that they know which color goes in which room. Many mistakes are made in this regard because of confusion over which bedroom is which.

Make sure you specify that the installers are to pick up and remove all scrap padding and carpet except for any large pieces that you want to keep as extra mats or future repair material. The scrap and waste from a carpet job can be substantial. You will still be left with a big vacuuming job because installers never clean up their work. A new car dealer won't give you your new car covered with mud and dirt, but a carpet dealer will give you a new carpet job covered with small scraps, thousands of threads and waste staples.

Lots and lots of fluff comes out of new carpet. If you vacuum with a conventional cleaner you will be emptying the bag every half a room. A commercial tank type vacuum is much better even if you have to rent one to clean up.

CHAPTER 32

PAINTING AND DECORATING

STAINING

In the final finishing, if there is to be any stained wood it should be done first so that any smears or drips can be painted over. Stains will act very differently depending on the wood they are applied to, and the method of application. If you have a particular look in mind, it should be tested on some scrap wood to see if it is what you really want. Some stain colors work better than others, and have the ability to look similar on various types of wood. Suppose you want to stain a birch door, with pine trim, and have it match. experimentation is definitely called for. A good painter, experienced in staining, will have some ideas on how to proceed.

If you want a dark stain look with rich highlights, such as you would do for a Tudor or Spanish design, I highly recommend a particular stain with which I have always had excellent results. The color is called "Jacobean" and it is made by "Minwax". This is a rich color with a lot of life.

Sometimes colors like "Walnut" for example, that look good on the sample, are dead and lifeless on architectural work, and are best reserved for furniture.

The best technique I have seen for staining flush doors is to apply the stain with a roller, but use the roller in your hand with a wiping stroke, don't actually roll it. This is an excellent method for attaining uniform application.

Stain tends to raise the grain in woods so for best results after the stain is dry the work should be lightly sanded or rubbed with a fine steel wool. A final coat of polyurethane will sharpen the colors and add life. You can use the urethane with a gloss finish or a satin finish. Most people will automatically say satin finish, but I have come around to the opinion that a gloss finish is better looking. Of course on rough sawn wood use only the stain. The stain on rough wood usually will be much darker so again, you should experiment first.

252

PAINTING CEILINGS

Light entering from windows usually casts across the ceiling and has the ability to make seams, joints and imperfections stand out. This effect is even more apparent on cathedral ceilings. Where clerestory windows are used it is the most apparent.

To hide this undesirable look it is common to use textured paint on ceilings. There are flock type spray paints that do a good job in this regard, but you might feel they give the ceilings a too commercial look. A good alternative is to use sand paint. That is ordinary ceiling white paint to which some fine sand has been added. When dry, the paint has a rough, slightly gritty look which is attractive. Sand paint however, is best applied by brush rather than roller, and should be done by someone experienced in sand painting, so that the brush strokes will appear in a random pattern.

WALL PAINT

The best advice is, use a good quality paint. Cheap paints are not washable and rub off easily.

By the time your job is done you will find that the newly painted walls have all kinds of smudges, marks and fingerprints. Touching up these marks using the paint will result in a detectable patch, because the paint will not dry to a perfect match on paint that has already been dry for a while.

The best procedure is to wash off all the smudges possible, and use touch up only when the mark will not wash off. I find a good spray cleaner like "Fantastick" and a damp sponge, will remove more than ninety percent of the marks. You will not believe how many of these marks there will be, but they will be everywhere in every room.

If you have used a good quality paint these marks will come off easily and will not leave any permanent sign.

COLOR

Nothing can make a house more attractive and interesting than the use of color, yet the vast majority of people are afraid to commit to a decision. They say, "I'll just use off white. I can always paint a color later on". Of course they never do. Look in your home magazines and Architectural Review, and you will see lots of ways to use color effectively.

The first area for color choice is in the carpeting. Try not to do the whole house in earth colors. Be a little bolder, you won't regret it. Lots of people choose a dark color carpeting because they think it will not show the dirt as much. Dark carpet is the worst. Every piece of lint and speck from the newspaper shows up on dark carpet and you'll be forever vacuuming. Don't be afraid of a light color in the living room. Today's miracle fibers resist soiling and are very easy to clean. Try to vary the colors in the bedrooms to make them distinctive and more interesting.

Here is one of my favorite color tricks: Choose a color that complements the carpet color and apply it in a pastel shade to the long wall in the room opposite the windows. Let's say for example that you have chosen a cinnamon color for the carpet. Use a complementary color like light coffee on the long wall and do the other walls in off white. You will find this adds a very nice color accent to the room without overwhelming it. If you want to change it later you only have to paint one wall. If you have used aluminum windows without wooden jambs, and your sheetrock returns to the window frame at right angles to the walls, paint the cheeks of the returns with the same color you used on the opposite wall. You will be amazed at how much more interesting the windows look, and how the color accent enhances the room.

BUYING COLORED PAINT

If you are going to use a colored paint try to choose your color from the paint chart of factory mixed colors. This paint will have a much better covering ability than a color you have mixed in the store. In order to facilitate the mixing, the paint base that is used in the store is not the same as the base used in the factory. Factory mixed paints should cover with no more than two coats while store mixed paints may require several more. I have found it necessary to use as many as five coats with a particular deep blue before the color was uniform and without streaks.

If you are going to use a store mixed color, use your regular off white for the first coat. This will cover most of the spackle marks and make the next coat of the color a lot more even and smoother.

When extra coats of paint are needed, the painter wants to get paid extra and he will be entitled to it.

Remember that off white paint is really a color and must be carefully chosen. Off whites are usually made with yellow and tan tones or gray and blue tones. If you have beautiful stained wood work, don't use an off white based on blue or gray, it won't look well. Use the one with the slight ecru tone. It may take a little looking and playing with the samples, but it's an important factor. Many a room has turned out as a disappointment because the wrong tone of off white was used, but nobody realized that was the reason.

WALL PAPER

Don't overlook the decorative beauty of wall paper. Nothing can make a richer looking dining room than a fine wall paper. If you want to be more conservative try wall paper in the half bath. You won't believe how great it will look and maybe you will be encouraged to use wall paper in the master bath.

If you are going to wall paper, give the walls a coat of your off white paint as a primer.

ARCHITECTURAL MIRRORS

This is another item that is almost always overlooked but can make a tremendous difference if used correctly. A full mirrored wall behind the whirlpool, blending with marble tile can be very very exciting.

If you have a fireplace that projects into the room, mirroring the walls to the left and right sides will make an outstanding effect.

CHAPTER 33

FINISHING UP

PATIOS

Patios are most feasible when your construction is a modified slab. They are usually positioned behind the house and accessed from the kitchen and/or dining room.

The most important requirement for a successful patio is that the ground is adequately compacted. A concrete patio for a house on slab can be poured at the same time as the slab is poured. The gravel fill and compaction should be exactly the same as for the slab. The patio is formed usually with 2x4s set to the proper size and elevation. I recommend that the elevation of the patio be six inches lower than the slab. This will make a comfortable step down.

If you are in a cold climate, a concrete patio can heave and crack. The best way to control this is to divide the patio into squares or rectangles about 6x6 or 6x8 feet. Half inch thick l x 4s of cedar make very good separators and will not rot out in the future. Plastic joint separators are also available. Make sure the masons put reinforcing wire in the patio. This is a step that is frequently left out as not being necessary. If you have cold winters it definitely is necessary.

Many masons like to finish patios and walks with what is called a broom finish, and is actually made by passing a stiff broom over the concrete. It is a lot easier to do than a smooth trowel finish. The rough surface is fine for walks where better traction when wet or slippery is desirable. However, if you like to walk out on your patio in your bare feet you may find the rough finish uncomfortable, so I recommend a smooth trowel finish. Make sure that the patio is constructed with a minimum of a quarter inch pitch to the foot sloping away from the house.

RULE 68

FINISHING UP

YOU MUST DOUBLE CHECK THE PITCH ON THE PATIO FORMS BEFORE POURING.

For some unknown reason patios frequently turn out without adequate pitch. Masons seem to be careless about this. There is nothing worse than a patio with a big puddle of water in the middle after it rains.

Patios can also be constructed of brick or flag stones. This is a lot more expensive than poured concrete but of course is a richer look. The best way is to set the brick or flagstone in mortar on top of a concrete base. Bricks are a special type called "Pavers" which are made to endure frost. Patio brick or pavers are available in a variety of colors and shapes which interlock forming many interesting patterns. They are laid tightly together with no mortar joints.

Flag stones are not perfect in size and are laid with conventional mortar joints.

A less costly option to laying a patio on concrete is to lay the bricks or stones on sand or fine stone chips which is carefully leveled and smoothed. It is essential that the material beneath the sand be a good layer of gravel to insure sufficient drainage.

A common problem with this installation that leads to heaving and uneven patios, is that the sub soil has too much clay and holds too much water which freezes and expands.

By far the biggest problem in laying this kind of patio and walkways as well, is that the underneath soil or ground, is not sufficiently settled and compacted. Many urban renewal projects have used brick paver sidewalks to simulate an older style. An examination of this work a few years later reveals the many instances where the walks have settled, sometimes creating dangerous conditions. This problem is frequently observed in the aprons built around newly constructed swimming pools. If possible, wait six months to a year to allow ground to fully settle before building this type of expensive surface.

WALKWAYS

The considerations described for patios apply equally to the construction of walkways. Walkways should have a joint approximately every four feet to keep them from cracking. In cold climates a certain amount of heaving and settling will take place with the walks. A good well drained gravel sub base at least eight inches thick will do a lot to minimize adverse effects.

Some people like to construct a more casual walkway by laying stones or concrete circles as sort of stepping stones. Sometimes the spaces in between are grass or crushed stone. Keeping this grass trimmed or the weeds out of the crushed stone can become a very burdensome task, and what seemed easy at first becomes an onerous problem later.

DECKS

In most ranch designs and bi-level designs the main living level is elevated above the final grade of the ground, and a patio is not an option. The popular solution is to build a wooden deck. Decks can be made in an endless variety of shapes and designs and are considerably more costly than a concrete patio.

Decks must be constructed from non rotting woods. Redwood is very good for durability but as previously mentioned it will discolor and blacken even if stained. Most people today use pressure treated lumber to build decks. Pressure treatment forces a solution of copper sulfate or other preservatives into the wood fibers which keeps them from rotting. If uncoated, pressure treated lumber will discolor and look very shabby in a short time. The problem is that the treated wood does not absorb paint and stain very well, and it tends to weather off in a few years. The vertical parts like the railings will hold the stain a lot longer, but the flat decking will loose the stain in about three years.

The best alternative I have found to these problems is to use a variety of eastern pine which has a very high resin content. I used it in full dimensional rough sawn form which I obtained from a rural saw mill. The heavy thick timbers and boards make a very impressive looking deck, far from the flimsy looking jobs you usually see. The rough sawn pine soaks in stain very well and will last a very long time without rot or decay.

CONCRETE RETAINING WALLS

When building on a sloping lot as was discussed in an earlier chapter, it may be useful to construct one or more retaining walls to control the changes in level from a higher area to a lower area. For example this might be where the ground behind a ranch house is higher but must be stepped down at the end of the house to come down to a driveway level that permits entry to a garage in the basement. Often the most useful way to build such a wall is to incorporate in it, a short flight of steps. The steps in the case given, would be at the corner of the foundation with a wall behind the steps running parallel to the axis of the house and gradually sloping downward.

The best possible way to construct such a wall and steps is to use poured concrete. It is important that the wall at the bottom or base be at least three times wider than at the top to prevent it tipping over from the action of frost.

Retaining walls that are built vertically and with the same thickness, if subjected to freezing temperatures will eventually fall over. Probably every body at some time or other has observed such a wall which is tipping forward and appears ready to fall.

When the face of a wall is exposed, the cold easily penetrates and freezes the soil behind the wall. The soil will expand with tremendous force and tip the wall slightly forward. The movement may be so slight that it is not noticed the first few years. When the frost behind the wall thaws out, the wall does not right itself, instead the dirt behind the wall just settles down into the space created by the shift in the wall. When the earth settles this forms a depression which will hold more water and allow it to soak down into the ground. The more water in the soil that freezes, the more expansion, and the more resultant movement in the wall. This process will repeat every year until the wall has been tilted so far that it falls over. Making the concrete wide at the bottom increases the weight and leverage of the wall so that if it has tipped slightly, when the frost thaws the wall will settle back to it's original plumb.

FIELDSTONE RETAINING WALLS

If the stone is available, in many ways laying up a field stone retaining wall is a lot easier than poured concrete. It can be done by hand as time permits. It can be curved or straight, sloped or level as the contours of the ground require.

The secret of building a successful fieldstone wall that will not eventually fall over is to tilt the wall back against the earth at least 15 or twenty degrees. In that way, if the wall has been pushed forward by the frost, it will settle back by it's weight to it's original position when the frost thaws. Depending upon the amount of patience you have, these walls can be very beautiful and require no mortar to set the stones. The best way is to lay out a lot of pieces of stone around you so that you can look them over, and select the piece of the best size and shape to fit in the next position. You might want to try more than one piece before you are satisfied. Patience is everything in achieving a good looking result.

THE DRIVEWAY

To have a good long lasting driveway it is important to have a good base. When first entering the site for development, we previously indicated that if the ground was soft and unstable, a base of rock tailings should be put down. On top of the tailings or the under level of soil if reasonably firm, a good base of ROB gravel should be put down. In place of the gravel a base of finely graded stone usually referred to as "Item 4" to identify it for road specifications, can be used.

The base should be put down early in the job so that the constant passage of trucks over it will compact it fully as the job progresses. When ready to pave, and I am assuming that we will pave with black top which is now almost universally used for this purpose, the base should be finally graded and pitched, material added if needed, and then rolled with a heavy paving roller.

For residential driveways the standard is a three inch thick black top layer of fine aggregate. The three inches should be the final thickness after placing and rolling. Sometimes a two inch base coat is put down of a coarser material, and then a one inch finishing layer of the finer material. This will increase the cost and is really not necessary for a residential driveway.

A new driveway should not be driven on for at least twenty four hours. Thereafter care should be taken not to turn the wheels of vehicles while standing stationary on the black top. This will cause a scuffing scar on the surface. For the first six months vehicles should be driven in and out in as straight a line as possible. If maneuvering is necessary, wheels should be turned gradually only while the vehicle is in motion.

Chair legs, bench legs, and kick stands of motorcycles will all indent new blacktop during the first six months.

Remember, if drainage or discharge from downspouts is directed onto the driveway, the driveway should be sloped or channeled to drain this water to the side so that in freezing weather the driveway will not become ice glazed from these runoffs.

LANDSCAPING

Nothing will finish off and beautify a new home more than good landscaping. If the budget can handle it, get the work done professionally. I strongly advise to use an established nursery landscaper to do the work. These people will guarantee the shrubs they put in, and are equipped to do the work in a proper and professional manner. They will have the equipment and the man power to get the job done in a reasonable time.

There are many independent landscapers around who operate out of a pick up truck. They may give you a little better price but often they don't have the manpower to get the job done and wind up coming and going and coming and going. You have put so much effort into building this house that you shouldn't fade out in the home stretch.

FINISHING UP

THE LAWN

The lawn should be put in by people who have the proper equipment to rake out the stones, and smooth and grade the lawn. The final result will only look as good as the preparation. A lawn that is sloped and graded smoothly is a thing of beauty. For best results the soil should be rolled after seeding. A lawn with rough spots, and ups and down will never look right. Remember doing it the second time will cost a lot more than doing it right the first time. Your nurseryman will know the variety or mix of grass seed that does well in your local climate.

When a new lawn is seeded it should be covered by mulch hay which will keep the moisture in the soil and help the seed germinate quickly. Fast development of the grass is desirable because it will prevent the erosion of the barren soil when it rains. Some contractors have equipment which spray on a seed and hay mixture. Others may seed by hand but have equipment to chop and blow on the hay. Either method is satisfactory.

Some small operators who don't have the equipment, will apply the hay by hand, by shaking it out. This is OK too but sometimes they will use straw instead of hay because it is cheaper. Straw is all right but it must be removed after the seed germinates, otherwise it will kill the new grass because it does not decompose. Good mulch hay is much finer, and will quickly decompose adding to the top soil, but straw will require a lot of raking and work to remove, which your landscaper has no intention of coming back to do.

To have a great lawn it is important to start right and don't let, crabgrass, weeds and dandelions get established. I highly recommend using a lawn service the first couple of years, that will come in and put down the necessary chemicals at the proper time to build a beautiful lawn.

FINAL CLEANUP

In many areas there are cleaning services that will come in an clean a new home at a reasonable price. If you want to do it yourself it usually amounts to a good days work for one person.

You will need a good vacuum cleaner with attachments, a spray cleaner such as Fantastik or 409, and a window cleaner like Windex. You will also need a razor scraper and a lot of paper towels.

Start with the vacuum attachment and clean from the top down. Take the dust off the tops of doors and door frames. clean the tops of the kitchen cabinets and vacuum out the insides of all the cabinets and drawers which will contain a lot of wood dust and chips from the installation.

If there is dried spackle in the bath tub, and on other fixtures do not scrape. Soak with water until it softens. For the marble and tile floors, wash them with plain water, then wipe and shine them with paper towels. For any dirt spots use the spray cleaner first. For chrome fixtures to look shiny, wipe them dry with paper towels.

Remove all the labels from the windows by pealing off as much as possible. If there is paper still stuck to the window do not scrape. All the glues used are water soluble. Spray them with the Windex, and then you will be able to scrape them off a few minutes later.

If there is spackle on the edges of your aluminum window frames do not scrape or you will remove the paint. Wipe with a wet sponge and the spackle will quickly soften. Wash it off and dry with paper towels.

Counter tops and appliances are easily cleaned with the spray cleaner and a damp sponge.

If you put down sheet vinyl on the floor it will probably have black printing on it. This ink is water soluble and comes off very easily. Clean all spots with the spray cleaner and then mop the floor down with clear water.

Vacuum off all the window sills and go around the base molding. When all the items above the floor are done you are ready to do the carpet.

Pick up all the scraps and small pieces you can so that they will not clog the vacuum. You need an edge wand attachment to run around the carpet at the base molding where it is secured on the tackless strip. Thousands of short threads will be in this groove from the cutting of the carpet. These threads are everywhere, but are easily vacuumed up. As mentioned before, a lot of fuzz and fluff comes out of new carpet and will fill your vacuum very fast. Small clippings lodged in the suction hose will collect this fuzz and clog the hose. You must constantly check that the suction is not clogged, and that the bag is not full. Otherwise you will do a lot of work for nothing. All of the dirt you have to clean up in a new house is dust and soil. there are no greasy deposits. That's why I recommend using clear water on the floors to avoid the extra work of getting up all the suds and the dull film which usually results when the floor dries. If the floors do look dull, run the vacuum cleaner over them. The rotating brushes do a good job in shining up a non greasy floor.

CHAPTER 34

SCHEDULING

Now that we have gone through the sequence of all the steps in building a house, we should turn our attention to the proper scheduling of steps and events so that the work is finished expeditiously, and well. Remember, the longer it takes, the more interest you will pay the bank, and the more taxes you will pay on a house you can't live in. If material prices are rising as they have done for lumber in recent years, your costs can grow higher than they should, if the job takes too long.

All amateurs, and most professionals do not use an organized progress schedule, and just run the job by the seat of their pants. How often have you noticed a construction job that seems to have stopped in the middle and then resumes a few weeks or even months later. The chances are that the delay was the result of poor planning.

THE CRITICAL PATH

Every construction job has what is called a critical path. The critical path is that sequence of events where each step to be performed cannot be commenced until a prior step has been completed. For example, you cannot build your foundation until your footings are finished. Those would be two items in the critical path.

In big construction projects there are sophisticated computer programs that plot the critical path and every item of the construction operation. Material delivery times are integrated with advance ordering times indicated. Many high rise building are started before all of the designs for the building are even completed.

Concomitant tasks and steps in the construction that can be done at the same time as a step in the critical path are done in parallel scheduling.

You don't need a computer to figure out your schedule. If you like, you can sit down with a large sheet of graph paper and plot out your entire schedule. It is not really difficult to do. Down the left side of your sheet list all of the individual steps of the construction. Across the top show the days during which the construction will take place, numbered in numerical order rather than calendar date. Place an X in each box on the line representing a particular part of the work, such as "Wiring", under the day or days on which that work is to be done. You can see immediately which trades you need to have ready to go, and that you need to know from them how long it will take to perform each part of the work that they are to do.

MAKING YOUR SCHEDULE

I considered preparing a critical path schedule and including it in this text, but I think that it will be much more instructional if you prepare the schedule, and I talk you through the steps. In this fashion you will have to participate in the thinking and the choices, and you will very easily learn the process.

For explanatory purposes I will assume that we are building on a gently sloping wooded lot requiring a well and septic system, and the construction will be on a modified slab.

THE CRITICAL PATH STEPS

These steps will each have an underlined heading. If a step is concomitant, it's heading will not be underlined.

GET THE BUILDING PERMIT

The obvious and necessary first step. Some locales don't even want you to cut a tree before you have your permit, and you don't want to get off on the wrong foot with the bureaucrats. So put this on your first line.

MARK OUT HOUSE AND DRIVEWAY LOCATION

In order to know where you are going, you need to get into the lot with your tapes, measure off from the lot line stakes that you have already had placed, and tie some surveyors ribbons in the trees and/or bushes to mark out the general area for the house, and the path of the driveway. This is line 2.

CLEAR AND GRADE FOR DRIVEWAY AND HOUSE

This is going to take a bulldozer so you need to have made your arrangements with the subcontractor that is going to do your excavating work. After a start on the driveway you can tell very quickly whether or not you will need any tailings. You definitely will need ROB gravel for the driveway bed. Order this material for the following day so that it can be placed and graded by the dozer. You will need a stable driveway to get your concrete truck in to pour your footings. Strip and save the top soil and prepare the "pad" for the house as previously described. (Line 3 etc.)

LAYOUT FOR FOOTINGS

SCHEDULING

This has been previously discussed.

EXCAVATE FOOTINGS

You need you excavator to bring in his backhoe and dig your footing trenches

SITE DEVELOPMENT

`This is concomitant work that can proceed while you are building the footings and foundation. Clear front and back areas for house. Dig tree disposal trench and garbage disposal trench. Cut up and pack trees in trench. Clear path to well location, add stabilizing gravel if needed. Clear area for septic system.

You want to get as much site work done while you can. If there is rain you will be delayed. If the ground freezes you will be delayed. Get done whatever you can as soon as you can. This will enable you to supervise more things on the site at the same time, and cut down the total time you must spend on the job.

SET GRADE STAKES

This procedure has been previously covered.

GET FOOTING INSPECTION

Don't pour without it or somebody will get mad at you.

POUR FOOTINGS

You need to have your arrangements made with your masonry contractor, and should order your concrete several days ahead to be sure you will get the delivery when you need it. You can always postpone or cancel the delivery if you have to.

LAY THE BLOCK

` If you have had your mason on the job for the footings you should schedule him to start the foundation the next day before he gets involved in another job and you have a delay waiting for him. Order your block, mortar and sand early enough to have it delivered the afternoon of the day you poured the footings. Remember, have the block distributed inside the foundation area but keep the mortar and sand outside.

INSULATE THE FOUNDATION

This is the step when you line the inside of the block foundation with 2 inch thick styrofoam. You can hold it in place by nailing it in the new mortar joints. On this day you should be having the ROB gravel delivered that you will backfill the foundation with.

BACKFILL THE FOUNDATION

The mortar of the foundation should be allowed to set for at least three days before starting to backfill. Hopefully this will come out over the week end and you can maintain the pace.

NOTE: You can see at this point that we are relentlessly following the critical path. We are especially trying to plan so that we do not have delays and breaks between the steps. You can see already that many things have to be ordered and arranged ahead of time so that they will be available when needed. This is where most people fall down and loose time. You must continually anticipate Now that you have got your schedule started from left to right, go back on each line and mark the point at which materials must be ordered. It is a little more difficult with the subcontractors because they have to schedule the start of your job with the finish of another job. Make your arrangements with them three to four weeks ahead and give them starting dates three or four days ahead of your schedule. you can always delay them for a day or two which is better than your waiting for them to finish the other job which did not end when they thought it would. As we progress along the critical path keep going back and putting in ordering dates.

WELL AND SEPTIC

This is concomitant work that can continue while the foundation is being finished. When you have the heavy machines on the job you want to use them to the best advantage. This will avoid delivery charges for the machines and keep the job moving. The excavator is working on the site work. Schedule in the septic system to keep him going. This will insure he is immediately available to back fill the foundation when needed. Arrange for the well drilling, and the excavator can dig the water line trench in his sequence. This work can continue during the time the framing is going on. The main object is to keep the contractor busy so he doesn't leave the job for another, and you will have to wait to get him back. This kind of scheduling is good for him and good for you.

WATER LINE

A concomitant job that is usually done by a separate pump contractor. Sometimes this may be the well driller or the plumber. Get the well line laid in so that the trench can be backfilled, and the line can be brought up in the appropriate place inside the foundation.

UNDER SLAB PLUMBING

This is the next step in the critical path. Arrange your plumber enough ahead so that he will make his debut on the job when you need him.

SITE WORK

At this point you should be ready to finish the site work. With the foundation done, all the rough grading can be finished around the outside so that the framers will have even ground to work on. This work is not in the critical path so it may stretch out a little without harm. The main thing is to get the work done while the machines are on the job. This will save you money and avoid delay later on if you have to wait to get them back. As soon as the plumber has brought the drain line out of the foundation you can go ahead with the setting of the septic tank and the connection to the distribution box. If the land is pretty level you may need the tank installed before finalizing the elevation of the distribution box and the fields.

UNDER SLAB PLUMBING INSPECTION

This may delay you a day or two waiting for the inspector. Use the time to schedule your concrete for the slab and have the plastic membrane and reinforcing wire delivered. The inside of the foundation should be compacted with a mechanical compactor. Use it as well for the location of the patio and front walk. They can be formed and poured when the slab is poured. I always like to pour the walk when I pour the slab because I will do it last. If I run short on concrete I can skip it and do it later or do just part of it.

POUR THE SLAB

If the weather is cold make sure you get inhibitors added to the concrete. If it is very cold, specify hot water mix. Have your plastic sheet and hay ready to cover the concrete after the troweling is finished. If the weather is hot make sure you have water to wet down the slab as it sets. Go back and flag in these arrangements on your slab pour line.

You are building your critical path and you see now how to anticipate and schedule ordering and delivery of materials. There are bound to be delays, from the weather if nothing else. The exact dates are not important. It is following the sequence that is important.

FRAMING

The next step is framing but at this point I would schedule in a weeks delay to allow things to catch up. If you get too far behind your schedule your projected delivery and trade start dates will be too far off to be useful.

Keep noting the calendar date above the sequential schedule date. If the ninth day of work scheduled is not reached until the fourteenth calendar day has elapsed mark the calendar date above the sequence date so that you can keep track of where you are. This will enable you to delay delivery dates and starting times by the number of days lag that have been accumulated. A computer can do all this automatically but it is more fun to do it yourself because it keeps you focused on the challenge.

You will need an estimate from the framers as to how long they will take. It depends on the design of the house and the number of men working. A simple raised ranch can be framed in three days, but a normal custom home will probably take four to eight weeks depending on the size of the crew.

You will want your windows on the job so the framers can set them. Window delivery may take anywhere from two to eight weeks, so it is important to go back on the framing line and flag in the time to order windows.

DUCT WORK

If you are going to have any duct work it can be started as soon as the floors are framed up. This will begin the mechanical sequence which is next in the critical path.

ROOFING AND SIDING

This is concomitant work which can continue as the mechanical trades work on the inside. Keep going back on the lines and scheduling in ordering and delivery dates for the materials.

PLUMBING AND ELECTRICAL WIRING

We want to get the duct work finished first so the plumber and electrician will know where it is and go around it. You don't want to find that your duct layout calls for work in a bay between beams where the plumber has already run a water line. A lot of builders don't schedule the plumber and electrician at the same time. Often these trades feel that the other one will be in his way. This is nonsense. The electrician has his service and panel work to do which is removed in location from the areas where the plumber will be working. The plumber will principally be occupied in and under the bathrooms. The electrician has work to do all over the house. If you meet with them when they start, which doesn't have to be on exactly the same day, you can set up a little coordination, and it should go fine. This should save you a week at least on your critical path.

ELECTRICAL AND PLUMBING INSPECTION

Lots of times your plumber and electrician do not schedule these inspections until they are done. Then you will waste two or three days waiting for inspectors to show up. Urge them to call for their inspection a few days ahead.

INSULATION

This is the next step in the critical path. It should not be started before the inspections are made because the plumbing and electrical work must be visible to the inspector.

EXTERIOR FINISHING

This concomitant work should continue while the interior work is being done. Roofing should be finished, front and back doors installed, garage doors installed, well pump and pressure system installed. Facias, soffits, shutters and all exterior trim should continue during this time. This work can continue to run while the interior work progresses so you have some flexibility in scheduling. The critical path is now on the inside. Set up your schedule lines for each one of these operations and schedule it according to the time estimates of the contractors.

INSULATION INSPECTION

Most jurisdictions require an inspection of the insulation work before it is concealed. Schedule your sheetrock delivery for this period while you are waiting for inspection.

DRYWALL INSTALLATION AND TAPING

These two tasks can be done concurrently to a degree but it usually works out only if the same contractor is doing both parts of the work. If the taping is being done by a separate contractor he will usually want to wait until the rockers are done and out of his way. If he has a lull in his work schedule he may ask to start sooner so as not to be idle.

UNDERLAYMENT AND INTERIOR TRIM

Next in the critical path, install underlayment. You trimmers can begin setting doors and installing trim. Your doors need to be ordered in time to be on the job by this step so go back on your interior trim line and mark in when to order the doors. Doors can take several weeks so check ahead with your supplier.

INSTALL INTERIOR STAIRS

This can be concomitant with interior trim but you want to be sure you ordered the stairs in plenty of time. Go back on the stair line and indicate the ordering date.

TILE WORK

Tile work can be installed during the trim phase but must be down before plumbing fixtures are set.

INSTALL CABINETRY

This is part of the interior finishing and should be done as part of it. It is in the critical path because cabinets and vanities must be set before sinks can be installed. If the floors are to be tiled it is better for the cabinets to be set first. Go back and set the date for ordering cabinets so they will arrive in time.

INTERIOR PAINTING

This is next in the critical path and should be finished before the mechanical trades return. My painter always liked to get in and do the ceilings during the interior trim phase. Then he would follow the trim work staining doors etc. If you can compress this with the finishing it will save time.

LANDSCAPING

The exterior finishing should be done along with any needed exterior painting and staining. There is no reason why the landscaping cannot be started so that it will be finished when the job is finished. Of course, depending on the climate and the season of the year, landscaping may have to be delayed.

VINYL FLOORING

If your kitchen flooring is to be vinyl you want to get it done next so that when appliances arrive they can be set right in place.

APPLIANCE DELIVERY

As soon as the kitchen floor is down you want the appliances delivered and set in place. This can be done by the deliverers if you make the right arrangements. You want the appliances in place so that when the plumber and electrician come back to finish they will be able to make the necessary final connections.

FINISH PLUMBING AND ELECTRIC

These two trades are next in the critical path and can be done simultaneously. The plumber will be setting toilets, sinks and completing final hookups for the meter if any, the hot water heater and the dish washer.

At the same time the electrician is installing the circuit breakers, the receptacle and switch devices, the finish plates, the range, the dish washer, the range hood, the water heater, and such HVAC equipment as is included in the job, such as a heat pump compressor and air handler.

HVAC EQUIPMENT

This can be concomitant with the above. The heat pump compressor and air handler must be set so the electrician can make final connections. If an oil burner is involved that should be set and completed concomitantly.

HANGING INTERIOR AND EXTERIOR LIGHTING FIXTURES

This step usually runs in the critical path after the other interior electrical and plumbing finishing is completed. Delivery and availability is important here. Many lighting fixtures take a while to get. Go back on this line and mark in an ordering date in accordance with your suppliers estimate.

CARPET INSTALLATION

This installation cannot be done while there are any other trades working in the house. It's best to make sure that all the plumbing and electrical work is finished so that the debris can be cleaned up and will not wind up on top of the new carpet. This does not always work out and sometimes you have an electrician finishing after the carpet is down.

DUCT LOUVERS AND TRIM

If there are any floor ducts this step must come last after the carpet is down. If there are no floor ducts it can be finished when the equipment is set up.

HARDWOOD FLOOR FINISHING

If there are hardwood floors they should be sanded and finished last.

FINAL INSPECTION FOR CERTIFICATE OF OCCUPANCY

This inspection depends on all electrical, plumbing and structural work being completed but does not require floor coverings to be complete.

You will probably want to schedule your final mortgage closing or settlement with the bank. Many banks will not set up a closing date unless you have provided them with a copy of the final C.O. You will also need a final electrical inspection precedent to the C.O. inspection. Both these inspections should be called for during the final flooring installation.

This should be the last step in the critical path. Final clean up as discussed earlier can now be done. All final outside landscaping work and clean up can now be completed while the paper work is in process.

After you have constructed your first schedule go back and do it again. Now you will have discovered all the lines you need for the various tasks and approximately the order in which they come. Do your left hand list in every other space so that you will have room to add other items that may arise.

The forgoing does not necessarily include every operation in your construction but it should be instructive to you in making your own schedule.

RULE 69

CONSTANTLY ANTICIPATE MATERIAL AND LABOR REQUIREMENTS.

The most important lesson is to schedule the ordering and delivery of materials and equipment far enough in advance so that they will be available when needed.

Above all, when in doubt, use common sense. Too soon is always better than too late. If you apply these principles you will cut the construction time in half. If you are running this job while making a living at your regular occupation, cutting the length of time in half also cuts your time spent on the job in half.